Globalization and Development in the Mekong Economies

Globalization and Development in the Mekong Economies

Edited by

Suiwah Leung

The Australian National University, Australia

Ben Bingham

International Monetary Fund, USA

Matt Davies

International Monetary Fund, USA

Edward Elgar

Cheltenham, UK • Northampton, MA, USA

Published by
Edward Elgar Publishing Limited
The Lypiatts
15 Lansdown Road
Cheltenham
Glos GL50 2JA
UK

Edward Elgar Publishing, Inc.
William Pratt House
9 Dewey Court
Northampton
Massachusetts 01060
USA

A catalogue record for this book
is available from the British Library

Library of Congress Control Number: 2009941161

Mixed Sources
Product group from well-managed
forests and other controlled sources
www.fsc.org Cert no. SA-COC-1565
© 1996 Forest Stewardship Council

ISBN 978 1 84844 482 9

Printed and bound by MPG Books Group, UK

Contents

PART I   DEVELOPMENTS IN EAST ASIA AND
THE WORLD ECONOMY

PART II   CASE STUDIES OF MEKONG COUNTRIES

Figures

Tables

Boxes

Contributors

Ben Bingham: International Monetary Fund, USA

Matt Davies: International Monetary Fund, USA

Hal Hill: College of Asia and the Pacific, Australian National University, Australia

Masahiro Hori: Economic and Social Research Centre, Cabinet Office, Tokyo, Japan (formerly International Monetary Fund)

Kotaro Ishi: International Monetary Fund, USA

Suiwah Leung: Crawford School of Economics and Government, Australian National University, Australia

Pritha Mitra: International Monetary Fund, USA

David Robertson: Trade Policy Expert, formerly University of Melbourne, Australia

Martin Stuart-Fox: University of Queensland, Australia

Leslie Teo: Singapore Investment Corporation Singapore (formerly International Monetary Fund)

Trevor Wilson: College of Asia and the Pacific, Australian National University, Australia

The views expressed are solely those of the authors and do not reflect the views of their employers or institutions to which they are affiliated.

Preface

This book is a result of and has benefited greatly from the international conference entitled *Globalization and the Mekong Economies* held at the Australian National University, Canberra, in 2008. Regional experts contributing to the conference include Vo Tri Thanh, Doan Quang, Adam McCarty and Ngo Huy Duc from Vietnam, Kem Reat Viseth and Chap Sotharith from Cambodia, Bounleua Sinxayvoravong from Lao PDR, Mya Than and U Myint of Myanmar, and Biswa Bhattacharyay of the Asian Development Bank. Discussants from the Australian National University who are experts in the region include Premachandra Athukorala, Ligang Song, Greg Cutbush and Peter Warr. Although the comments and discussions from these and other participants at the conference are not specifically published in this book, they certainly impacted on the thinking of the authors and the final shape of the chapters.

The conference was supported financially by the Australian Agency for International Development (AusAID) and the International Monetary Fund. Organizational and staff support was provided by the Australian National University. As the world economy recovers from a crisis unprecedented since the Great Depression, the lessons of development through global participation remain for the latecomers to industrialization in the Mekong region. The sponsors and organizers are therefore to be thanked for their foresight in supporting policy studies of an important region of developing Asia. Furthermore, as many of the participants are former graduates of Australian universities, this conference and book represent an important activity in furthering the links between Australians and the people in the region. It is through goodwill and exchange of ideas amongst people that world peace and prosperity could be advanced.

Suiwah Leung
Canberra, Australia

PART I

Developments in East Asia and the world
economy

1. Globalization and development in the Mekong economies: Vietnam, Lao PDR, Cambodia and Myanmar

Suiwah Leung, Ben Bingham and Matt Davies

Post World War II developments in the four Mekong economies of Vietnam, Laos, Cambodia and Myanmar show similarities and differences. All four emerged from colonialism in the late 1940s/early 1950s with varying qualities of physical and social infrastructure. Except for Myanmar, all experienced war and conflict and by the mid-1970s all adopted some form of socialist central planning. Vietnam and Laos implemented Soviet-style central planning. Myanmar embraced isolationism from the West, with its economy under central government control in the hands of the military. Meanwhile, the Khmer Rouge in Cambodia enforced a severe form of central planning, resulting in the destruction of all business and market activities.

By the end of the 1980s, four 'lost decades' of economic development left the living standards of Mekong 4 citizens considerably below those of the fast-growing outward-looking East Asian economies. With the collapse of the former Soviet Union and the withdrawal of Vietnamese troops from Cambodia in 1989, the Mekong 4 embarked on market-oriented reforms to take advantage of the benefits of trade and investment with the world economy. Vietnam implemented *Doi Moi* (or 'Economic Renovation') in 1989; Laos adopted the *NEM* (New Economic Mechanism) in 1990; Myanmar began opening up its economy to foreign investment and tourism in 1988, and Cambodia embarked on serious reforms and resumption of relations with international financial institutions in 1993. All four economies became members of ASEAN.

With the exception of Myanmar, the initial successes of market reforms soon became evident. Although starting from a low base, Vietnam's average annual GDP growth (close to 8 percent per annum) prior to the Asian financial crisis of 1997 exceeded that of the ASEAN 5 and those of Laos and Cambodia were approaching the ASEAN 5.[1] Inflation rates before 1997 were also declining rapidly. Furthermore, economic growth has been accompanied by significant reductions in poverty. Even in Myanmar, GDP growth averaged around 5 percent between 1989 and 1998. Inflation, however, remained high (over 25 percent per annum) reflecting deep-seated problems with government finances, resulting in macroeconomic instability, which has continued to plague the economy.

Previously, the Vietnamese government showed a strong bias towards the state sector in international trade and investment. In the new millennium, concerted efforts to redress the bias resulted in a strong rebound in economic growth and foreign direct investment (FDI). Vietnam also started more active participation in globalization by embarking on the production and assembly of parts and components of certain manufactured goods that have become the hallmark of the production networks of East Asia. Although economic reform and development in Cambodia and Laos were less advanced than in Vietnam, FDI flows were still robust, albeit to a more limited range of sectors, principally electricity generation and mining in Laos, and tourism and garments in Cambodia. Only in Myanmar have reforms stagnated, with economic policies placing greater emphasis on control and security than on developing a domestic private sector. Consequently, not only did Myanmar have the lowest levels of FDI inflows amongst the Mekong 4 but, in contrast to the other three Mekong economies, the share going to manufacturing in total FDI inflows in Myanmar fell during the 2000s.

However, by 2007, even in Vietnam, not to mention the other three Mekong economies, transition was incomplete. In addition to continued bottlenecks in infrastructure and human capital, reform of public institutions lagged behind the needs of an increasingly entrepreneurial and market-oriented private sector. Institutional weaknesses ranged from the need to build stronger macroeconomic institutions (central banks and ministries of finance) to judiciary and public administration reforms. Lack of institutional reform, especially in Vietnam, became a key impediment to improving long-term competitiveness.

For the Mekong 4 the need to improve long-term competitiveness increased during the global recession following the financial crisis of 2008. Exports and capital inflows fell sharply, resulting in a slowdown in growth for all of the Mekong 4 in 2009. With limited resources available for fiscal stimuli, it has been difficult for the Mekong 4 to avert the full impact of the global recession, although Vietnam and Laos are currently weathering the crisis better than many of their neighbours in the region. Although distracted by the short-term economic challenges posed by the global recession, countries are again focusing on the longer-term reforms needed to secure new export markets and future investments once the global economy recovers. This is especially true in Vietnam and Laos, where the next set of five-year plans are being prepared for the forthcoming Party congresses in 2011.

With this in view, the book is divided into three parts. Part I, Chapters 2–6, canvasses the opportunities and threats of globalization for the Mekong 4. Chapter 2 discusses the opportunities that the production networks of East Asia provide for the Mekong 4 to expand their manufacturing base quickly by utilizing their large quantities of unskilled labour at the component assembly end of the supply chain. It also points out the danger of being trapped at the bottom of the chain, and hence the need to continually improve the economies' long-term competitiveness, enabling entrepreneurs to move up the value chain. Chapter 3 focuses on China, which is a major participant in the regional production networks, acting both as a competitor and an investor to the Mekong 4. Chapter 4 looks at the globalization of financial services. Despite the 2008 financial meltdown in the US and the EU, the less sophisticated end of the financial services spectrum offers opportunities for the Mekong 4 to open their financial sectors to regional and global foreign direct investment and associated skills transfer. Chapter 5 examines the alignment of fiscal incentives in the region for attracting FDI while Chapter 6 looks at the 'noodle bowl' of preferential trade agreements and indicates some guidelines by which the Mekong 4 could navigate through them.

Part II analyses each of the four Mekong economies. Chapters 7–10 argue the need for better public institutions to strengthen economic management and enhance the business environment and competitiveness in the longer term. Priorities include modernizing central banks, ministries of finance, and ministries of planning and investment as well as upgrading professional staff. Longer-term judiciary and public administration reforms are needed to address, *inter alia*, land titling and land use rights, particularly in the ability to use these as collateral for the financing of domestic small–medium-sized enterprises. All countries need to develop financial sectors in a sustainable manner. Judicial reform to protect the rights of lenders and investors in Cambodia should also be high on the policy agenda. With the short-term prospect of reduced growth, increased unemployment and poverty resulting in possible social unrest, the political will to focus on longer-term structural reform will undoubtedly be sorely tested.

The political economy of structural reform is the subject of Part III. Chapter 11 examines the political cultures of each of the Mekong 4 economies, while Chapter 12 (the final chapter) assesses the likelihood of reforms being implemented in the medium term future. In addition to the long-standing *political* objections to globalization, the current global recession has engendered fears of a new wave of protectionist policies on the part of industrialized developed countries. These can take different forms ranging from jingoism ('buy local products') to protectionist financing policies ('lend domestically') to halts in migration ('jobs for our own people'). This is a difficult context in which to convince developing countries of the benefits of continued globalization. At the same time, the case studies in Part II show that, with the exception of Myanmar, the Mekong economies are already very open economies. Unlike China, they are too small to rely on domestic demand to generate growth. International trade and investment (possibly with China playing a bigger role) will continue to be the order of the day. Only deeper structural reforms will convince domestic and international investors that the Mekong 4 will be truly competitive and business-friendly investment locations. No doubt, the political economy of reforms differs from country to country, with Vietnam judged as having the best prospects, followed by Cambodia and then Laos. It is hoped that the military regime in Myanmar will come to appreciate the benefits to themselves of faster growth and a stronger economy, and will therefore proceed to integrate more with the vibrant region that is Asia today.

NOTE

1. ASEAN 5 comprises Indonesia, Philippines, Thailand, Malaysia and Singapore.

2. Innovation and economic development: the role of production networks

Ben Bingham

1 INTRODUCTION

Recent literature points to the role of 'economic discovery' in economic development.[1] Hausman and Rodrik (2003) were among the first to suggest that a capacity to discover new economic activities might drive development. Imbs and Wacziarg (2003), and more recently Klinger and Liederman (2006), subsequently confirmed a robust relationship between economic diversification and economic development.

This chapter explores the link between economic discovery and the spread of international production networks. The literature (Baldwin 2006; Kimura 2006) suggests that these networks might promote economic discovery in developing countries because production fragmentation increases the potential range of activities in which developing countries have a comparative advantage. A synergy also exists between the desire of advanced economy firms to improve their competitiveness by offshoring activities and developing countries' interest in promoting economic discovery. Developing countries that recognize these opportunities and exploit them are likely to have a significant edge over those that do not.

Thus there may be a link between the rapid pace of economic discovery in East Asia over the past quarter century and the spread of regional production networks. These reflect, in part, greater openness to globalization and the unbundling of production processes. In turn, the development divide within East Asia may partly reflect the fact that the Mekong 4[2] were slower to adapt to these changes than their more developed ASEAN counterparts.

The chapter concludes with a word of caution. While production networks can help start industrialization, it is not a panacea. Escaping the middle-income trap, which implies moving up the value chain, is not straightforward and has stumped many aspiring countries. Moreover, life on the bottom rung of production networks – the so-called 'bleeding edge' – is uncomfortable. Nevertheless participating in production networks does at least appear to provide opportunities for rapid economic discovery that might not otherwise be available for developing countries.

Section 2 discusses the incentive to innovate, and its implications for the process of economic discovery. Section 3 discusses how participating in international production might lower barriers to economic discovery. Section 4 discusses some of the determinants that make a country an attractive location for production networks. Section 5 concludes.

2   INNOVATION AND DEVELOPMENT

Imbs and Wacziarg (20003) found that economies become more diversified as countries get richer and that this process continues until relatively late in the development process. This pattern held above and beyond shifts of factors of production from agriculture to manufacturing and on to services and could be observed even within sectors, such as manufacturing. Klinger and Lederman (2006) found the same result in their analysis of export patterns. Both papers point to countries diversifying until they reach a fairly high level of per capita GDP,[3] which suggested that discovering a comparative advantage in new activities might be integral to the development process.

These findings are consistent with a Schumpeterian view of development in which growth depends on the rate of innovation in an economy. In this case the relevant form of innovation is economic discovery – broadening the economic base through the introduction of new activities. As Aghion and Howitt (2006) demonstrate: long-run growth ultimately depends on the rate of innovation (Box 2.1).

2.1   The Incentive to Innovate

Why are some countries better than others at economic discovery? Or more pertinently, what hinders economic discovery in poorly performing countries? Recent research has focused on the role of the entrepreneur in the innovation process; if entrepreneurs are unwilling to risk investing in innovation new productive activities are unlikely to emerge or only emerge very slowly.

The following framework, adapted from Aghion and Howitt (2006), helps explore what drives entrepreneurs to invest in innovation. It illustrate entrepreneurs' decision framework under two conditions: (i) innovation in activities in which they are potentially competitive (Case A); and

BOX 2.1   SCHUMPETERIAN GROWTH FRAMEWORK

Aghion and Howitt (2006) develop a model in which economic growth depends on the process of innovation.

Basic Model

The model starts with a production function specified at the industry level:

$$Y_{it} = A_{it}^{1-\alpha} K_{it}^{\alpha} \qquad (1)$$

In this function, A_{it} is a productivity parameter attached to the most recent technology used in industry i at time t, and K_{it} is the flow of a unique intermediate product used in sector i, each unit of which is produced one-for-one by capital.

Each intermediate product is produced and sold exclusively by an incumbent monopolist who possesses the most advanced technology. If a new entrant improves the technology parameter A_{it}, then he is able to displace the incumbent monopolist and dominate the industry, until he is displaced by the next technologically dominant new entrant.

Aggregate output is the sum of the industry specific outputs Y_{it}, and under certain simplifying assumptions can be represented by a simple Cobb–Douglas aggregate per-worker production function:

$$Y_t = A_t^{1-\alpha} K_t^{\alpha}, \text{ where } A_t = \Sigma A_{it} \qquad (2)$$

Innovation and Growth

The economy's long-run growth rate is given by the growth of A_t, which depends on endogenously on the economy-wide rate of innovation. The theory is flexible in modeling innovation. It encompasses 'frontier' innovations that result in a new global technology parameter $(\bar{A}_{it})$, where $\bar{A}_{it} = \gamma \bar{A}_{it-1}$, as well as 'within-frontier' innovations that bring domestic technology up to the global frontier.

Consider a country in which 'frontier' innovations take place at frequency μ_n and 'within-frontier' innovations at frequency μ_m. The change in the economy's productivity frontier is given by:

$$A_{t+1} - A_t = \mu_n (\gamma - 1) A_t + \mu_m(\bar{A}_t - A_t) \qquad (3)$$

and, hence the growth rate would be:

$$g_t = \mu_n (\gamma - 1) + \mu_m(a_t^{-1} - 1), \text{ where: } a_t = A_t/\bar{A}_t \qquad (4)$$

Thus long-run economic growth depends on the frequency of innovation and imitation, the impact of innovations on the stock of technology, and the distance of a country from the technology frontier.

(ii) innovation in activities in which they are vulnerable to competition from a technologically superior competitor (Case B).

Case A

Consider a model in which each sector of the economy has a front-runner who uses the most advanced technology available locally (A_{it}). There are also followers using slightly outdated technology (A_{it-1}). The front-runner currently earns a profit $\pi^*_{it} = \delta A_{it}$, while followers earn a profit $\pi_{it} = \alpha \delta A_{it-1}$, where $\alpha < 1$.[4] If the front-runner innovates and raises A_{it} by γ, he can use a first-mover advantage to remain the front-runner. If not he risks, with probability p, becoming a follower with reduced profitability.

The decision to innovate will depend on the marginal benefit, v_{it} that the front-runner expects to gain from innovation. This is the difference between the profit he will earn with certainty if he innovates, and the expected profit if he does not. Thus:

$$v_{it+1} = \delta \gamma A_{it} - [p\alpha\delta A_{it} + (1 - p)\delta A_{it}]$$
$$v_{it+1} = [(\gamma - 1) + p(1 - \alpha)] \delta A_{it} \qquad (2.1)$$

The marginal benefit v_{it} therefore depends on the threat of competition p, the hit to profits (α) if the front-runner loses his position of primacy, as well as the return on innovating ($\gamma - 1)\delta A_{it1}$. The higher p and α, the greater the incentive to innovate to escape the threat of competition. Indeed, if p and α are sufficiently high it may be worth innovating even if γ is less than one – that is, reduces rents – if it staves off the threat of competition. The threat of competition applies to all forms of innovation, including economic discoveries that introduce new activities. Any discovery, if sufficiently large, will impact on the rents of existing activities either directly on price, if the new activity is a close substitute, or by bidding up the price of scarce factors and non-tradable goods.

The core intuition of Aghion and Howitt's analysis is that competition is likely to be a spur to innovation in an environment where competitors are fairly evenly matched. Although competition may reduce rents associated with innovation, the loss of rents associated with not innovating may be greater. Indeed limiting competition could hinder innovation, as it would make it easier for firms to earn rents without incurring the expense of innovation.

Case B

The outlook is different if an entrepreneur is considering entering an activity where she is far from the technological frontier.[5] In this situation the likelihood is that she will remain behind the frontier, even if she manages to imitate the latest technology because the frontier will have moved on. Most likely, industry leaders will wipe her out if she enters into this new activity.

The decision facing the entrepreneur is as follows: if she invests in this new activity she could earn a rent, say δA_{it}, but it will only materialize if she does not face competition from an industry leader. If she does face such competition, let the probability be p, then her profit will be zero. Under these circumstances the benefit from investing in such an innovation would be:

$$v_{it+1} = (1 - p)\delta A_i$$

Thus, the higher the probability of competition from an industry leader, the less likely that it will be worthwhile investing in this new activity.

There are a couple of implications. Firstly it suggests that at any given time there is a boundary to the set of potential economic discoveries for a developing country. In principle, raising trade barriers or otherwise limiting competition might extend the set, as would subsidies. However, this will be costly, especially in countries with small domestic markets where the scope for learning by doing is more limited. Moreover, the risk of failure rises exponentially the further a country is from the technology frontier. Secondly, it suggests that investing in human capital is an imperative. While exploiting existing opportunities for economic discovery is important, over the long haul expanding the set of activities in which a country is potentially competitive is crucial for development.

2.2   The Cost of Discovery

High costs can also be a barrier to economic discovery. The greater the cost the lower the rate of discovery, especially if the costs are economy-wide rather than firm-specific.[6] This is the central thesis of Hausman and Rodrik (2003) who point out that economic discovery is not a costless undertaking; it involves significant investment by entrepreneurs. Costs include researching potential new activities, learning the characteristics of foreign demand, matching that with the domestic economy's cost structure, adapting technologies from abroad to local conditions and mastering domestic and foreign regulations.

Countries able to reduce the cost of investing in economic discovery clearly have a comparative advantage. As discussed below, one possible explanation of the success of East Asian economies is that they have been particularly successful in exploiting the strategies of advanced economy firms that were seeking to enhance their own competitiveness by off-shoring activities to low-cost locations. The most successful countries not only attracted inbound investment by advanced economy firms but also established conditions that encouraged those firms to establish local supply chains.

3   GLOBALIZATION AND INNOVATION

How might globalization stimulate economic discovery in developing countries? There are two channels. Firstly, globalization expands potential economic discoveries by increasing the range of activities in which developing countries have a comparative advantage. Secondly, globalization expands the potential role of foreign investors helping countries that provide a conducive investment climate overcome the costs associated with economic discovery.

The following analysis, adapted from Baldwin (2006) and Kimura (2006), illustrates how production fragmentation can alter the comparative advantage of a low-income developing country.

3.1   Pre-Globalization

Consider first the relative comparative advantage of advanced (North) and developing (South) countries in a pre-globalization scenario. Figure 2.1 shows the global set of activities along the horizontal axis ranked according to the size of productivity gap between North and South economies. The activities in which the North has the largest productivity gap

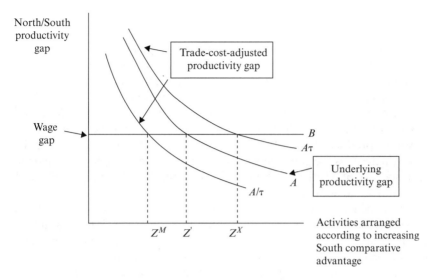

Source: Baldwin (2006, p. 17). (reproduced courtesy of R. Baldwin)

Figure 2.1   A pre-globalization scenario

(say, R&D) are on the far left. Those where the North has the smallest productivity gap (for example, manual labor) are on the far right. It is important to note that low-skill activities that are bundled, that is, used jointly, with high-skilled activities in the production of a good or service would be on the left. Assembly of computers in the 1970s would have been one such example.

Curve A shows the decline in the productivity gap as one moves from left to right across the range of activities. The horizontal line B marks the point where the productivity gap between North and South equals the wage gap. In the absence of trade costs, the border-line activity would be at Z'. Activities to the left of Z' would be undertaken in the North and embodied in exports to the South. Those to the right of Z' would be undertaken in the South and exported to the North.

Trade costs reduce the competitive edge of southern firms in northern markets and vice versa. Thus, the trade-cost-adjusted productivity gap for southern firms shifts to the right, to $A\tau$, while the curve for northern firms shifts to the left, to A/τ. The South can only export activities to the right of Z^X, while the North can only export activities to the left of Z^M. The activities in between are non-traded.

3.2   Post-globalization

Looking now at the impact of production fragmentation on the comparative advantage of developing countries, consider a production process involving five activities (Figure 2.2). Pre-fragmentation these activities are carried out in a single production site because the cost savings from locating them in different sites is more than offset by 'service link costs'.[7] Note that in this state the productivity gap for each activity is equal to the average productivity gap for all five activities. If that average exceeds the North–South wage gap then all five activities will be located in the North, irrespective of whether the South has a comparative advantage in some of the individual activities.

Now consider an innovation in an advanced economy that reduces service link costs. The innovation could be technological, for example, a reduction in communication costs, or reflect an advancement in management technology that increases the capacity of firms to manage activities spread across different geographical locations. Most likely it will be a combination of both. Let us suppose that the reduction in service link

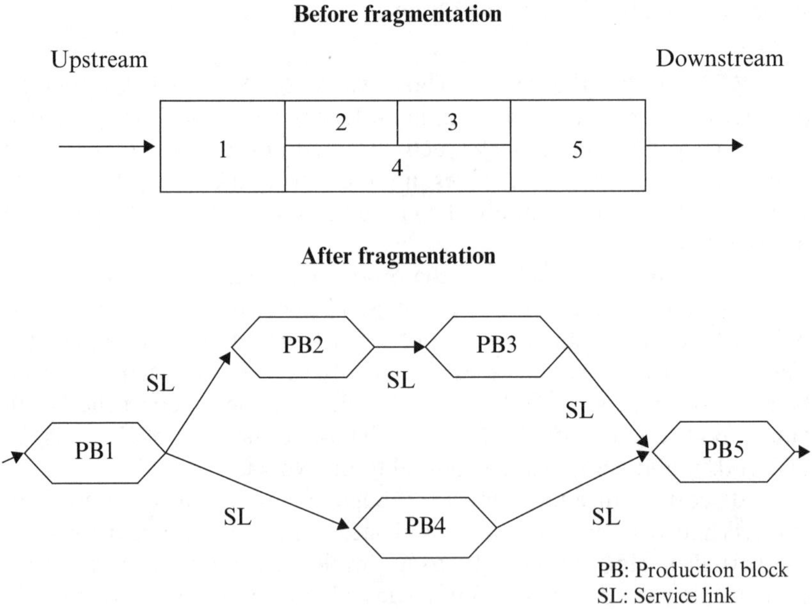

Before fragmentation

Upstream   Downstream

After fragmentation

PB: Production block
SL: Service link

Source: Kimura (2006, p. 335). (reproduced courtesy of F. Kimura)

Figure 2.2   Production process before and after fragmentation

costs is sufficient to make it cost-efficient to unbundle this set of activities and locate them in different production sites, as shown in the bottom panel of Figure 2.2.

The impact on developing countries could be quite significant. No longer is the location of an activity determined by the average productivity of the combined set. The productivity gap for low-skill activities (for example, assembly operations or call centers) will shrink rapidly, making it profitable to offshore those activities. In contrast, the productivity gap for high-skill activities will rise, potentially opening up new export opportunities for advanced economies.

These changes in relative comparative advantage are illustrated in Figure 2.3. Baldwin wished to emphasize here that the shifts in comparative advantage were not only likely to be large, but unpredictable as well. This is important for industrial strategy as it implies that picking winners would be much harder in a fast-moving post-globalization age where the implications of shifts in management, information and production technology will be hard to predict. Instead, government's role will increasingly need to focus on fostering conditions that help entrepreneurs exploit opportunities for economic discovery.

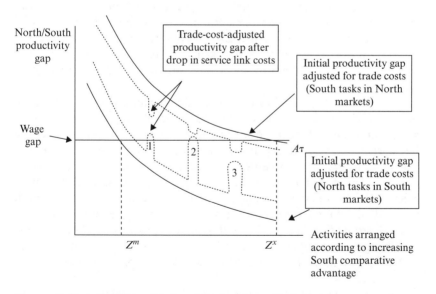

Source: Baldwin R. (2006, p. 26). (reproduced courtesy of R. Baldwin)

Figure 2.3 Changes in relative comparative advantage

4 WHAT MAKES A COUNTRY ATTRACTIVE TO PRODUCTION NETWORKS?

The answer involves looking more deeply into the fragmentation theory that we touched on above. First proposed by Jones and Kierkowski (1990), this theory explores the conditions under which firms find it optimal to fragment their production process, either geographically, by locating blocks of their production process in different locations[8] or by outsourcing blocks to an entity outside of the firm (or both).

4.1 Some Theory

The intuition behind production fragmentation is relatively straightforward: firms will fragment their production process when the savings from offshoring or outsourcing an activity outweigh the increased cost associated with coordination production activities across different sites, the so-called service link costs. The duality between production and service link costs is essential to understanding the formation of production networks. The greater the savings in the former, relative to increases in the latter, the greater the incentive for firms to fragment their production processes and develop production networks. Frequently the motivating force is an exogenous event that either increases production costs at the factory – for example an appreciation of the exchange rate[9] – or lower service link costs, for example an improvement in information and/or management technology.

Ando and Kimura (2003) and Kimura (2006) emphasize the importance of low service link costs, given that many developing countries offer a comparative advantage in unskilled labor. The lower a country's service link costs the more attractive it will be to potential investors. First-movers will have an advantage, because service link costs tend to show economies of scale. The denser the network of suppliers and customers the more efficient it is to operate a production process.[10] Countries that establish regional minima in service link costs tend to attract large numbers of fragmented production blocks. The industrial clusters in East Asia, such as the Shanghai-Jiangsu corridor and Guangzhou in China, Samut Prakan in Thailand, and Shah Alam in Malaysia are examples of agglomeration forces in action.

There is a clear overlap between this theory of production networks and the literature on knowledge-capital models of MNEs (Markusen and Maskus 2002). The central intuition of these models is that knowledge is geographically mobile and can be a joint input into multiple production facilities. Vertical MNE's[11] are motivated by efficiency gains that can be realized by unbundling skill-intensive headquarter services from lower-skill production services. These efficiency gains are realized by undertaking the latter in unskilled-labor-abundant countries. These knowledge–capital models predict that vertical MNEs are most likely to come into existence when: (i) the parent and host economies have large differences in skilled and unskilled labor endowments; (ii) foreign plant set-up costs – and associated risks – are low; and (iii) trade and communication costs are not a significant barrier.

What makes a location attractive to investors according to these theoretical frameworks? Firstly, the cost advantages have to be high, as offshoring is inevitably accompanied by substantial service link costs.[12] In addition to low-cost labor other elements of the business climate, for example access to high-quality and low-cost infrastructure services, will be important. Secondly, service link costs must not be prohibitive. A premium will be placed on good transport and communication, efficient distribution systems as well as low trade barriers. Thirdly, the level of risk is a significant factor, given that investors are operating outside of their domestic environment. Sound macroeconomic policies, stable and transparent legal and regulatory regimes, as well as mature dispute settlement mechanisms will be important considerations. The presence of strong local business networks, preferably with regional links, may also help mitigate the risk of moving to a new environment.

Can lagging economies overcome the disadvantages of not being first-movers and carve out a niche for themselves in production networks? The literature on economic geography suggests that they can: agglomeration generates centrifugal as well as centripetal forces. The former include congestion effects, such as more costly/less efficient transport services, increased labor costs, labor and human capital shortages. These centrifugal forces provide lagging economies in the neighborhood an opportunity to enjoy spin-offs from the agglomeration forces that concentrated activity in major economic centers. Another centrifugal force is the risk of relying too heavily on one region for key chains in its production process – in effect the risk of putting all of one's eggs in one basket. The desire to minimize such risks also provides opportunities for countries that can provide sufficiently attractive service link and production conditions.

4.2   Empirical Literature

Ng and Yeats (1999) started a body of literature that shows which countries have a comparative advantage in production networks. There are few surprises. East Asia dominates production networks, dominating global trade in components (Bingham 2008, Table 1) and in measures of revealed comparative advantage (Bingham 2008, Table 2). Within East Asia, China[13] and the ASEAN 4[14] are the strongest performers, with the Mekong 4 lagging the rest of ASEAN by a considerable margin. Of the four, only Vietnam has made progress over the last 15 years. Outside of East Asia, Costa Rica, Mexico and Brazil are competitive among Latin American countries, while Hungary, (former) Czechoslovakia and Poland are most competitive in Europe.

Measures that gauge whether countries are punching above their weight in terms of their share of component trade show similar results (Bingham 2008, Table 3). However, there are a couple of notable exceptions. The most interesting is China, whose share of trade in machinery goods and components is relatively low given the huge size of its labor force.[15] This likely reflects the fact that China's industrial activity has been concentrated in its coastal provinces, with participation by the labor force of inland provinces constrained by impediments to internal labor mobility and a lack of competitive infrastructure in these provinces. Considering only coastal provinces, which account for about 30 percent of China's labor force, China's competitiveness becomes more readily apparent. One implication is that the real competitors for other countries in East Asia may be China's inland provinces and the pace with which these provinces are integrated into the global production networks.

The empirical literature on what drives this pattern of comparative advantage, however, is relatively sparse. What is clear is that some of the standard variables suggested by the theoretical literature, such as remoteness from regional economic centers, differentials in labor endowments, barriers to investment and country risk provide only a partial explanation of the global pattern of competitiveness in production networks (Bingham 2008). One can make a fairly compelling case that East Asia's substantial endowment in low-cost labor, as well as the significant intra-regional variations in labor costs and endowments, provided a fertile ground for the expansion for production networks in that region. Similarly, the Mekong 4's relatively limited engagement in production networks so far can be fairly convincingly linked to a low ranking in competitiveness variables. But such casual empiricism is less than satisfactory if one is looking for a more universal model of production networks.

There is a compelling case for a more systematic modeling of the factors that drive country competitiveness in production networks, especially as the theory of production networks provides a relatively rich set of potential explanatory factors. One that may deserve particularly close attention is the importance of low trade barriers as logic would suggest that this must be a prerequisite for participation in production networks.

Baldwin (2006) suggests the ASEAN 4 quickly recognized this reality and unilaterally cut tariffs on network-related trade from the mid-1980s onwards to compete for investment by offshoring multinational enterprises. In the early days the reduction in tariffs often came in the form of duty drawbacks and duty-free treatment located in export processing zones, but over time these duty concessions were converted into straightforward tariff reductions. While the Mekong 4 initially responded slowly, the proliferation of recent trade initiatives suggest that they too have recognized the need for low tariff barriers to compete for foreign direct investment

What is perhaps less appreciated is that tariff barriers now constitute only a relatively small proportion of trade costs. This point was highlighted by the World Bank in its 2001 report, *Making Trade Work for the Poor*, which provided evidence that transport cost barriers outweigh tariff cost barriers by a wide margin. While part of the transport cost barrier is exogenous, being inextricably linked to a country's location, two recent studies have suggested that trade costs have a significant home grown component.

Insights of relevance to the Mekong 4 come from Dee (2007) and Djankov et al., (2006). Dee's paper posits that auxiliary charges, mainly port handling costs, explain the bulk of the variability of shipping costs between pairs of destinations. Moreover, while ocean freight charges have tended to fall over time, auxiliary charges have tended to rise, offsetting the gains from technological advancement (for example, bigger vessels) and lower tariffs. This suggest that differences across countries in auxiliary charges, over which governments have a measure of control, are a source of absolute and comparative advantage, and that reducing these charges would have a great impact on reducing barriers to trade.

Djankov et al.'s study focuses on the time cost of moving goods from the factory gate to the nearest port. They found that each additional day a product is delayed prior to being shipped reduces trade by at least 1 percent. The impact of delays was even greater for time-sensitive goods, with a day's delay reducing trade by 6 percent. These findings may explain why seemingly remote countries such as Mauritius still enjoy success as an exporter. Mauritius' trade infrastructure is as efficient as that of the United Kingdom and more efficient than France. Reducing the substantial time costs of trade in the developing countries such as the Mekong 4 would likely have a substantial impact on these countries' comparative advantage in tradable goods.

5 CONCLUSION

This chapter has explored the potential link between economic discovery and the spread of international production networks. It suggests that participating in these production networks can lower barriers to economic discovery in developing countries. It does so through two channels. Firstly, by providing greater opportunities for specialization, production fragmentation increases the potential range of activities in which developing countries have a comparative advantage. Secondly, partnerships with advanced economy firms seeking to offshore low-skill activities can significantly reduce the cost of economic discovery for developing country entrepreneurs.

The chapter has also explored some of the factors that might make a country a competitive investment destination for international production networks. While much more work needs to be done, especially on the empirical side, the theories on production networks and multinational enterprises appear to provide some insights into the preferred location for production networks.

At the global level, East Asia's substantial endowment in low-cost unskilled labor appear to have given it a significant competitive edge over other regions. Moreover, significant differences in labor costs and endowments among countries in East Asia provide fertile ground for the expansion of production networks. Within East Asia, significant investment barriers, poor infrastructure and high risk appear to have been significant barriers to the participation by the Mekong 4 in the spread of production networks, despite their competitive labor endowments and relative proximity to the major economic centers in the region. The gap between Vietnam and the other Mekong 3 is also explained, at least in part, by Vietnam's more favorable investment conditions.

At a more general level, one of the reasons East Asia was so successful in developing new industries may lie in the fact that it took better advantage of the changes brought about by production fragmentation and the competitive strategies pursued by advanced economy firms seeking offshore low-skilled activities. By making themselves attractive to multinational investors, they secured a partner that helped them significantly accelerate economic discovery. If correct, it would imply that countries within East Asia that responded promptly to this new reality had a considerable advantage over those that did not.

However, there is one caveat. While engagement with international production networks can help start industrialization, the literature suggests that moving beyond simple assembly operations is far from smooth in practice.[16] Local firms have to overcome a wide array of challenges if they are to proceed up the value chain.[17]

Nevertheless, participation in production networks does at least provide opportunities for rapid innovation – in terms of an expansion of activities – that might not otherwise be available to developing countries.

NOTES

1. Coined by Hausman and Rodrik, economic discovery describes the process through which new activities are introduced into an economy.
2. Cambodia, Lao PDR, Myanmar, Vietnam.
3. Imbs and Wacziarg (2003) estimated the transition point at about $15000 in 1996 US dollars. Klinger and Lederman (2006) found that the transition point using export data was higher (around $20 000).
4. The follower catches up with the front-runner with one period lag, but the profit is lower than the front-runner received, because the technology is no longer state-of-the-art.
5. For example, consider the incentives facing a developing country entrepreneur pondering the merits of entering the aircraft industry.
6. If the costs are economy-wide the threat of competitors' innovating is also reduced.
7. This is a term, initially coined by Kimura (2006) to describe the cost of coordinating ('linking') production blocks located at different geographical sites.
8. For simplicity, this chapter will refer to this as offshoring, although the production blocks do not necessarily have to be relocated to another country.
9. The sharp appreciation of the Yen following the Plaza agreement in 1985 is considered one of the initial driving forces behind the rapid spread of production networks in East Asia.
10. The greater the proximity of potential customers and suppliers, the lower the cost of identifying them, consulting with them, enforcing quality control and timeliness, and resolving disputes.
11. These models distinguish between horizontal MNEs that have multiple plants replicating similar activities in many locations and vertical MNEs that geographically fragment production into stages on the basis of countries' relative factor endowments.
12. National border effects include: trade impediments, customs clearance and immigration procedures, higher transport costs and the risks associated with operating in an alien policy environment (Kimura 2006).
13. Includes Hong-Kong and Macao.
14. Indonesia, Malaysia, Philippines and Thailand.
15. For example, although China accounts for around 23 percent of non-industrial trade in components, its labor force is close to 30 percent of the non-industrial world.
16. See Sturgeon and Lester (2003). They argue that process of engaging with production networks is sometimes oversimplified. Specifically, portraits of a smooth trajectory that starts with simple assembly, progresses towards more sophisticated manufacturing, and culminates in firms having the capacity to produce and sell their own branded products on world markets, greatly underestimate the difficulty of moving up the value chain.
17. Sturgeon and Lester cite the example of Taiwanese computer suppliers in the late 1990s. When Compaq decided in 1997 to market a complete PC for less than $1000 – a strategy followed by its competitors – many small PC manufacturers in Taiwan were forced to close. Those that remained only survived by shifting production to mainland China.

REFERENCES

Aghion, P. and P. Howitt (2005), 'Appropriate growth policy, a unifying framework', The 2005 Joseph Schumpeter Lecture, presented to the 20th Annual Congress of the European Economic Association, 25 August, Amsterdam.

Ando, M. and F. Kimura (2003), 'The formation of international production and distribution networks in East Asia', National Bureau for Economic Research working paper 10167.

Baldwin, R. (2006), 'Globalization: the great unbundling(s)', paper prepared for Globalisation challenges for Europe and Finland project, September, Economic Council of Finland.

Bingham, B. (2008), 'Innovation and economic development: the role of production networks', paper presented at the Conference on Globalization and Mekong Economies, The Australian National University, Canberra, 31 March–1 April.

Dee, P. (2007), 'Impact of trade costs on trade: empirical evidence from Asian countries', Asia-Pacific Research and Training Network on Trade (ARTNeT) working paper no. 2707.

Djankov, S., C. Freund and C. Pham (2006), 'Trading on time', World Bank policy research working paper.

Hausman, R. and D. Rodrik (2003), 'Economic development as self-discovery', *Journal of Development Economics*, **72**(2), 603–33.

Imbs, Jean and Romain Wacziarg (2003), 'Stages of diversification', *The American Economic Review*, **93**(1), 63–86.

Jones, R. and H. Kierkowski (1990), 'The role of services in production and international trade: a theoretical framework', in R. Jones and A. Kreuger (eds), *The Political Economy of International Trade*, Oxford: Blackwell, pp. 31–48.

Kimura, F. (2006), 'International production and distribution networks in East Asia: eighteen facts, mechanics, and policy implications', *Asian Economic Policy Review*, 1, 326–44

Klinger, B. and D. Lederman (2006), 'Diversification, innovation, and imitation inside the global technology frontier', World Bank research policy working paper no. 3872.

Markusen, J. and K. Maskus (2002), 'Discriminating among alternative theories of the multinational enterprise', *Review of International Economics*, **10**, 694–707.

Ng F. and A. Yeats (1999), 'Production sharing in East Asia: who does what for whom, and why?', World Bank policy research paper no. 2197.

Sturgeon, T. and R. Lester (2003), 'The new global supply-base: new challenges for local suppliers in East Asia', Massachusetts Institute of Technology IPC working paper series.

3. The rise of China: implications for the Mekong countries

Matt Davies[1]

1 INTRODUCTION AND BACKGROUND

This chapter concentrates on the effects of China's rapid economic growth on the Mekong countries. It focuses on the post-1995 period, which covers emergence from conflict and intensive reform in the Mekong, and the meteoric period of China's rise, including its World Trade Organization (WTO) entry in 2001.[2]

Section 2 provides a brief overview of the nature of China's rise. Section 3 looks at how China's presence has affected the Mekong countries' exports to third markets. Section 4 looks at how China's rise has provided an opportunity for the Mekong countries as a market for exports and a source of external finance. It also reviews how China's impact on world markets has affected their terms of trade. Section 5 looks at the likely future implications of China's continuing growth and Section 6 draws tentative conclusions and identifies policy priorities for the Mekong countries.

2 THE RISE OF CHINA[3]

Driven by an export-led development strategy, China is now the world's third largest exporter. This growth appears dramatic but is similar in magnitude to the surges in trade associated with earlier integration of other rapidly growing East Asian economies into the global trading system.

More reliant on foreign finance than its East Asian predecessors, foreign-financed firms account for around half of China's exports as compared to 20–25 percent of Taiwan POC and South Korea's manufactured exports in the 1970s. By 2003, China's Asian trading partners collectively accounted for about 70 percent of the cumulative FDI in China (Branstetter and Lardy, 2006).

Although the center of complex production networks in East Asia (reviewed in Chapter 2, and see also Soesastro, 2006), the networks are not, per se, a facet of the rise in China. Rather, the development of just-in-time production techniques and rapidly falling communications costs provided the necessary conditions for their development (Baldwin, 2006). The availability of a growing, increasingly outward-looking China with its abundant, low-cost and well-educated workforce, however, was key to the development of the triangular trade pattern and strengthening of regional competitiveness.

China's exports have moved rapidly up the value chain. Originally concentrating in low value-added labor-intensive commodities, China has emerged as a major producer and exporter of electronic and IT products. It now exports products more in common with capital and skill-abundant OECD members than economies with comparable income levels (Branstetter and Lardy, 2006). Beginning with the assembly of finished goods from imported components, China is now increasingly sourcing the components for final assembly domestically (Cui and Syed, 2007).

Imports have also grown rapidly, increasing from 6 percent of GDP in 1980 to 29 percent of GDP in 2006 and increasing by 90 percent in dollar terms between 2003 and 2006. Imports reflect the need for more components and intermediate goods (including power and energy) to produce final export goods (around two-thirds of imports) and the growing demand for final consumption goods in the rapidly growing domestic economy. China also accounts for a large and rising share of world trade in key primary commodities, stimulating the rapid price rises seen in these commodities in recent years (Deutsche Bank, 2006; United States International Trade Commission, 2006).

The heavy concentration of China's manufacturing industries within the coastal provinces reflects[4]: (i) an explicitly incrementalist development policy on the part of the Chinese authorities (for instance, Special Enterprise Zones were initially established in the costal provinces); (ii) the sizeable transport cost and time advantages for investors in locating close to a port; and (iii) tendencies in industrial development towards the agglomeration of similar activities in geographic areas.

Little evidence supports the view that increases in China's exports significantly reduce exports of other emerging Asian economies or crowd out FDI flows into the rest of the region (Ahearne et al., 2003). Most Asian economies have significant and growing complementarity with China, ensuring they benefit from China's continuing economic growth. The share of China's imports from the region has risen dramatically, reflecting the impact of the production networks described above, and it has replaced the United States as the most important destination for the exports of all East Asian economies (Gill and Kharas, 2006).[5]

Nor have China's gains come about at the expense of the labor-intensive ASEAN-4 economies. Rather, China and the ASEAN-4 have together displaced the newly industrialized economies in industries – such as apparel, footwear, and household products – that these more advanced economies were relinquishing (Loungani, 2000).

Recent World Bank (2006) work suggests that manufacturing industries in some western hemisphere countries, particularly in Mexico and to a lesser extent in Central America and the Caribbean, have been negatively affected by Chinese competition in third markets and competition from Chinese imports has been associated with modest unemployment and adjustment costs in manufacturing industries. Overall however, the fear of major costs to other countries from China's dynamic rise appears to have been overstated.

Under the 'Going Global' slogan, China's outward FDI has gathered pace since WTO accession in 2001. Chinese outward FDI remains relatively small though, and is mostly concentrated in Asia (around 60 percent), with Hong Kong SAR being the largest recipient (around three-quarters of total outflows to Asia) – although a significant portion of this investment is likely to be roundtripping back into China to take advantage of investment incentives. Africa and Latin America are also becoming significant destinations, in particular due to natural resource investments (Deutsche Bank, 2006a).

As a result of its spectacular growth, high savings rates, low consumption and intervention in foreign exchange markets, China has amassed considerable official reserves. These reserves have been used to significantly increase its foreign aid program particularly in countries in which China has strong strategic interests, in Asia, but also increasingly in Africa, where China has strengthened relations with natural resource producers through direct investment and development finance, particularly in the infrastructure areas from which traditional donors have been tending to withdraw.

3   CHINA AS A COMPETITOR FOR THE MEKONG COUNTRIES

This section looks at the extent to which China's rise has restricted the growth of exports from the Mekong countries. It utilizes trade data from the UNCTAD World Integrated Trade Solutions (WITS) database using the SITC (revision 3) three-digit classification during the period 1995–2005. Although not without shortcomings, the three-digit classification remains the most appropriate data source.

3.1   Export Structure of the Mekong Countries

The exports of the Mekong countries grew rapidly over the period, from an average of 20 percent of GDP in 1995 to over 40 percent in 2005. Around 80 percent of Cambodia and Vietnam's exports and 70 percent of Laos's exports are to markets outside of Asia, predominately the United States and European Union. Myanmar, by contrast, exports mostly within Asia and, in particular, to Thailand.

Export structure, however, remained quite concentrated for all the countries. The top five product classes at the three-digit level account for two-thirds to three-quarters of Cambodia's, Laos's, and Myanmar's exports. Table 3.3 shows that Cambodia's are entirely concentrated in garments while Myanmar's are concentrated in natural gas and wood. Copper, electricity, wood and garments dominate Laos's exports. Vietnam has a more diversified bundle, split between energy, agricultural products and footwear/garments. Beyond its top ten export groups, Vietnam has a further nine groups with at least a 1 percent share in its 2005 exports, and these include electrical and computer equipment as well as primary goods and textiles.

The number of different classes of exports of the Mekong countries and, in particular, those of Cambodia, Vietnam and Myanmar, have remained remarkably stable over recent years, at least at the three-digit level (Table 3.1). All countries have expanded their range of exports but, for the most part, new products have remained a very small proportion of overall export value. Laos made the greatest strides, which reflects the surge in energy and mineral exports. The apparent lack of progress in diversification in Vietnam reflects the gains the country made in earlier periods and the relatively aggregated level of the trade data used for the analysis. When a longer time period and more disaggregated data are used, Vietnam is seen to have diversified particularly rapidly between 1990 and 1995 (IMF 2008).

3.2   Competition with China

An often-used measure of potential competition between countries in export markets is an export similarity index – the nearer 100 percent the index the more similar are export structures. Table 3.2 shows that Vietnam has the most similarity to China, with an index of around 40 percent. The largest contributors are garments and footwear – accounting for around one-quarter of the similarity – but more sophisticated exports such as electrical circuit equipment, computers and telecommunications equipment also make significant contributions. The other countries have much lower indices – in line with those found in African countries (Jenkins and Edwards, 2006). Cambodia's index is only 16 percent despite the fact that

Table 3.1   Mekong countries: number of exported products

	Cambodia	Myanmar	Laos	Vietnam
2000	172	202	137	247
2001	179	201	164	246
2002	186	204	160	247
2003	181	208	174	249
2004	181	200	187	251
2005	195	207	188	250

Source: World Integrated Trade Solution Database, 3-digit classification.

Table 3.2   Mekong countries: export similarity indices with China

	Cambodia	Myanmar	Laos	Vietnam
1995	18	13	18	39
2000	21	20	16	40
2005	16	12	16	38

Source: World Integrated Trade Solution Database, SITC rev. 3-digit classification.

its main exports are in markets in which China is dominant. This last point reflects the fact that the export similarity index is not particularly effective in assessing the threat of a large diversified exporter to a small concentrated exporter. In these cases, it will tend to measure the lack of diversification of small countries rather than the similarity of their exports. A relatively small Chinese export could, in fact, pose a major threat to the Mekong countries in third markets, but would not show up as a major factor in the export similarity index that takes the minimum of the product in the two countries' share of exports.

We, therefore, take an alternative approach, similar to the one proposed by Jenkins and Edwards (2006), by looking at the extent to which the exports in which the Mekong countries have specialized are competing in markets in which China is successful.

Table 3.3 shows that, despite its low export similarity index, Cambodia appears most at threat from China. Its top ten exports are all in categories that China has expanded its market share over the period 2000–05. Laos has some significant exports, particularly electricity, which are not threatened by China, but the majority of its exports – over two-thirds – are in areas where China has expanded its market share. Myanmar, whose exports are most oriented to primary products, appears to be least

Table 3.3   Mekong countries: competition with China in key export markets, 2005

A. Cambodia

Product	Share in Total Exports 2005 (%)	Growth in Market Share (%)	Growth in China's Market Share (%) 2000–05
Articles of apparel nes	32	57	31
Women/girl clothing woven	20	56	42
Women/girl wear knit/croch	13	226	37
Men/boy wear, woven	11	−13	32
Men/boy wear knit/croch	6	156	13
Footwear	5	3	10
Natural rubber/latex/etc	2	−29	162
Wood simply worked	2	511	88
Golf non-monetary ex ore	1	73050	301
Fruits/nuts, fresh/dried	1	662	20

B. Myanmar

Product	Share in Total Exports 2005 (%)	Growth in Market Share (%)	Growth in China's Market Share (%) 2000–05
Natural gas	40	461	−62
Wood in rough/squared	15	34	−46
Vegetables, frsh/chld/froz	10	93	−3
Men/boy wear, woven	4	−8	32
Wood simply worked	4	31	88
Crustaceans molluscs, etc	4	−12	31
Copper	3	19	54
Articles of apparel nes	2	−84	31
Fish, live/frsh/chld/froz	2	88	35
Petrol./bitum. oil, crude	2	−100	−47

C. Lao PDR

Product	Share in Total Exports 2005 (%)	Growth in Market Share (%)	Growth in China's Market Share (%) 2000–05
Wood simply worked	21	116	88
Copper	14	–	54
Articles of apparel nes	12	0	31
Electric current	11	–	−65
Men/boy wear, woven	9	−2	32
Wood in rough/squared	6	−58	−46

Table 3.3   (continued)

Product	Share in Total Exports 2005 (%)	Growth in Market Share (%)	Growth in China's Market Share (%) 2000–05
Women/girl clothing woven	4	34	42
Men/boy wear knit/croch	3	29	13
Coffee/coffee substitute	3	−35	154
Veneer/plywood/etc	1	207	329

D. Vietnam

Product	Share in Total Exports 2005 (%)	Growth in Market Share (%)	Growth in China's Market Share (%) 2000–05
Petrol./bitum. oil, crude	22	1	−47
Footwear	15	52	10
Furniture/stuff furnishing	6	164	71
Articles of apparel nes	4	125	31
Crustaceans molluscs, etc	4	49	31
Men/boy wear, woven	4	46	31
Women/girl clothing woven	4	145	42
Rice	3	73	−73
Coffee/coffee substitute	3	16	154
Coal non-agglomerated	2	94	−2

Source: World Integrated Trade Solution Database.

threatened, with two-thirds of its imports in areas where China's market share has decreased.

Vietnam, with its more varied export bundle, has a mixed story; its large primary product exports are in areas where China's export share has declined (due primarily to its rapidly rising domestic demand for these products). However, its manufactured exports are all in areas where China has increased its market share. Outside of the top ten product lines listed in Table 3.3, the pattern is similar.

Overall, it is clear that China's increasing market share in a particular product class has not inhibited significant growth in market share for the Mekong countries. In fact, in most cases in Table 3.3, a growth in China's market share is associated with a larger – in proportionate terms – growth in the market share of the Mekong countries. The Mekong countries have thus far been able to compete effectively in the (limited number of) areas in which they specialize. The rise of China appears to have opened up opportunities in third markets rather than eroded the competitive space within them for the Mekong countries.

This point is illustrated by the continued growth in the garment industry in the Mekong region, and particularly in Cambodia and Vietnam, following the expiry of the Multi-Fiber Agreement quotas in 2005. Prior to the expiry of these quotas there was widespread nervousness among small garment producers that China's future unfettered access to major markets would all but destroy their industries. In reality, however, this has not occurred, although there have been some reallocations at the margin (for instance, there has been very little growth in the Laos garment industry in recent years). This was aided in part by the safeguard measures placed on China by the United States and the European Union. It also likely reflects a demand for diversification of production location on the part of both buyers and producers.

The garment industry also provides a good illustration of another notable point from Table 3.3: the degree of crossover between the main exports of the Mekong countries. The countries in the region are not just competing against China and beyond, they are competing against each other, particularly in the garment sector. With Vietnam's recent accession to the WTO, and thus quota-free access to the key US garment market, this competition has become more evident. Cambodia, which had enjoyed rapid, mainly double-digit growth in its garment exports to the United States, saw its growth slip markedly in the latter part of 2007 as Vietnam's market share grew.

4   CHINA AS A PARTNER FOR THE MEKONG COUNTRIES

4.1   China as a Trading Partner

Now the largest single source of imports for the Mekong region, China accounted for around 18 percent of total imports in 2005, compared to around 10 percent in 1995 and 2000 (Table 3.4).

To a large extent, growth in imports represents an increasing demand for intermediate goods arising from the growing export industries of the Mekong countries (Table 3.5). A key element of this is machinery and inputs for assembly style manufacturing industries, in particular in the manufacturing (Vietnam) and garments (Cambodia) sector. It also is affected by the development of the Mekong countries and the consequent increasing demand for manufactured and consumer goods, particularly vehicle and engines (Laos and Myanmar).

China has not, as yet, become a significant export market for the

Table 3.4   Mekong countries' trade with China

	1995	2000	2005
Percentage of imports			
Cambodia	4	8	17
Vietnam	4	9	16
Laos	4	5	9
Myanmar	29	18	29
Percentage of exports			
Cambodia	1	2	0
Vietnam	6	11	9
Laos	3	1	3
Myanmar	11	6	7

Source: IMF, Direction of Trade Statistics (n.d.).

Table 3.5   Composition of imports from China, 2005 (in percent of total imports)

Import type[1]	Cambodia	Laos	Myanmar	Vietnam
Primary goods	5	2	14	22
Intermediate goods	80	53	63	63
Finished goods	15	45	23	16

Note: 1.   Author's classification based on three-digit trade classification.

Source: World Integrated Trade Statistics, SITC, rev. 3.

Mekong countries. It accounts on average for around 5 percent of their exports. Cambodia's exports are minimal as are Laos's – which are mainly concentrated in crude materials and manufactures. Vietnam has the largest share of exports to China, which have been mainly concentrated in petroleum products and coal. However, there has also been a growing role for manufactures and machinery, which have all grown by over 100 percent between 2003 and 2006 suggesting that Vietnam may be beginning to become integrated into Chinese production networks.

4.2   Terms of Trade Impact

China's increasing role in world trade also affects the Mekong countries' terms of trade. China's success – and the related rise of efficient Asian production networks – has put downward pressure on the prices of manufactured goods, in particular electronics and textiles. On the other hand,

China's voracious appetite for primary products, particularly oil, minerals and certain foodstuffs, has been a significant contributor to international price rises (Kaplinsky, 2006).

For Cambodia, which has almost no primary exports and substantial imports, the effect has most likely been negative. The opposite holds true in Myanmar, whose trade is dominated by primary exports. For Laos and Vietnam, whose imports and exports contain both primary and finished goods, the effect is likely to have been more balanced.

4.3 China as a Source of External Finance

Export industries in the Mekong countries are, like China's, largely financed by FDI. Although data is limited, there are indications that China is becoming an increasing source of FDI into the Mekong region, mainly in the natural resources areas but also in manufacturing.

The main beneficiary of the increasing Chinese FDI into the Mekong region has been Cambodia – China accounts for around one-third of all FDI, mainly in the garment and tourism industries. China has also become more active in Laos and Myanmar but remains only a peripheral investor in Vietnam. In Laos investments have largely been in the rubber and agribusiness sectors but levels of investment remain much lower than in Cambodia (*Asia Times*, 2007).

Major Chinese investments in Myanmar have been concentrated in the natural gas and primary resource sectors. However, an increasing number of small traders and enterprises from China establishing themselves in Myanmar, largely beyond the scope of formal FDI statistics, provide much of the technology and knowledge transfer into the Myanmar private sector.

Chinese aid has also become more significant in the Mekong region, particularly in Cambodia reflecting, in part, the strong political ties between the two countries dating back to the Khmer Rouge period. Cambodia also shares with the other major African recipients of China's aid potentially significant petroleum resources and, in addition, holds a strategic geographic position. In the other Mekong countries, China does not appear, as yet, to have emerged as a significant formal aid donor.

5 POTENTIAL FUTURE IMPACTS

5.1 The Continuing Rise of China

As the Chinese economy develops and accumulates physical and human capital and technological knowledge, the export mix should gradually change away from the labor-intensive end of the product spectrum in the direction of more knowledge- and capital-intensive activities.

Rising costs, particularly in the coastal areas where manufacturing is agglomerated, are forcing manufacturers to consider alternative destinations for low-cost assembly operations (Fujita and Hamaguchi, 2006; *Economist*, 2007, 2008). The movement could be to other less-developed Asian economies or to inland China where there are greater reserves of relatively cheap surplus labor, but where other operating costs are higher. These alternatives, however, need to be highly attractive as the competitiveness of Chinese exports remains very strong. Key factors in investment decisions would include the availability of cheap effective labor, good infrastructure, easy access to low-cost efficient shipping, and stable political and economic environments.

Chinese demand for imports is also likely to keep growing, both for intermediate goods for the manufacturing industries and for consumer goods for the growing middle class (including services). However, perhaps the most significant changes and developments are likely to be in China's demand for primary products. Demand for food and agricultural imports is likely to increase markedly as labor continues to move out of farming into industry and tariffs are reduced as part of China's WTO commitments. China's demand for metal ores will also continue to add significantly to world demand and prices (Deutsche Bank, 2006).

Energy demands, however, will dominate. The International Energy Association (2007) estimated that China will become the largest energy user in the world in 2010, overtaking the United States. This need for reliable sources of oil and energy is likely to continue to influence China's outward looking policies.

5.2 Implications for the Mekong Countries

China's growing demand for primary products and its upward influence on world prices perhaps represents the most significant short-term opportunity for the Mekong countries to increase their exports. With their fertile agricultural land, water resources and high potential for further mineral and oil discoveries, the Mekong countries are well set to increase their share in many of the key primary product markets.

All the Mekong countries produce rice. Vietnam is one of the world's largest rice exporters and Cambodia has been steadily increasing its exports in recent years. Rubber is also produced – Cambodian production has been decreasing recently, while production has been increasing rapidly in Laos, much of it under Chinese investment.

In fuel and energy too, the Mekong countries are all well placed to maintain and expand exports. Myanmar and Vietnam have substantial resources of oil and natural gas. Cambodia has potentially significant offshore oil and natural gas resources under exploration, although none are under development as yet. Laos will over the coming years produce significant volumes of electricity from the large hydro projects currently under development.

China's demand for other resources both renewable and non-renewable such as wood products and minerals could also be an opportunity for the Mekong countries. All the countries have substantial forested areas that could, if well managed, provide a sustainable export income for years to come. Mineral companies are also currently prospecting or producing a number of products across the region.

While a growing market in primary products with improving terms of trade could significantly improve the medium-term external position of the Mekong countries, it is not sufficient to enable them to catch up economically and socially with their ASEAN peers. This requires development of the manufacturing and, ultimately, service industries sectors. A key element of this strategy is likely to be establishing policies that enable them to participate more in the East Asian production networks.

For the Mekong countries, in particular the three smaller and poorer countries, their main competitive weapon is their low-wage levels (Table 3.6, panel B). All have relatively low levels but are not significantly lower than their main competitors for new investment including China. Wages also need to be reinforced by productivity, which is dependent, in part, on public investment in education and training. With the exception of Vietnam, the Mekong countries fare much worse in this area than most of their competitors. Nevertheless, in Vietnam, skilled managerial workers remain scarce and the premium placed on them is reflected in the wages shown in Table 3.6 – over five times the rate for similar workers in coastal China.

A key factor for integrating into the East Asian production networks is the ease of shipping, as most components are transferred between network participants by sea. One of the reasons for the agglomeration of industry in China is the simplicity of shipping from the coastal cities. Landlocked Laos faces the greatest barrier among the Mekong countries in this regard. Nevertheless, in utilizing cheap Thai gateways it has been able to keep shipping costs relatively low. Vietnam, with its long accessible coastline and reasonably low cost ports, is strongly advantaged in this area, while Cambodia and Myanmar have a theoretic advantage which is only being partially utilized at present.

Macroeconomic stability and management of economic and fiscal policies is a key element of competitiveness. It has improved markedly in

Vietnam and Cambodia and, somewhat more recently, in Laos. Myanmar has also made some progress, but remains well behind the other Mekong countries and the more industrialized ASEAN countries in this regard.[6] All four countries exhibit high levels of political stability, with *de jure* or *de facto* one-party political systems.

Weak public administrations and widespread problems in the quality and reliability of governance, including widespread corruption, hamper the Mekong countries' competitiveness (panel C of Table 3.6). The Mekong countries all rank in the bottom third of the Transparency International Corruption Perceptions Index with Cambodia, Laos and Myanmar all in the bottom 10 percent.

A useful summary indicator of the impact of the quality of governance on business costs is the World Bank's cost of doing business index (panel A of Table 3.6). This ranks 178 countries on a number of categories. The database covers three of the four Mekong countries (Myanmar is excluded) and all of their main competitors for investment in export-oriented industries. Cambodia and Laos rank very poorly at 145 and 164. Vietnam, however, performs much better on the doing business indicators, outperforming most of the regional competitors with a ranking close to that of China.

6 CONCLUSIONS

The rise of China has not, as yet, impeded the growth of the Mekong countries. In fact, as China was accelerating its growth and trade, three of the Mekong countries – Cambodia, Laos and Vietnam – also underwent successful periods of economic and trade growth. The reasons behind the slower growth in Myanmar are largely unrelated to China's rise and derive from domestic political and governance issues.

Continued growth in China's demand for primary products will likely continue to advantage the Mekong countries. Increased exports of these products in a global environment of rising prices should provide a firm foundation for the Mekong countries' external position over the medium term.

Increasing the scale and scope of manufacturing exports is, however, key to enabling the Mekong countries to catch up economically and socially with their ASEAN peers. The continued rise of China will present some opportunities here, particularly as investors – including from China – look for new locations to source their assembly operations as costs continue to rise in coastal China. However, competition in this area will be intense, both from inland China and other Asian countries.

Table 3.6   Mekong countries: indicators of competitiveness

	Cambodia	Laos	Myanmar	Vietnam	China
A. World Bank Cost of Doing Business Index, 2007 (Ranking)					
Overall rank	145	164	–	91	83
Starting a business	162	78	–	97	135
Dealing with licenses	144	111	–	63	175
Employing workers	133	82	–	84	86
Registering properly	98	149	–	38	29
Getting credit	177	170	–	48	84
Protecting investors	64	176	–	165	83
Paying taxes	21	114	–	128	168
Trading across borders	139	158	–	63	42
Enforcing contracts	134	111	–	40	20
B. JETRO Investments-Related Cost Comparisons Survey, 2007 (In US dollars)					
Wages (monthly)					
Workers	100	69	25	169	111
Engineers	170	217	51	391	215
Managers	300	417	114	1526	334
Rent (per square meter)					
Industrial estate	1.8	1.0	0.3	0.2	1.5
Office	8.0	7.5	15.0	35.2	32.0
Electricity (Business use, kWh)	0.16	0.07	0.08	0.08	0.10
Gasoline (per liter)	1.0	0.9	0.3	0.7	0.7
Transport (per container)					
Japan (Yokohama)	1755	1255	1800	750	300
United States (Los Angeles)	3806	4306	–	2450	2000
International phone call (per minute)	2.7	1.8	8.1	1.6	3
C. Transparency International (Ranking)					
Perceptions of Corruption Index, 2007	162	168	179	123	72

Sources: World Bank (2007); Overseas Research Department (n.d.), Japan External Trade Organization (2007).

India	Bangladesh	Philippines	Indonesia	Sri Lanka	Pakistan
120	107	133	123	101	76
111	92	144	168	29	59
134	116	77	99	160	93
85	129	122	153	111	132
112	171	86	121	134	88
36	48	97	68	97	68
33	15	141	51	64	19
165	81	126	110	158	146
79	112	57	41	60	94
177	175	113	141	133	154
267	57	283	113	96	179
463	126	359	299	184	474
1011	310	843	753	453	865
7.2	0.1	1.0	5.5	0.9	0.0
14.9	7.1	7.5	10.9	9.5	18.2
0.09	0.18	0.10	0.09	0.18	0.08
1.2	0.9	0.8	0.5	0.9	1.0
834	1650	950	1205	700	700
2824	3400	2525	3900	3900	6000
0.8	1.1	1.2	1.2	0.6	0.3
72	162	131	143	94	138

Working to the Mekong countries' advantage in this process is their geographic position (they are strategically located at the heart of the East Asian production networks), their membership of ASEAN and WTO (for all but Laos) – which provides relatively good access to final markets, including the United States and the European Union – and their low wage levels. These are all strong factors in investment decisions. Vietnam has the added advantage that it has a relatively large domestic market in which final products can be sold. However its wage levels do not provide significant advantages over Chinese levels. The Mekong countries also all have relatively high non-wage business costs that could hamper their competitiveness going forward. Governance and corruption are particular concerns here.

It is important, therefore, that the Mekong countries devise and implement policies that improve their competitiveness. Not doing so would not only reduce their prospects of increasing their share in future regional and global growth, but also could jeopardize recent gains. Many of the export industries in the Mekong countries, and particularly the important garment industry, are relatively footloose and can move rapidly to other locations if the current host countries' competitiveness begins to erode. In the near future, the expiry of safeguards measures of the United States and the European Union on China will provide a stern test of the real underlying competitiveness of the garment industries in the Mekong region.

Four broad policy areas should be priorities in this regard.

Firstly, continued strengthening of macroeconomic policies is required to promote growth and low inflation in a more complex global economic environment. This is essential to attract investors and maintain export competitiveness. However, the more integrated with the global economy a country becomes, the more challenging setting these policies becomes. The three rapidly growing Mekong economies that are reasonably integrated with the global economy – Cambodia, Laos and Vietnam – are beginning to find this out. All are currently observing, to a greater or lesser extent, the problems that are playing out on a larger stage in China: coping with surging inflation and rapid monetary growth fueled by foreign inflows while maintaining real exchange rate competitiveness.

Secondly, financial sectors, particularly in the three poorer countries, need development to assist in macroeconomic policy implementation and facilitate inward portfolio investment, which at present is only a feature of Vietnam's external financing.

Thirdly, both public and private investment in physical infrastructure, particularly ports and roads, needs to be increased to lower operating costs for investors. Investment in improving human capital, through enhanced education and training of the workforce, is also required to improve future productivity. This will require improved fiscal policy and wise utilization of available external aid, including from China.

Finally, improving governance and reducing corruption is essential. The low ranking of the Mekong countries on all major indices of governance is a reflection of current weaknesses and a very public signal to potential investors of the difficulties in doing business in the region.

NOTES

1. The author is greatly indebted to Messrs Murtaza Syed, Masahiko Takeda, Ben Bingham and Lazaros Molho for guidance in the early stages of this chapter, Ms Suchitra Kumarapathy for her invaluable research assistance and Deb Loucks for editorial support. All views and errors remain, of course, those of the author and do not necessarily represent the views of the IMF.
2. See country case studies (Chapters 7–10) for details on the nature of the Mekong countries' development over this period.
3. This section provides a stylized rather than exhaustive overview of the key features of the rise of China and the impact it has had on other countries in Asia; for more detailed accounts see Eichengreen et al. (2004), IMF (2004), Gill and Kharas (2006), and World Bank (2006)
4. See Gill and Kharas (2006, chapter 5) for a more detailed description of this process.
5. China's expanding trade surplus with the United States to some extent mirrors its large deficit with the rest of East Asia.
6. See country case studies for detail on macroeconomic progress and policy issues.

REFERENCES

Ahearne, A., J. Fernald, P. Loungani and J. Schindler (2003), 'China and emerging Asia: comrades or competitors?', Board of Governors of the Federal Reserve System international finance discussion paper no. 789, Washington DC.

Asia Times (2007), 'China rubber demand stretches Laos', *Asia Times Online*, 19 December.

Baldwin, R. (2006), 'Globalisation: the great unbundling(s)', paper prepared for Globalisation Challenges for Europe and Finland project, September, Economic Council of Finland.

Branstetter, L. and N. Lardy (2006), 'China's embrace of globalization', National Bureau of Economic Research working paper no. 12373, Cambridge, MA.

Cui, L. and M. Syed (2007), 'The Shifting Structure of China's Trade and Production', International Monetary Fund working paper no.07/214, Washington DC.

Deutsche Bank (2006), 'China's commodity hunger: implications for Africa and Latin America', Deutsche Bank Research, *Current Issues*, 13 June.

Deutsche Bank (2006a), 'Global champions in waiting: perspectives on China's overseas direct investment', Deutsche Bank Research, *Current Issues*, 4 August.

Eichengreen, B., Y. Rhee and H. Tong (2004), 'The impact of China on the exports of other Asian countries', National Bureau of Economic Research working paper no.10768, Cambridge, MA.

Fujita, M. and N. Hamaguchi (2006), 'The coming age of China-plus-one: the Japanese perspective on East Asian production networks', draft paper for the World Bank–IPS Research Project on the Rise of China and India.

Gill, I. and H. Kharas (2006), *An East Asian Renaissance: Ideas for Economic Growth*, Washington DC: World Bank.

International Energy Association (IEA) (2007), *World Energy Outlook 2007: China and India Insights*, Paris: IEA.

International Monetary Fund (IMF) (2004), 'China's emergence and its impact in the global economy', *World Economic Outlook*, April, Washington DC.

IMF (2008), 'Bangladesh: selected issues', IMF country report no. 08/335, Washington DC.

Jenkins, R. and C. Edwards (2006), 'The Asian drivers and Sub-Saharan Africa', *IDS Bulletin*, **37** (1), 23–32.

Kaplinsky, R. (2006), 'China and the global terms of trade', *IDS Bulletin*, **37** (1), 43–53.

Loungani, P. (2000), 'Comrades or competitors?: Trade links between China and other East Asian economies', *Finance & Development*, **37** (2), June.

Soesastro, H. (2006), 'Regional integration in East Asia: achievements and future prospects', *Asian Economic Policy Review*, **1**, 215–34.

The Economist (2007), 'The problem with made in China', 11 January, US edn.

The Economist (2008), 'No fun and games', 10 January, US edn.

United States International Trade Commission (2006), *The Effects of Increasing Chinese Demand on Global Commodity Markets*, publication no. 3864, June.

World Bank (2006), *Dancing with Giants: China, India and the Global Economy*, Washington, DC: World Bank, chapters 2 and 3.

4. Finance, trade and development in East Asia: opportunities for Mekong economies

Suiwah Leung

1 INTRODUCTION

Before the financial crisis in 1997 most East Asian countries relegated financial development to the policy back-burner. Even the early 1980s debt crisis, which sparked a spate of financial deregulation, left the conventional wisdom that finance followed and complemented trade unexamined. Government policies needed to focus only on export-led growth and financial development would follow.

In the early days of the Japan-centred production network from the 1980s through to the mid-1990s, Japanese banks supported Japanese companies in financing trade in Taiwan, South Korea and the ASEAN 4 (Malaysia, Philippines, Thailand and Indonesia). Japanese bank finance was usually intermediated through domestic banks because of the latter's superior local knowledge (Gill and Kharas 2007). Concurrently, central banks pursued exchange rate stability by pegging the region's currencies to a US dollar-dominated basket (Frankel and Wei 1994). Hence, Asian banks managed the credit risk while Asian governments managed the exchange rate risk (Gill and Kharas 2007). The failure of this strategy became painfully apparent during the 1997 banking and currency crisis (the Asian financial crisis).

The economic and political consequences of the crisis re-focused government attention on financial development. Reform concentrated on clearing non-performing loans, better managing the region's accumulated international reserves and building sound securities markets. Consequently, the 2008 global financial crisis has had a relatively small impact on the region's banking and financial sector, although the negative fallout in trade and the real economy has necessarily been larger (McGuire and Tarashev 2008).

The wealth of theoretical and empirical evidence on the positive contribution of financial development to economic growth also motivated reform (see Levine 2004). Section 2 briefly examines this literature while highlighting the issues relevant for the Mekong 4. Section 3 looks at financial development in emerging East Asia since the Asian financial crisis, and discusses the implications for countries in the Mekong sub-region. Section 4 discusses the regional initiatives in the light of developments in the market. The concluding section discusses some of the policy priorities for financial sector development in the Mekong 4.

2   WHY FINANCIAL DEVELOPMENT?

In the *Wealth of Nations* (1776) Adam Smith emphasized the importance of innovation through specialization for increased productivity. The use of money as a medium of exchange significantly reduced the information and transactions costs associated with barter, making specialization and exchange easier.

Component production and assembly within a vertically-integrated supply chain (the production network) is an elaborate version of Smith's pin factory where the production process is broken down into its components enabling specialization of labour, capital and technology in the production of parts and in the assembly of the final product. Such specialization enables developing countries to participate in this trade at the lower end of the technological spectrum (Baldwin 2006). This increases the range of economic activities in which low-income developing countries can participate (see Chapter 2).

However, increased specialization of production processes increases transactions costs ('service link' costs),[1] which include costs associated with payments – both financial and 'time costs'. Lowering payments costs increases the range of 'on the shelf' production processes that are economically attractive for investors (Greenwood and Smith 1996). Developing countries with a sound banking and payments system can better lower the transactions costs associated with payments and hence participate in the intra-regional components trade.

The importance of financial development extends beyond providing an efficient payments system.[2] Financial intermediaries (commercial banks, pension funds, stock brokers, investment banks, and so on) undertake the costly business of finding out about firms and their management and help direct investment capital towards those enterprises with the best chance of success.[3]

This important feature of a well-functioning financial system is supported by studies using firm-level data to examine the effect of financial sector reforms in Ecuador and Indonesia on the allocation of credit (Caprio et al. 1994). On a panel of several hundred Ecuadorian firms and over two hundred Indonesian firms, financial liberalization resulted in a flow of credit to the more efficient firms.

Underdeveloped financial systems fail to allocate scarce capital efficiently and result in credit rationing, which constrains the development of the private sector. Lack of access to finance is a constant complaint on the part of small–medium-sized enterprises (SMEs) in several Mekong countries. As shown by Boyd and Smith (1992), poor financial development in developing countries could actually result in scarce capital flowing out to capital-rich countries with higher quality financial systems. This is consistent with the observation that an estimated 54 percent of bank credit in Cambodia went to investments overseas. The lack of legal protection for lenders and inadequate dispute resolution mechanism grossly undermine the resource allocation function of the country's banking system (Leung 2009). Often, where legal infrastructure is weak, informal finance takes up the vacuum left by the formal finance sector (in the case of Vietnam, for example, see McMillan and Woodruff 1999). But in the absence of government subsidies informal financial markets generally have high costs of funds resulting in high interest rates to borrowers (Ghate 1992).

Remittances provide a further link between financial development and economic growth in developing countries. Econometric evidence indicates that remittances are driven as much by profit as by altruism (Lueth and Ruiz-Arranz 2006). Consequently, lowering transactions costs – via improved financial development and reductions in barriers to current account transactions – raises the flow of remittances back to home countries. Certainly, policies in Vietnam to reduce barriers to current account transactions probably resulted in significant increases in receipts of remittances from 2005 through 2007.[4] The likelihood of profit, as well as anecdotal evidence, indicates such receipts could fund family enterprises engaged in production networks.[5] However, systematic analyses of the actual use of remittances are presently unavailable.

A well-functioning financial system also helps countries finance large 'lumpy, investment projects, particularly in ports, roads, railways and telecommunication projects essential to improving developing countries' 'connectivity' with the international economy. While governments of some low-income developing countries can reasonably expect funding from aid donors, the ability of these governments to raise investment funds on their own will enhance the likelihood of donor contributions to these infrastructure projects. The Vietnamese government has had some success in recent years in borrowing on the international market by issuing US dollar-denominated bonds. This type of borrowing, however, exposes the government to exchange rate risks. A well-functioning domestic bond market would enable the government to tap into domestic savings by issuing bonds denominated in its domestic currency, thus reducing the exchange rate risks involved in issuing US dollar bonds. This would also provide additional channels for household and domestic corporate investments and help diversify away from real estate and stock markets, which have been responsible for much of the asset price bubbles and macroeconomic turbulence of early to mid-2008.

There are therefore several cogent reasons for developing countries to focus on financial development. These include facilitating ease of payments resulting in enhanced foreign direct investment (FDI) and remittances inflows, efficient allocation of scarce capital leading to a reduction of the credit constraint on the domestic private sector and pooling of savings for the public funding of large infrastructure projects.

3 FINANCIAL DEVELOPMENT SINCE THE CRISIS OF 1997

3.1 Continued Importance of Banks in Emerging East Asia

As seen in Table 4.1, commercial bank loans to non-financial sectors as a percentage of GDP are generally much higher in East Asia compared with Latin America and Eastern Europe.[6] Financial development in the Mekong 4, however, is uneven. While commercial bank loans as a percentage of GDP has more than doubled in Vietnam over the past five years, and is approaching the levels of the other emerging East Asian countries, the banking sectors of the other three economies are grossly under-developed (for more detailed discussion, see Chapters 7–10).

3.2 FDI in Banking Relatively Low but Increasing Rapidly in Emerging East Asia

The Asian financial crisis represents a watershed in terms of policy changes towards FDI in banking. With the notable exception of Malaysia, all the other countries relaxed restrictions against FDI in their banking sectors. Together with substantial write-downs of capital due to non-performing loans of local banks, this meant that foreign ownership in banking increased, particularly in Thailand and South Korea. FDI in Indonesia's banking sector has also grown considerably since the financial crisis, albeit from a very low base.[7] Furthermore, given that Indonesia has had the greatest degree of liberalization in terms of foreign bank entry into

Table 4.1 Some features of bank systems in emerging market economies

Country	Commercial bank loans (percent of GDP)[1]	Three largest banks' share of all commercial banks' assets[2]
East Asia		
China	213[3]	65
Hong Kong	148	76
Singapore	111	94
Korea	108	53
Malaysia	107	47
Thailand	94	47
Philippines	36	56
Indonesia	32	58
Mekong 4		
Cambodia	14	89
Lao	9	96
Myanmar	6	100
Vietnam	85	57
Latin America		
Argentina	23	43
Brazil	78	66
Chile	67	56
Mexico	30	63
Peru	20	79
Venezuela	23	42
Eastern Europe		
Czech	56	67
Poland	46	63
Russia	35	16
Estonia	84	94
Bulgaria	59	53
Hungary	71	75
Slovakia	53	75

Notes and sources
Data are shown for the latest year available, which are mainly 2007.
(1) Commercial bank loans to non-financial sectors. *Source*: Beck et al. (2000). Data updated by authors up to 2007 (see: http://econ.worldbank.org/WBSITE/ EXTERNAL/EXTDEC/EXTRESEARCH/0,,contentMDK:20696167~pagePK:64214 825~piPK:64214943~theSitePK:469382,00.html).
(2) *Source:* secondary source as above. Primary source, *Fitch's BankScope database*.
(3) *Source:* the China Banking Regulatory Commission, accessed 11 April 2009: (http:// www.cbrc.gov.cn/english/home/jsp/docView.jsp?docID=20071112169537BCC40F1A9 5FF169F0FB9383B00).

the sector, its growth in financial sector FDI does not seem to have been commensurate with policy changes in this area.

In China several foreign financial institutions have recently taken minority stakes (between 10 and 25 percent) in the country's three largest banks, amounting to US$18 billion (Domanski 2005). With China's commitments to WTO, particularly the reduction in barriers to trade in services, the trend towards FDI in banking (and financial services more generally) is expected to continue and accelerate.

3.3   Changing Character of Foreign Banks in Emerging East Asia

There is evidence that non-Japanese Asian banks are beginning to invest actively in the region. Chua (2003) cites the acquisition of major stakes in two Thai banks by DBS and UOB (both Singapore-based banks); the interest by Taiwan and Hong Kong banks in several Filipino banks; and Hong Kong and Singapore banks acquiring interests in mainland Chinese banks and some Vietnamese joint stock banks.[8] Also, several non-Japanese Asian banks are interested in the bank divestment and privatization programme in Indonesia. Possibly one-quarter of financial sector FDI in emerging Asia comes from banks that are domiciled in the region excluding Japan (Domanski 2005).

Recapitalization of weak banks in the wake of the Asian financial crisis and the subsequent divestment and privatization programmes form a natural vehicle for FDI in banking through mergers, acquisitions and the establishment of subsidiaries.[9] Mergers and acquisitions, in turn, mean that foreign banks have almost instant access to the retail branch networks of the local banks. Consequently, foreign banks pursue business in local markets rather than passively service the needs of the multinationals. Local currency loans of Bank of International Settlements (BIS) reporting banks in the region have, for example, overtaken the amount of foreign loans in recent years (Wooldridge et al. 2003; Hohl et al. 2007). Furthermore, as in the case of Thailand, fee-based incomes from consumer finance and investment banking services are forming a substantial part of the incomes of local banks that are merged with foreign banks (Okuda and Rungsomboon 2006).

3.4   Implications of Increased FDI in Banking for Domestic Economies

Mergers and acquisitions inevitably involve greater linkages with parent banks, resulting not only in the transfer of skilled human resources, but also back office routines, credit control systems and other infrastructures, including IT systems. Empirical analyses of microeconomic bank-level data of Thailand shows that the four foreign-acquired banks performed significantly better in terms of improved technology, superior risk management, and generally increased efficiency. These four Thai banks also increased their fee-based incomes while retaining their share of interest incomes via traditional intermediation functions. In summary, increased foreign penetration of the Thai banking sector increased economies of scale as well as economies of scope, with significant benefits to the consumers (Okuda and Rungsomboon 2006).

At the same time, the continuing US credit crisis shows that, as globalization and deregulation in finance continues, significantly increased complexity in financial products can outstrip the financial literacy of consumers. The implications of this for system stability and hence for the role of the central bank is only starting to surface in policy debates (Adams 2008).

Nevertheless, evidence suggests that at the less complex end of the financial spectrum increased foreign penetration into the banking sectors of emerging East Asian economies produces positive results. These are salutary lessons for the Mekong 4 seeking rapid transformations of their largely backward banking sectors. Such transformations are particularly necessary for those developing countries taking part in the regional production networks.

Three types of finance are needed for participation in the production network (Gill and Kharas 2007):

- FDI in manufacturing for capital investments in building, machinery, and relevant infrastructure;
- Short-term trade credit;[10]
- More 'patient' capital for firms to undertake innovation necessary to move up the value chain in these networks.

In the case of Vietnam, registered as well as disbursed FDI has picked up since 2002 and is estimated to exceed the peak levels in 1996/97, despite expected falls in 2009 due to the global recession. In spite of some pick-up in recent years in Lao and Cambodia, the levels of FDI are very much lower than that of Vietnam (see Figure 4.1).

Given the relatively low (albeit increasing) levels of per capita income in the Mekong 4, bank credit will probably remain a main source of finance for industry for the foreseeable future.[11] Finally, at the levels at which the Mekong 4 are likely to participate in the production networks, the sort of innovations required would be more in the nature of marginal improvements or economic discoveries rather than significant breakthroughs in product designs or production techniques. Thus, bank finance rather than

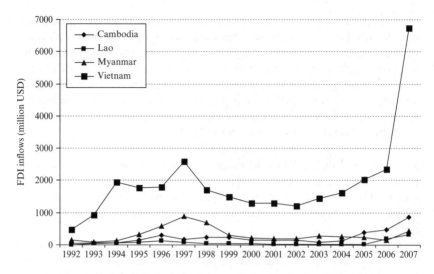

Source: UNCTAD Foreign Direct Investment database: accessed 11 April 2009.

Figure 4.1   Disbursed FDI inflows into Mekong economies

capital raisings in the securities markets is likely to remain important and, indeed, desirable, as bank managers would be responsible for monitoring loans to such businesses and applying necessary financial disciplines (Gill and Kharas 2007). Furthermore, given the evidence of profit motive in remittances and the fact that reductions in transactions costs significantly increase the flow of remittances (see the discussion in Section 2 on Lueth and Ruiz-Arranz 2006), an efficient banking sector with linkages to banks in the Asian region and the world could considerably ease the financial constraints involved in the production networks. For these reasons, rapid improvement in their domestic banking sector through increased FDI in banking would seem to be a priority for the Mekong 4.[12]

3.5   Securities Markets

Stock market capitalization in the region has grown 3.5 times in the past decade, mostly in the financial centres of Hong Kong and Singapore. Cross-listing by international firms is relatively low, and by other Asian firms even lower (Belaisch and Zanello 2006).[13] Cross-listing in the major financial centres and of the region (and the world) could be encouraged and would improve the corporate governance of firms in emerging East Asia, including the fledgling private firms in the Mekong 4. To the extent that these firms could enhance their reputation by listing on well-established stock exchanges they would also find it easier to gain access to bank finance. Bank-based and market-based systems reinforce each other in the early stages of financial development (Demirgüç-Kunt and Maksimovic 1996).

Since the 1997 crisis domestic currency bonds have also grown almost three-fold in emerging East Asia but these are supported primarily by government bond-raisings in all countries except Hong Kong.[14] The negative impact of the crisis on government budgets, together with the need to re-capitalize banks in some crisis countries, created the need for substantial government bond-raisings.

Corporate bond raisings are not common and even where they do occur (as in Malaysia), they are generally associated with semi-government authorities backed by government guarantees. Cross-border impediments such as capital controls, as well as local market impediments including withholding taxes, taxes on financial transactions and lack of market development generally have been identified as major challenges to the continued growth of regional bond markets (Gyntelberg et al. 2006). To the extent that regional initiatives such as the Asian Bond Fund II are able to remove some of the above impediments they will contribute to continued bond market development in the region (see Section 4).

Government bond-raisings in the Mekong 4 for major infrastructure investments are important for economic development generally and for domestic firms participating in the production networks in particular. Therefore, reducing impediments to the growth of bond markets should also benefit the Mekong 4, although at this stage of economic development their participation in corporate bonds could only be a longer-term goal.

In conclusion, the improved banking environment together with the trend towards increased FDI in banking could be beneficial for the Mekong 4 in helping transform their backward banking sectors.[15] Continued development of equities and bond markets would be necessary for firms in emerging East Asia to gain finance for significant innovations in order to move up the value chain in the regional production networks. However, with the possible exception of Vietnam, the value of securities markets at this stage seems more limited for the latecomers in the Mekong.

4 REGIONAL INITIATIVES TO SUPPORT MARKET DEVELOPMENTS

Increased FDI in banking requires cooperation between prudential supervisors across national jurisdictions.[16] An incident involving a bank's subsidiary may have serious ramifications, resulting in systemic risk in the host country, but only relatively minor impact on the bank's headquarter country. Supervisors in the two countries could differ in their decisions as to whether the subsidiary should be rescued and by whom. This problem is acute if the banking subsidiary is a major institution in a small developing country (such as in the Mekong 4), but the parent-bank is a relatively minor concern headquartered in an advanced industrialized country.[17]

Indeed, continuing dialogue and cooperation amongst supervisors would not only help in situations of crisis, but would also assist in the implementation of Basel II. As Basel II stresses the assessment of capital adequacy based on an individual bank's own assessment of risks in its asset portfolio, Asian countries have seen this as a way of enhancing their banks' risk management and reducing the reliance on collaterals (Hohl et al. 2006). However, effective implementation of Basel II requires a level of expertise from both banks and their supervisors that is, at times, not observed even in developed, let alone developing countries. The 2007–08 subprime crisis in the US reflects, at least in part, a failure in prudential supervision.[18] The smooth functioning of the world banking system is a public good that requires the combined efforts of national governments.

As for development of government bond markets in the region, the Asian Bond Funds 1 and 2 (ABF1 and ABF2) are in place. In June 2003, the 11 EMEAP central banks pooled international reserves of $1 billion and invested in bonds issued by sovereign and quasi-sovereign borrowers from eight of the 11 EMEAP countries.[19] ABF1 bonds are denominated in US dollars. The intention is to enable Asian emerging market governments to learn how to issue bonds to international investors.[20] In 2005, the ABF2 was launched, drawing on combined international reserves of $2 billion from the EMEAP central banks to be invested in local-currency-denominated bonds.

After the Asian financial crisis concern grew that Asian governments were only able to borrow internationally in securities denominated in US dollars, leaving them bearing all the exchange rate risks (the so-called 'original sin' problem, see Eichengreen 1999). Hence, from this point of view, ABF2 is meant to open the way for Asian governments to borrow in securities denominated in their own currencies. However, the small size and the illiquidity of the ABF secondary markets adds little if issuing debt in their own currencies was the sole intention of the ABF initiative.

On the other hand, in getting the EMEAP central banks to participate in the market via the ABFs, authorities actually learn at first hand about the impediments faced by international investors with regard to investing in domestic-currency bonds. These include not only the obvious ones associated with capital controls such as bureaucratic approvals for the repatriation of capital and interest, but also other barriers such as with-holding taxes, taxes on financial transactions, and inefficient clearing and payments systems. This type of hands-on learning has been effective in promoting the lowering and eventual removal of a number of barriers amongst the governments in emerging East Asia (Ma and Remolona 2005). In addition, the ABF Pan Asian Bond Index provides a regional benchmark for the development of bond markets generally. In this sense the ABFs may indeed have been a useful market-supporting exercise with potentially valuable lessons for the Mekong 4 as well.

Stock markets worldwide are prone to bubbles – often with adverse consequences for the real economy. In emerging Asia, Korea (Feb. 1986–Jan. 1988), Indonesia (Jan.–Dec. 1988), China (Mar. 1992–Feb. 1993), and more recently, Vietnam (Mar. 2006–Feb. 2007) have all seen double- and triple-digit annual percentage increases in stock prices.[21] In these circumstances, rapid portfolio inflows, coupled with undisciplined domestic bank lending, could increase the risks of banking and currency crises. Macroeconomic monitoring and regional peer review associated with the Chiang Mai Initiative could prove helpful for the Mekong 4, in addition, of course, to the regular surveillance and monitoring on the part of the IMF. From the viewpoint of longer-term market development (as distinct from management of 'bubbles'), regional initiatives for compa-nies to cross-list in the Hong Kong and Singapore exchanges would be beneficial in terms of improved corporate governance and could assist in minimization of 'bubbles' in emerging market countries where corporate governance is generally weak.

5 CONCLUSIONS – IMPLICATIONS FOR LATECOMERS IN THE MEKONG REGION

The growth of production networks in East Asia since the 1980s had relied on foreign direct investment by multinational companies in countries with low wages and large pools of unskilled labour to produce manufacturing goods for export to the developed OECD countries. This occurred against the backdrop of a global multilateral trading system and relatively stable exchange rate regimes. The transactions costs involved in inefficient pay-ments systems and the financing costs of making economic discoveries for domestic firms to move up the value chain in the production networks were considered relatively insignificant.

With the challenges to the multilateral trading system and the growth of various preferential trading agreements in the new millennium (see Chapter 6), the outlook for latecomers to the network is uncertain. In addition, the 1997 Asian financial crisis and the pressing need for a number of the original ASEAN-6 to remain competitive in the networks re-focused attention on financial development. Section 2 of this chapter identifies the importance of financial development as a means of lowering transactions/ service link costs within the network, of financing domestic firms in moving up the value chain within the network and of funding physical infrastructure projects to reduce further the service link costs of the networks. Faced with a considerably more competitive environment, the latecomers of the Mekong need to develop their financial sectors rapidly.

Section 3 points out that FDI in banking services could result in rapid transformation of the largely backward banking sectors in the Mekong 4. With the possible exception of Vietnam, the level of monetization in the other three countries is low, less than 10 percent of GDP. This is largely a result of immature banking sectors and lack of confidence in the use of banking services. Even in Vietnam, the state-owned commercial banks (SOCBs) occupy over 50 percent of the total assets of the banking sector and the historical ties to the state-owned enterprises (SOEs) are still strong. Nevertheless, lowering barriers to entry for foreign banks would increase the competition for the domestic banks (both state-owned and private) as well as help increase the public's confidence in the use of banking services.

In Cambodia, two foreign banking subsidiaries were established in 2005 and attracted large shares of deposits from the single Cambodian domestic private bank.[22] In Lao PDR, a number of foreign banking subsidiaries have also been established in recent years and there are several branches of Thai-owned banks. Nevertheless, the state-owned banks still play a dominant role. As an extreme case, no foreign bank operates in Myanmar at all, and since the banking crisis of 2003, domestic banks provide only payments services and do not currently operate as financial intermediaries (see Chapter 9 below).

It is clear that there is considerable scope for lowering barriers to entry in their banking sectors in order for the Mekong 4 to take advantage of the growth in FDI in banking services both globally and within the Asian region. This could range from raising the stakes (from 30 percent) available for foreign investment in domestic banks in Vietnam, to permitting foreign banks to open branches, take local deposits, and service mining companies in Lao PDR. Lowering entry barriers would, of course, have to be done in conjunction with measures to strengthen financial markets more generally, such as improved legal framework for accessing collateral, some form of credit information system for the assessment of risks, and an interbank mechanism to allow banks to compete as well as to collaborate in order to spread risks more evenly throughout the system. Increased financial literacy amongst consumers is also beginning to be recognized as an element contributing to financial system stability. The entry of foreign banks can add to the pressure to modernize the financial infrastructure whilst at the same time, foreign entrants bring with them technical know-how and human resources to enable such modernization to take place.

Strengthening the financial infrastructure would also help in the development of equities markets and bond markets. As discussed in Section 4, equities markets are subject to speculative bubbles, and careful management is needed to avoid spillovers into macroeconomic instability. Furthermore, development of securities markets has implications for exchange control arrangements of these countries, in addition to the streamlining of withholding taxes and financial institutions' taxes.

In short, for the latecomers in the Mekong to integrate rapidly into the regional trading and financial arrangements, considerable deepening of reforms in their own economies are needed. Precise measures depend on the stage of economic transformation of each individual country and will be examined in the case studies (Chapters 7–10).

NOTES

1. First identified by Kimura and Ando (2003)
2. Hicks (1969) maintains that the technological discoveries responsible for the Industrial Revolution were made decades earlier, but the 'lumpiness' of the capital investments needed to bring those discoveries on stream meant that financial development such as the advent of the joint-stock firm was needed in order to pool savings and spread the risks before the application of new technologies could be funded.
3. Initially, much of the investment capital for the expansion of production networks to a new country is likely to be provided through foreign direct investment and suppliers' credit. However, these sources will only finance a relatively limited role for domestic entrepreneurs. In particular, innovation by domestic entrepreneurs is likely to be constrained in the absence of access to domestic finance.
4. These policies include removal of tax on remittances (1997), removal of restrictions that remittances could only be taken out in VN dong (1999) and removal of restrictions on the type of financial institutions qualified to handle remittances (2002). Remittances rose from about 5.5 percent of GDP in 2001 to almost 8 percent of GDP in 2007.
5. At the end of 2007 overseas Vietnamese had invested in about 3000 small–medium-sized projects worth about US$2 billion (Committee for Overseas Vietnamese Affairs 17/1/2008).
6. As at 2005, holdings of government assets in Indonesian and Philippine banks amounted to around 15 percent of GDP, reflecting partly the subdued investment climate and partly the very risk-averse nature of these banks (Ghosh 2006).
7. Average foreign ownership in the top ten Indonesian banks grew from zero percent in 1997–99 to 16.7 percent in 2004 (Ghosh 2006).
8. For details on minority foreign stakes in Vietnamese joint stock banks, see Appendix Table 4A.1.
9. Recapitalization of failed banks initially occurred mainly through domestic investors – namely government-owned asset management companies established for the purposes

of dealing with non-performing loans. The subsequent divestment and privatization process, however, attracted foreign investors, particularly in Korea and Thailand.

10. Prior to the financial crisis of 1997 this would most often be in the form of letters of credit from banks. However, evidence from South Korea in the 1960s and '70s showed that even large enterprises would borrow from banks for fixed investment but access the informal sector for part of their working capital (Cole and Park 1983). The modern day informal sector could include established brokerage houses such as Li and Fung in Hong Kong who would broker deals between large clients in the US and Europe (for example Disneyland Co. Ltd) and small toy manufacturers in China for whom they would provide working capital.

11. In developing countries there will always be a role for informal finance for the poor and those with no collateral. However, for small manufacturing concerns, banks have the advantage of lower costs of funds, even though informal markets may have lower information/transactions costs. Therefore, it is possible to have banks lending to traders who then on-lend to SMEs, thereby exploiting the comparative advantages of both the formal and informal financial sectors (Ghate 1992).

12. This would appear to be so despite the fact that the 2008 financial crisis in the US and Europe has revealed the possible risks associated with global banks trying to reduce funding of their own offices in local markets when pressed for funds in foreign markets. In the same manner that the Asian financial crisis a decade ago has resulted in strengthened banking sectors in the region, it could be expected that the 2008 financial crisis will result in better-managed global banks so that the risks of sudden disruptions to local markets would diminish.

13. Listing by international firms in Hong Kong amounted to about 36 percent of trading in 2004. Of that, listing by other Asian firms constituted only about 7 percent.

14. Source, see http://asiabondsonline.adb.org/asiabondindicators. Shortly after the crisis, there was also a desire to diversify away from reliance on banks towards raisings in the bond markets. Government bond raisings provide a benchmark yield for corporate bonds.

15. Banks in the Asian region seem to have managed to weather the financial storm in the US during 2008.

16. This is highlighted by the 2008 financial crisis in the US and Europe, and is very much on the agenda of current attempts to strengthen prudential supervision of banks in the relevant countries.

17. Having said this, at the time of incorporation of foreign-invested joint venture banks, there could well be some protections put in place by banking regulators to limit these entities from risk exposures to the headquarters' balance sheets. Hence, the challenges faced by these domestic banks with part foreign ownership could be less than those faced by 'free-wheeling' private joint stock banks in countries such as Vietnam.

18. Internationally reputable rating agencies are often relied upon for assessing the credit risks of mortgage and other asset-backed securities issued by banks and other financial institutions. However, the independence of assessments could be in question as some of these rating agencies are also consultants to the financial institutions issuing the asset-backed securities (Thirlwell 2007).

19. The 11 EMEAP participants comprise the central banks and monetary authorities of the five 'original ASEANs' (Singapore, Malaysia, Thailand, Philippines and Indonesia) plus Japan, Korea, Hong Kong and China, plus Australia and New Zealand. Australia, Japan and New Zealand are the three EMEAP countries in which investments were expressly excluded.

20. The Vietnamese government has, in recent years, successfully issued around $US750 million dollar-denominated bonds in the international market, but no dong-denominated bond issues have yet been attempted.

21. For detailed discussion on Vietnam, see IMF Country Report No. 07/385, 2007.

22. Merger of the Canadia Bank and the Foreign Trade Bank (IMF Country Report, Cambodia, 2007).

REFERENCES

Adams, S. (2008), 'Asymmetric information and central banks' role in consumer protection: financial literacy from the top down', Pacific Financial Technical Assistance Centre working paper, 25–26 August, Suva, Fiji.

Baldwin, R. (2006), 'Globalisation: the great unbundling(s)', paper presented for the Globalisation Challenges for Europe and Finland project, Prime Minister's Office, Economic Council of Finland, accessed at www.vnk.fi/hankkeet/talousneuvosto/tyo-kokoukset/globalisaatioselvitys-9-2006/artikkelit/Baldwin_06-09-20.pdf.

Beck, Thorsten, Asli Demirgüç-Kunt and Ross Levine (2000), 'A new database on financial development and structure', *World Bank Economic Review*, **14**, 597–605.

Belaisch, Agnès and Alessandro Zanello (2006), 'Deepening financial ties', *Finance and Development*, **43** (2), 16–19.

Boyd, J.H. and B.D. Smith (1992), 'Intermediation and the equilibrium allocation of investment capital', *Journal of Monetary Economics*, **30**, 409–32.

Caprio, G. Jr., Izak Atiyas and James A. Hanson (1994), *Financial Reform: Theory and Experience*, Cambridge: Cambridge University Press.

Chua, Hak Bin (2003), 'FDI in the financial sector: the experience of ASEAN countries over the last decade', Monetary Authority of Singapore paper submitted to Bank for International Settlement CGFS publications no. 22: *Foreign Direct Investment in the Financial Sector of Emerging Market Economies*.

Cole, D. and Y.C. Park (1983), *Financial Development in Korea, 1945–1978*, Cambridge, MA: Harvard University Press.

Demirgüç-Kunt, A. and V. Maksimovic (1996), 'Stock market development and financing choices of firms', *The World Bank Economic Review*, **19** (2), 341–69.

Domanski, Dietrich (2005), 'Foreign banks in emerging market economies: changing players, changing issues', *BIS Quarterly Review*, December, 69–81.

Eichengreen, B. (1999), *Toward a New International Financial Architecture: A Practical Post-Asia Agenda*, Washington, DC: Institute for International Economics.

Frankel, J.S. and S.J. Wei (1994), 'Yen bloc or dollar bloc – exchange rate policies of East Asian economies', in Takatoshi Ito and Anne O. Krueger (eds), *Macroeconomic Linkage: Savings, Exchange Rates, and Capital Flows*, Chicago, IL: University of Chicago Press.

Ghate, P.B. (1992), 'Interaction between the formal and informal financial sectors: the Asian experience', *World Development*, **20** (6), 859–72.

Gill, I.S. and Homi Kharas (2007), *An East Asian Renaissance: Ideas for Economic Growth*, Washington, DC: The World Bank, cf. Chapter 4 on 'Finance'.

Ghosh, Swati R. (2006), *East Asian Finance: the Road to Robust Markets*, Washington DC: The World Bank.

Greenwood, J. and B.D. Smith (1996), 'Financial markets in development, and the development of financial markets', *Journal of Economic Dynamics and Control*, **21**, 145–81.

Gyntelberg, Jacob, Guonan Ma and Eli Remolona (2006), 'Developing corporate bond markets in Asia', in Bank for International Settlement paper no. 26, 13–21.

Hicks, J. (1969), *A Theory of Economic History*, Oxford: Clarendon Press.

Hohl, Stefan, Patrick McGuire and Eli Remolona (2006), 'Cross-border banking in Asia: Basel 2 and other prudential issues', in G. Caprio, D. Evanoff and G. Kaufman (eds), *Cross-Border Banking: Regulatory Challenges*, Singapore: World Scientific accessed at www.bis.org/repofficepubl/apresearch0603.pdf.

International Monetary Fund (IMF) (2007), 'Vietnam: selected issues', IMF country report no. 07/385.

Kimura, Fukunari and Mitsuyo Ando (2003), 'Fragmentation and agglomeration matter: Japanese multinationals in Latin America and East Asia', *The North American Journal of Economics and Finance*, **14** (3), 287–317.

Leung, Suiwah E. (2009), 'Integration and transition: Vietnam, Cambodia and Lao PDR', in Timo Henckel (ed.), *Sustaining Development and Growth in East Asia*, London: Routledge.

Levine, R. (2004), 'Finance and growth: theory and evidence', National Bureau for Economic Research working paper 10766, Cambridge, MA.

Lueth, E. and Marta Ruiz-Arranz (2006), 'A gravity model of workers' remittances', International Monetary Fund working paper WP/06/290.

Ma, G. and Remolona, E.M. (2005), 'Opening markets through a regional bond fund: lessons from ABF2', *BIS Quarterly Review*, June, 81–92.

McGuire, P. and N. Tarashev (2008), 'Bank health and lending to emerging markets' *BIS Quarterly Review*, December, 67–80.

McMillan, J. and C. Woodruff (1999), 'Interfirm relationships and informal credit in Vietnam', *The Quarterly Journal of Economics*, **114** (4), 1285–320.

Okuda, Hidenobu and Suvadee Rungsomboon (2006), 'Comparative cost study of foreign and Thai domestic banks in 1990–2002: its policy implications for a desirable banking industry structure', *Journal of Asian Economics*, **17** (4), 714–37.

Smith, A. (1776), *An Inquiry into the Nature and Causes of the Wealth of Nations*, London: W. Stahan & T. Cadell.

Thirlwell, M. (2007), 'Crunched lessons for the 2007 TLA crisis', Lowey Institute, Sydney, Australia.

Wooldridge, Philip D., Dietrich Domanski and Anna Cobau (2003), 'Changing links between mature and emerging financial markets', *BIS Quarterly Review*, September, 45–54.

APPENDIX

Table 4A.1   FDI in Vietnamese joint stock banks

Joint stock bank	Acquirer	Date of acquisition	Stake acquired (%)	Deal value (USD million)
Sacombank	Dragon Financial Holding	2001	10	n.a
	IFC	2002	10	3
	ANZ	Mar 2005	10	27
Asia Commercial Bank	Standard Chartered Bank	Jun 2005	8.6	22
Techcombank	HSBC	Dec 2005	10	17
		Jan 2007	+ 5	33.7
VP Bank	OCBC	Mar 2006	10	15.7
Oriental Commercial Bank	BNP Parisbas	Nov 2006	10	n.a
Southern Bank	UOB	Jan 2007	10	30
Habubank	Deutsche Bank	Oct 2007	10 (+10% awaiting central bank's approval)	n.a

Notes:
1. The IFC has reduced its holding in Sacombank to 5.6 percent in Dec 2007 but total foreign holding in the bank is still nearly 30 percent.
2. Sacombank is listed on Hochiminh city stock exchange market. Asia Commercial Bank is listed on Hanoi stock exchange market.
3. In 7 March 2008 the Ministry of Finance increased the ratio of foreign holding in non-listed companies which included non-listed banks from 30 percent to 40 percent.

5. How can regional public expenditure stimulate FDI in the Mekong?

Pritha Mitra

1 INTRODUCTION

Cross-country experiences show that foreign direct investment (FDI) accelerates growth in developing countries through contribution of capital, technical know-how, organizational, managerial and marketing practices, and global production networks (Lall, 2000).[1] Properly targeted public expenditures can boost the attractiveness of traditional factors that draw in FDI such as natural or human resources, markets, efficiency gains, low production costs and strategic assets.[2]

FDI-attracting public initiatives are more successful under regionally coordinated public programs. Public expenditures creating an attractive environment for FDI span a variety of areas from infrastructure and human capital to public subsidies and low administrative barriers. Coordination and cooperation across countries can help reduce costs in each of these key areas. Competition for FDI across countries in a region can become destructive resulting in detrimental FDI gains for any individual country. For example, competition across neighboring countries in FDI-targeted tax incentives can result in fiscal revenue losses for all countries. In contrast, regional coordination of public expenditure initiatives can eliminate destructive competition.

How can the Mekong attract FDI through regionally coordinated public expenditures?[3] Having already taken the first steps towards regionally coordinated public expenditure to attract investment, the Mekong can induce significant FDI by pushing further coordination in areas of public subsidies, infrastructure and human capital development and institutional reform. The Greater Mekong Subregion Strategic Framework (GMS-SF), a program of subregional economic cooperation designed to enhance economic linkages across borders, has already made significant progress in coordinating infrastructure across the region.[4] For example, GMS-built roads and bridges creating priority transport corridors have increased cross-border trade and FDI in the Mekong. However, progress in other FDI-attracting areas, including human capital development and legal and regulatory reforms have been more measured.[5]

The findings of this chapter suggest that under the umbrella of the GMS-SF, Mekong countries should pursue greater coordination and coopera-tion in priority FDI attracting areas: public subsidies, human capital and infrastructure development, improving the institutional environment and finally investment promotion. Section 2 provides background informa-tion on coordination of economic policies in the Mekong and FDI trends. Section 3 discusses ways in which public expenditure can attract FDI. Section 4 presents cross-country experiences in attracting FDI through participation in regional agreements. Section 5 addresses implications for the Mekong, while Section 6 concludes.

2 REGIONAL COORDINATION AND FDI IN THE MEKONG: STYLIZED FACTS

FDI flows into the Mekong have risen substantially in recent years. Driven by natural resource investments, Lao PDR's 2007 FDI as a percentage of GDP was over six times its value five years before. Increased political stability has set the stage for substantial FDI in Cambodia's tourism and garment industries. Vietnam's FDI, having remained stable at around 5 percent of GDP for most of this decade, picked up substantially in 2007 and 2008. Even prior to this increase, the foreign-invested sector had emerged as the most dynamic segment of the economy, with the foreign-invested sector's contribution to GDP growth more than doubling between 2002 and 2007.[6]

Realizing the benefits of regional coordination in increasing FDI and more generally economic growth, the Mekong countries in conjunction with Thailand and China have established a forum for coordination of economic policies.[7] In 2002, the Greater Mekong Subregion Strategic Framework (GMS-SF) was launched identifying the following areas for cooperation: (i) strengthen infrastructure linkages, (ii) facilitate cross-border trade and investment, (iii) enhance private sector participation and improve its competitiveness, (iv) develop human resources and skills competencies and (v) environmental protection and sustainable use of shared resources.

The GMS-SF has already made significant progress in coordinating infrastructure across the Mekong. Roads and bridges built under the GMF-SF have already created priority transport corridors, increasing cross-border trade and FDI in the Mekong. Institutional changes through harmonization of cross-border issues (for example, document requirements) have reduced trading costs and thus improved FDI prospects in some parts of the Mekong.[8] Energy sector coordination has begun with the establishment of a framework for power trade. Meanwhile, the joint initiative on implementing optical fiber infrastructure is in its final stages. Once complete, Mekong telecommunications costs are expected to reduce dramatically.

Progress in non-infrastructure FDI-promoting areas have been more gradual. Implementation of initiatives to address education and skills development have been mixed. Regional civil service management training and networking is underway, yet comprehensive action plans for human capital development have not yet emerged. Strengthening institutional and policy frameworks to promote investment and cooperation amongst investment promotion agencies has been limited to organizing road shows, conferences and discussions of a regional guarantee facility. Currently, there is no formal initiative on coordination of public subsidies.

3   HOW PUBLIC EXPENDITURE ATTRACTS FDI

What can Mekong policy-makers do to substantially influence FDI? Public policies can influence significant determinants of FDI in developing countries including trade openness, low labor costs, natural resources, market size, macroeconomic stability, tax incentives, infrastructure, human capital and institutional environment.[9] Incentives such as public subsidies and improved human capital will further encourage FDI, while reforms in infrastructure and institutions will reduce investors' costs. Active investment promotion will alert foreign investors of the incentives and reduced costs of investment in the Mekong.

3.1   Public Subsidies

Foreign investors enjoy a large range of public subsidies, including reduced corporate income taxes, tax holidays, investment allowances and tax credits, exemptions from selected indirect taxes (for example, import tariffs on inputs), loss write-offs, accelerated depreciation and export processing zones. Indirect public subsidies such as subsidized loans, dedicated infrastructure, government equity stakes in large ventures, training and subsidized pricing of land and utilities are also gaining popularity.[10]

The ultimate impact of public subsidies in developing countries remains unresolved.[11] Besides providing immediate benefits to foreign investors, public subsidies also signal a welcoming attitude towards foreign investors (Tanzi and Shome, 1992). A 1 percent reduction in corporate income tax rates increases FDI by approximately 2 percent, favoring reduced rates to attract FDI (Hines, 1999).[12] In contrast, Hasset and Hubbard (1997) argue a transparent and simple tax regime with uniformly low rates for all investors (domestic and foreign), as is found in Hong Kong, is most effective in boosting private investment. The OECD (2003a) notes that multinationals apply sophisticated tax planning and are not in need of tax holidays or exemptions and recommends lower labor taxes, accelerated depreciation, five-year loss carry-forward rules for domestic and foreign investors and strengthening thin-capitalization rules and regulations on transfer pricing. Complex and unpredictable public subsidy schemes, granted on an ad hoc basis, increase administrative costs, raise possibilities for corruption and create an uncertain business environment.

Competing public subsidies across countries may result in substantial revenue losses and increases in unproductive public expenditure across the region.[13] Instead, regionally coordinated public subsidies will benefit all its members, especially since public subsidies cannot substitute for an attractive overall investment climate characterized by human capital, infrastructure and a stable institutional environment.

3.2 Human Capital

FDI and human capital reinforce one another, where human capital attracts FDI, FDI then raises the level of human capital, attracting greater FDI.[14] Human capital develops not only through training provided by foreign investors, but also through positive spillover effects.[15] The skills learnt in FDI industries spreads through movement of labor from FDI to domestic industries. Spillovers grow with improved human capital, enhancing the ability of domestic investors to absorb FDI-related technology transfers (OECD, 2002).

Public policies play an important role at each stage of the evolving relationship between human capital and FDI. Adequate and effective public educational expenditures is crucial to human capital development. Governments emphasizing flexible demand-driven human resource development strategies, targeting multinationals in high value-added areas and coordinating education and training policies are most likely to attract FDI. Once FDI has arrived, government policies have been important in facilitating training and promoting multinationals to invest in human resource development (Miyamoto, 2003). The most successful policies were created in coordination with multinationals and foreign academic institutions, focusing on technology and business administration ties.

3.3   Infrastructure

Reducing costs from high quality physical infrastructure raises investors' (foreign and domestic) rate of return, improving the investment climate. Appropriate infrastructure also reflects an advancing economy, sending a positive signal to foreign investors. A recent UNCTAD survey found the quality of telecommunications as the third largest barrier for FDI in developing countries where macroeconomic and political stability were the first and second (UNCTAD, 2007).

Increased public investment in infrastructure raises concerns over public investment crowding-out private investment, by reducing private sector financing and incentives.[16] Public expenditures in infrastructure, however, do not necessarily crowd-out more productive private investment. It can have positive externalities on private investment, or crowd-in private investment, through the provision of infrastructure necessary for private sector growth. Mitra (2007) finds public investment has crowded-in private investment, particularly FDI, in Vietnam.

FDI involvement in large developing country infrastructure projects has alleviated some of the pressures on public expenditure, providing financing and operational expertise. In the past decade, over 80 percent of developing country private infrastructure investment initiatives involved FDI (Sader, 2000). Successfully obtaining FDI participation in large infrastructure investments, however, often depends on accompanying institutional reforms that ease the administrative costs and create a stable operating environment.

3.4   Institutional Environment

A stable and well-functioning institutional environment attracts and retains FDI. Predictability of future regulatory policies can be as significant to investment decisions as the standards enforced (OECD, 2001). Regulatory frameworks tend to be politically dependent on line ministries creating an unpredictable future operating environment for investors (Sader, 2000). Low institutional development, structural rigidities and poor governance are a tax on investment, adding to the statistically and economically negative nexus between administrative costs and FDI after controlling for other factors (Morisset and Neso 2002). The impact of reduced corruption exceeds that of lowering taxes. For example reducing the level of corruption from that of Mexico to Singapore would have approximately the same impact on FDI as a reduction of 30 percentage points in the corporate income tax rate (Wei, 2000). Inadequate intellectual property rights safeguards have resulted in a diversion of investment from technology-intensive industries, production and distribution (Smarzynska, 2002).

Public policies should focus on improved dispute resolution, protection of private property and a stable regulatory environment. Practical areas where policies might focus include strengthening the judiciary (including commercial courts and expedient resolution of commercial disputes), improving access to land and construction permits, dismantling barriers to free entry and exit of firms, reducing transaction costs of doing business (investment approvals, customs clearance), enforcing labor laws and eliminating discriminatory provisions against foreign investors. Benassy-Quere et al. (2005) quantitatively determine a detailed list of institutional reforms that attract FDI – capital and credit regulations are especially important.[17]

3.5 Investment Promotion

Investment promotion makes foreign investors aware of opportunities and services as well as the ease of doing business in a country or region. Without skillful marketing, despite all the elements of a business-friendly environment being in place, foreign investors may not be aware of the changes in the country. Empirical evidence suggests a positive relationship between FDI promotion expenditures and FDI flows. Singapore and Ireland, for example, outspent (per capita) most countries in investment promotion (Velde, 2001; Rajan, 2003).

Investment promotion includes a variety of activities.[18] Firstly, image-building activities promote the country and its regions and states as favorable locations for investment. Secondly, direct targeting of firms by promotion of specific sectors and industries and personal selling and establishing direct contacts with prospective investors generate investment. Thirdly, investment promotion tailors investment service activities to prospective and current investors' needs. And fourthly, investment promotion includes the monitoring and evaluation of such measures as the realization ratio (percentage of FDI approvals translated into actual flows).[19]

Investment promotion agencies (IPAs) have been popular exhibiting mixed results and sometimes increasing the regulatory burden for FDI. In the absence of a regulatory environment with simple rules, and where the IPA has the authority to negotiate with the regulatory system, one-stop investment promotion agencies become yet another stop (Lall, 2000). An empirical analysis of 58 countries (Morisset, 2003) finds the positive impact of IPAs on FDI is highly correlated with IPAs that have: (i), a high degree of political visibility (such as links to the prime minister or president's office), (ii), active private sector involvement (for example, private sector participation on the IPA's board) and (iii), operate in a country with an overall solid investment environment. The study also finds IPAs are most effective in functions such as image building, investor facilitation and servicing, investor generation and policy advocacy, as opposed to generating sector-specific investments.

4 EXPERIENCES FROM REGIONAL AGREEMENTS

4.1 Regional Trade Agreements

Regional trade agreements (RTA) can benefit member countries by encouraging reforms leading to improved regional investment environments and sending positive signals to investors. RTA membership can also strengthen commitment to domestic reform attractive to FDI (Park and Park, 2007). Domestic reform creates more investment than RTA membership. Participation in an RTA alone cannot raise FDI, especially in developing countries. Domestic reform is defined as the degree to which policies and institutions are supportive of economic freedom in terms of government size, legal structure, protection of property rights, access to sound money, international exchange and regulation. Reforms associated with a regional trade agreement are also seen as a cost-reducing signal for FDI (Dee and Gali, 2003).

4.2 European Union

Evidence from the experiences of accession to the European Union confirms that public subsidies, human capital and institutional reform are critical to augmenting FDI. Marin (2004) finds that Austrian and German companies are increasingly outsourcing skill-intensive activities to Central and Southeastern European countries to take advantage of their relatively inexpensive skilled labor. In Southeastern Europe higher degrees of liberalization of trade and foreign exchange regime and reforms in infrastructure encourage FDI (Demekas et al., 2005). In contrast, high levels of unit labor costs, corporate tax burdens and import tariffs discourage FDI. Above a threshold level of FDI, tariffs, the business environment and institutional and infrastructure development are much more important than labor costs, hinting that 'successful host countries' are able to attract increasingly high value-added and sophisticated foreign investment.

Institutional reforms often played the most important role in attracting FDI. Despite many reforms and low-cost high-skilled labor, Bulgaria and

Romania performed poorly in attracting FDI until new privatization laws were introduced (Carstensen and Toubal, 2003). Privatization through sales to outside owners was found much more effective in attracting FDI than manager-employee buyouts. Carstensen and Toubal (2003) also find that risks associated with non-payment, non-servicing payment for goods and services loans, trade-related finance and non-repatriation of capital were significant barriers to FDI in Central and Eastern European countries. More generally, Bevan et al. (2001) and Braconier and Ekholm (2001) show that steps towards integration with the EU, especially institutional reforms, have a positive effect on FDI flows.[20] The OECD (2003b and 2004) describes how the reforms tied to European Union accession were the engine for inward FDI.[21]

Southeastern European countries have adopted a regional approach to shaping their foreign investment environment through the South-East Europe Investment Compact. To avoid destructive competition for FDI, this compact aims at regional reform, investment, integrity and growth through a unified approach towards foreign investors across countries on the principle of equal treatment with domestic investors. The Investment Compact describes the existing exceptions from national treatment for foreign investors (that is, when treatment is less favorable than for domestic investors) by country, with the objective that these exceptions be eliminated over time. In accordance with the pact, member countries will work towards: (i) unifying FDI registration and approval procedures with those for domestic firms, (ii) permitting acquisition of real estate by foreign investors for FDI purposes, (iii) minimizing FDI-related requirements on statistical reporting, work and residence permits, (iv) eliminating discrimination in access to government procurement contracts, and (v) removing obstacles to FDI in financial and professional services.

4.3 NAFTA

The reform-creating environment that lead to Mexico's inclusion in the North American Free Trade Agreement (NAFTA), initially propelled FDI inflows into Mexico.[22] Waldkirch (2003a) emphasizes the important role of reform for more FDI inflows to less developed countries based on analysis of the empirical determinants of FDI in Mexico under NAFTA. In preparation for NAFTA, Mexico undertook substantial structural reforms including trade liberalization, sovereign debt restructuring, financial liberalization and privatization. Especially important for investors were protection of corporate property and access to domestic markets (OECD, 2001).

FDI flows to Mexico some years after entering NAFTA, although significant, were less than anticipated. Cuevas et al. (2005) attribute this to a decline in competitiveness in the later half of the 1990s, resulting from the limited size and early end to the privatization program and a halt in reforms which were the consequence of the inability of Congress to pass reform laws.[23]

5   IMPLICATIONS FOR THE MEKONG[24]

Strategic coordination across the Mekong can bring together the unique offerings of each country, under the umbrella of a 'Mekong FDI strategy', creating a regionally attractive package for FDI. For example, vertically-oriented FDI, occurring when a multinational corporation chooses a regional location for each link of its production chain to minimize global costs, may thrive in the Mekong. Vietnam's more advanced infrastructure and inexpensive skilled labor can be combined with Lao PDR and Cambodia's inexpensive low-skilled labor and natural resources.[25] Based on the cross-country experiences described earlier in the chapter, this section suggests cooperative strategies that are likely to benefit the Mekong.

5.1   Public Subsidies

The Mekong countries would benefit from coordinated public subsidies. Currently the nature of public subsidies across Cambodia, Lao PDR and Vietnam are similar (see Table 5.1). Primary incentives include tax holidays, reduced corporate income tax rates, investment allowances or accelerated depreciation and special exemptions for import duties and other indirect taxes. These subsidies are targeted towards foreign investors and exporters, creating differential treatment across domestic and foreign investors. The differences in subsidies, not necessarily large in magnitude, could lead to destructive competition. Alignment of incentives, for example standardized corporate tax rates across the Mekong, would avoid any revenue loss through destructive competition. Even where there is little risk of destructive competition, reflecting each country targeting a different type of FDI, the common nature of the incentives would serve as a positive signal. Risk-averse foreign investors would perceive common tax incentives as a sign of greater stability of these incentives in the future. Coordination would, however, entail upfront financial costs of changing tax laws and administrative costs involving coordination across countries.

In deciding the magnitudes of coordinated public subsidies, weighing the costs and benefits, policymakers may find a low level of incentives set

Table 5.1 Tax incentives

Tax incentive	Cambodia	Lao PDR	Thailand	Vietnam
Corporate income tax (standard)	20 percent	35 percent or 1 percent turnover	30 percent	28 percent
Corporate income tax (reduced)	9 percent (phased out in 2008)	20 percent (designated areas); 15 percent (lowland companies); 10 percent (remote	Investment promotion zones with 50 percent reduction of CIT for five years	10, 15 or 20 percent
Dividend withholding tax	CIT rate	10 percent	10 percent except domestic intercompany dividends which are exempt	None
Tax holidays	Nine years (maximum)	Seven years (maximum)	Eight years (maximum)	Nine years (maximum)
Tax incentive sectors	High-tech, export, tourism, infrastructure, energy, rural development, environmental protection	None	Exporters	High-tech, energy, agriculture, research and development, labor-intensive industries, infrastructure, large-scale industrial projects, traditional crafts, professional development, other.
Investment allowances	None	None	25 percent for infrastructure	None

Table 5.1 (continued)

Tax incentive	Cambodia	Lao PDR	Thailand	Vietnam
Accelerated depreciation	Plant and equipment investment financed from reinvested profit	None	None	Yes
Import duty and VAT exemptions	Import duty exemptions on promoted investments	Reduced import duties on inputs of foreign investors and exporters	Exemptions and reduced import duty and VAT rates on inputs of exporters	Exemptions from import duty and VAT in certain sectors
Export promotion zones	Enjoy special depreciation of 40 percent in the first year of operation as an alternative to the tax holiday.	–	50 percent reduction of CIT for five years after tax holiday in specific zones.	Businesses in industrial zones, export-processing zones, high-tech zones and economic zones can enjoy tax incentives.
Other	–	Special incentives on case-by-case basis	Exempt dividend distributions during tax holiday period	–

Source: PriceWaterhouseCoopers (2006), Botman et al. (2006), Authorities of respective countries.

uniformly across domestic and foreign investors most beneficial. Large incentives can lead to large losses and increased corruption. The potential losses from FDI tax incentives in Vietnamese tax revenues alone are estimated to be close to 0.7 percent of GDP per annum (Fletcher, 2002). Large subsidies also make investors weary of their continuation in the future. A transparent and simple public subsidy scheme, small in size but uniform in nature across all investors, domestic and foreign, signals stability to investors for whom frequent changes in tax regimes is costly. The low magnitude of incentives and transparency of a regionally coordinated system also reduces possibilities for official corruption and other rent-seeking behavior.

5.2 Human Capital

Mekong coordination on human capital development would reduce costs for any individual country. Economies of scale may be exploited through regional training centers, where all Mekong countries share the training costs. The GMS-SF has already begun this initiative through joint training of civil servants in management. Future training could usefully seek to include areas of regulatory and financial sector administration, thereby reducing the costs of investors in dealing with public administration. The Mekong could carry the training initiative further to the private sector. Learning from the experiences of the European transition economies, the Mekong can offer inexpensive skilled labor to its Asian neighbors. Training could be geared towards vertically-integrated industries targeted under a 'Mekong FDI strategy'. Linking this type of training with foreign academic institutions will also create another gateway to industries linked with these institutions.

5.3 Infrastructure

The momentum of the current commendable collaboration in improvement of transport infrastructure should continue in other essential infrastructure. Adequate industrial infrastructure has been a crucial element in attracting FDI to the developing world. It is crucial that the optical fiber network currently completed in Vietnam, Thailand and China under the GMS-SF is extended to Lao PDR, Cambodia and Myanmar as soon as possible. In order to be fully effective in reducing telecommunications costs, the accompanying regulations need to be adequately addressed and coordinated across the GMS-SF countries. Coordinated infrastructure improvements will not only reduce costs but also ensure minimum quality standards, providing more confidence to investors.

Vietnam has successfully crowded-in FDI with public expenditures in infrastructure. Vietnam's recently improved infrastructure has successfully attracted infrastructure-sensitive and technologically-intensive FDI. Lao PDR and Cambodia's infrastructure in energy, water, sanitation, ports and storage require significant improvements to reach the level of Vietnam. These two Mekong countries may find it helpful to begin by targeting similar infrastructure standards and development process as that of Vietnam, with heavy public expenditures in the above-mentioned key areas of infrastructure.

The pressure on public finances from large-scale infrastructure investment may be moderated through FDI in infrastructure itself. Lao PDR, for example, has received sizeable FDI in hydropower development, a renewable natural resource. Attracting FDI to infrastructure unrelated with natural resources, however, poses a challenge in the absence of appropriate regulatory and legal frameworks. Development of a stable operating environment will be key for the Mekong countries to attract FDI in non-resource-based infrastructure.

5.4 Institutional Environment

Regionally coordinated regulatory and legal frameworks in all FDI-related areas will reduce institutional costs while reducing investors' perceived risk of ad hoc regulatory and legal changes. Reforms induced through a regional commitment were a primary factor in boosting investor confidence for transition economies joining the European Union and for Mexico joining NAFTA. Investors are concerned over the stability of regulatory frameworks that are politically dependent on line ministries, as is currently the case for Mekong countries. A common comprehensive regulatory framework across the Mekong will reduce political influence, increase transparency and predictability, while removing destructive competition, resulting in a better institutional environment across the region. As Vietnam already adheres to WTO rules on international regulatory standards, it may be useful to apply the Vietnamese structure across the Mekong as a starting point. The region should move towards meeting international best practices, beyond WTO standards, in order to remain globally competitive. Cost-sharing in creating and administering a common framework will eliminate redundant costs, reducing the overall cost for each country.[26]

Standardized institutional frameworks across the Mekong should address a wide range of areas. Financial sector reform, a stated concern of foreign investors in Vietnam, will be important. It was a significant barrier for Central and Eastern European countries joining the European

Union. Removal and rationalization of investment regulations should be emphasized. Improved governance and intellectual property rights as well as common safeguards will be especially central in attracting higher quality FDI, such as technology-intensive industries. Appropriate regulations governing transport, energy, telecommunications and other major infrastructure will be necessary for the success of the associated physical infrastructure.

An important aspect of Mekong institutional reforms will be the privatization of state-owned enterprises. Privatization has played an integral role in creating a more attractive institutional environment for FDI in Romania, Bulgaria and Mexico. In Mexico, even after entering NAFTA, the halt of reform in privatization was a barrier to FDI. Based on the experiences of these countries, immediate attention to reforms in privatization and focusing on methods of privatization would benefit FDI flows in the Mekong. Recently investors remarked that state-owned enterprise reform remains a challenge for Vietnam. A harmonized approach across the Mekong will facilitate FDI, especially vertically-integrated FDI which may operate a chain of production across the Mekong.

5.5 Investment Promotion

Dynamic and effective regionally integrated investment promotion is crucial to further enticing FDI in the Mekong. Under the GMS-SF, coordination amongst IPAs has been limited. This may be a consequence of investment promotion ranking low in priorities for the GMS-SF, given the success and large resources devoted to individual IPAs of China and Thailand. The Mekong countries, with relatively limited resources for their IPAs, could greatly benefit from more intense coordination. Collaborative Mekong investment promotion will not only reduce marketing costs for individual countries but will also provide a platform to promote vertically-integrated FDI as well as country-specific opportunities for FDI. Regular monitoring of the success of joint investment promotion activities, through movements in realization ratios, will maintain motivation for the initiative. Based on cross-country experiences, the initiative will be most successful through focus on marketing and image-building activities as opposed to interfering in the regulatory environment.

In the transition towards attracting FDI through uniform public subsidies and a harmonized institutional environment, the South-East European investment compact may serve as a guide in communicating these changes to investors. In a similar spirit to the compact, clearly describing the harmonization objectives and priorities in one simple document will encourage investor confidence. Differences in public subsidies and institutions across Mekong countries and targeted synchronization dates should also be included.

6 CONCLUSION

Greater coordination in public expenditures to attract FDI will benefit all Mekong countries, enhancing the region's growth potential. Although the first steps towards a regionally integrated approach in attracting FDI have been taken in infrastructure, accelerated coordination in other areas is required. Regional coordination will significantly reduce FDI-attracting public expenditures for individual countries. In addition, cooperation will eliminate destructive competition across the Mekong, particularly in public subsidies.

Given the importance of institutional changes in boosting investor confidence, an initial emphasis on improving the institutional environment may be warranted. As the experiences of the European Union and NAFTA have demonstrated, institutional reforms approached through regional coordination signals a stronger commitment to reforms than individual initiatives. Particular attention should be paid to privatization laws and methods, critical for ensuing FDI.

Institutional reforms will both supplement and complement other FDI-conducive public expenditure areas. A better institutional environment would attract FDI in various areas, including infrastructure relieving some of the public financial burden of infrastructure investment. Public expenditures in training for public and private sector employees will further supplement improved institutions and infrastructure in attracting a greater volume and quality of FDI. Uniform and low public subsidies will work hand-in-hand with institutional reforms in signaling a stable operating environment. Marketing these improvements under a united 'Mekong FDI' strategy will alert and entice foreign investors.

NOTES

1. The literature generally finds that FDI enhances growth, where overall the benefits outweigh the costs. Lim (2001) provides a survey of the literature.
2. Morisset and Neso (2002) provide a summary of factors attracting FDI.
3. For the purposes of this chapter, Mekong is defined as Lao PDR, Cambodia and Vietnam. Due to limited information Myanmar is not included.
4. The GMS-SF consists of Cambodia, China, Lao PDR, Myanmar, Thailand and Vietnam. This paper focuses on aspects of the GMS-SF relevant to Cambodia, Lao PDR and Vietnam only.
5. ADB (2007) provides a detailed review on progress of the GMS-SF.

6. See Chapters 7–10 below for more detail on FDI of individual countries.
7. In 1992, with the assistance of the Asian Development Bank, the Greater Mekong Subregion (GMS) countries initialized a program of subregional cooperation. Until 2002, the program did not have an explicit development strategy.
8. Some areas of the Mekong, including Cambodia, are still in the process of piloting this harmonized approach. The Cross-Border Transport Agreement covers all aspects of cross-border transport facilitation in one document. See ADB (2007) for details.
9. Comprehensive reviews of the literature on determinants of FDI include Blonigen (2005) and Nonnemberg and Mendonca (2004).
10. Details on public subsidies provided to investors are found in OECD (2002) and World Bank (2003).
11. See Wells et al. (2001) and Zee et al. (2002) for summaries of opposing views in the empirical literature on the costs and benefits of public subsidies.
12. These results correspond to a tax elasticity of -0.6 and a CIT rate of 30 percent.
13. See Wells et al. (2001) and Nunnenkamp (2002) for more details.
14. Jaumotte (2004) emphasizes the importance of education and financial stability of host countries relative to regional trade agreement membership.
15. Borensztein et al. (1995) find that the more educated the labor force, the greater the net positive impact of FDI on growth.
16. Aschauer (1989a and b), Ghali (1998), Voss (2002) and Mitra (2006) provide empirical evidence pointing to crowding out of private investment in a variety of industrialized and developing countries.
17. These include existence and security of formal property rights, market capitalization, credit market regulations, support to R&D and innovation, information on firms, ability of bank executives, evolution of government efficiency, efficiency of the tax system, lack of corruption, bank and financial supervision, bankruptcy law, ability of the society to adapt and innovate, government transparency, efficiency of justice, regulation of competition, respect of intellectual property and security of private contracts. See Rajan (2004) for details.
18. See Rajan (2004) for details.
19. MIGA provides a comprehensive compilation of international best practices in investment promotion (see http://www.fdipromotion.com/toolkit/user/index.cfm).
20. A part of the positive impact may also reflect the increased political stability associated with European Union accession.
21. OECD (2003b) also supports positive investment creation from EU membership.
22. NAFTA contains provisions for liberalizing international investment and creating a legal and economic environment conducive to FDI.
23. The 1997 elections resulted in a Congress where no party held the majority. Consequently no party could pass a law on its own and reforms were held up.
24. Owing to limited information Myanmar has not been included in the analysis.
25. Based on Mexican industry-level data, Waldkirch (2003b) demonstrates that when there are large skill differences between the FDI-originating country and the FDI-receiving country, FDI flows into sectors that are intensive in both skilled and unskilled labor.
26. Redundant costs include, for example, the cost of hiring regulatory experts and drafting legislation.

REFERENCES

Asian Development Bank (ADB) (2007), *Midterm Review of the Greater Mekong Subregion Strategic Framework (2002–12)*, Manila: ADB.
Aschauer, D.A. (1989a), 'Is public expenditure productive?', *Journal of Monetary Economics*, **23**, 177–200.

Aschauer, D.A. (1989b), 'Does public capital crowd out private capital?', _Journal of Monetary Economics_, **24**, 171–88.
Benassy-Quere, A., M. Coupet and T. Mayer (2005), 'Institutional determinants of foreign direct investment', Centre d'Etudes Prospectives et d'Informations Internationales working paper no 2005-05, Paris.
Bevan, A., S. Estrin and H. Grabbe (2001), 'The impact of EU accession prospects on FDI inflows to Central and Eastern Europe', University of Sussex, Sussex European Institute Policy paper no 06/01.
Blonigen, B. (2005), 'A review of the empirical literature on FDI determinants', National Bureau of Economic Research working paper no 11299, Cambridge, MA.
Borensztein, E., J. De Gregorio and J.W. Lee (1995), 'How does foreign direct investment affect economic growth?' National Bureau of Economic Research working paper no 5057, Cambridge, MA.
Botman, D.P.J., A. Klemm and R. Baqir (2008), 'Investment incentives and effective tax rates in the Philippines: a comparison with neighboring countries', International Monetary Fund working paper no 08/207.
Braconier, B.H. and K. Ekholm (2001), 'Foreign direct investment in Central and Eastern Europe: employment effects in the EU', Center for Economic Policy Research discussion paper no 3052, London.
Carstensen, K. and F. Toubal (2003), 'Foreign direct investment in Central and Eastern European countries: a dynamic panel analysis', Kiel Institute for World Economics working paper no 1143, Kiel, Germany.
Cuevas, A., M. Messmacher and A.Werner (2005), 'Foreign direct investment in Mexico since the approval of NAFTA', _World Bank Economic Review_, **19** (3), 473–488.
Dee, P. and J. Gali (2003), 'The trade and investment effects of preferential trading arrangements', National Bureau for Economic Research working paper series 10160.
Demekas, D.G., B. Horvath, E. Ribakova and Y. Wu (2005), 'Foreign direct investment in Southeastern Europe: how (and how much) can policies help?', International Monetary Fund working paper no WP/05/110.
Fletcher, K. (2002), 'Tax Incentives in Cambodia, Lao PDR, and Vietnam', presentation for the IMF Conference on Foreign Direct Investment: Opportunities and Challenges for Cambodia, Lao PDR and Vietnam, August 16–17, Hanoi.
Ghali, K.H. (1998), 'Public investment and private capital formation in a vector-error correction model of growth', _Applied Economics_, **30**, 837–44.
Hassett, K.A. and R.G. Hubbard (1997), 'Tax policy and investment', in A.J. Auerbach (ed.), _Fiscal Policy: Lessons from Economic Research_, Cambridge, MA: MIT Press, pp. 339–85.
Hines, J.R., Jr (1999), 'Lessons from behavioral responses to international taxation', _National Tax Journal_, **52**, 305–22.
Jaumotte, F. (2004), 'Foreign direct investment and regional trade agreements: the market size effect revisited', International Monetary Fund working paper 04/206.
Lall, S. (2000), 'FDI and development: policy and research issues in the emerging context', Queen Elizabeth House, University of Oxford and Organisation for Economic Co-operation and Development working paper no 43.
Lim, E.-G. (2001), 'Detriments of, and the relation between, foreign direct

investment and growth: a summary of the recent literature', International Monetary Fund working paper no 01/75.

Marin, D. (2004), 'A Nation of Poets and Thinkers – Less So with Eastern Enlargement? Austria and Germany', Centre for Economic Policy Research discussion paper series no 4358, London.

Mitra, P. (2006), 'Has government investment crowded out private investment in India?' *American Economic Review, Papers and Proceedings*, **96** (2), 337–41.

Mitra, P. (2007), 'Has public investment crowded in or crowded out private investment in Vietnam?', International Monetary Fund Selected Issues Paper SM/07/341.

Miyamoto, Koji (2003), 'Human capital formation and foreign direct investment in developing countries', Organisation for Economic Co-operation and Development, Development Centre working paper no 211.

Morisset, J. (2003), 'Does a country need a promotion agency to attract foreign direct investment? A small analytical model applied to 58 countries', World Bank Policy Research working paper no 3028.

Morisset, J. and O.L. Neso (2002), 'Administrative barriers to foreign investment in developing countries', *Transnational Corporations*, **11**, 99–121.

Nonnemberg, M. and M.J. Cardoso de Mendonca (2004), 'The determinants of foreign direct investment in developing countries', paper 061 presented to the 32nd Brazilian Economics Meeting, Sao Paolo, Brazil.

Nunnenkamp, P. (2002), 'Determinants of FDI in developing countries: has globalization changed the rules of the game?', Kiel Institute for World Economics working paper no 1122, Kiel, Germany.

Organisation for Economic Co-operation and Development (OECD) (2001), *Regulatory Investment Incentives*, Paris: OECD.

OECD (2002), *Foreign Direct Investment for Development: Maximising Benefits, Minimising Costs*, Paris: OECD

OECD (2003a), *Tax Policy Assessment and Design in Support of Direct Investment*, Paris: OECD.

OECD (2003b), *Policies and International Integration: Influences on Trade and Foreign Direct Investment*, Paris: OECD.

OECD (2004), *Regulatory Reform and Market Openness: Understanding the Links to Enhance Economic Performance*, Paris: OECD.

Park, I. and S. Park (2007), 'Reform-creating regional trade agreements and foreign direct investment: applications for East Asia', The International Centre for the Study of East Asian Development working paper series vol. 2007–01.

Price Waterhouse Coopers (2006), *International Tax Review*, September.

Rajan, R.S. (2003), 'Sustaining competitiveness in the new global economy: introduction and overview', in R. Rajan (ed.), *Sustaining Competitiveness in the New Global Economy: A Case Study of Singapore*, Cheltenham, UK and Northampton, MA, USA: Edward Elgar.

Rajan, Ramkishen S. (2004), 'Measures to attract FDI', *Economic and Political Weekly*, 3 January.

Sader, F. (2000), 'Attracting foreign direct investment into infrastructure', International Finance Corporation Foreign Investment Advisory Service occasional paper 12, Washington, DC.

Smarzynska, B.K. (2002), 'Composition of foreign direct investment and protection of intellectual property rights: evidence from transition economies', World Bank policy research working paper no 2786, February.

Tanzi V. and P. Shome (1992), 'The role of taxation in the development of East Asian countries', in T. Ito and A. Krueger (eds), *The Political Economy of Tax Reform*, Chicago, IL: University of Chicago Press.

United Nations Conference on Trade and Development (UNCTAD) (2007), *UNCTAD Investment Brief No. 3*, Geneva: Investment Issues Analysis Branch.

Velde, T.D.W. (2001), 'Policies towards foreign direct investment in developing countries: emerging issues and outstanding issues', mimeo, Overseas Development Institute, London.

Voss, G.M. (2002), 'Public and private investment in the United States and Canada', *Economic Modelling*, **19**, 641–64.

Waldkirch, A. (2003a), 'The "New Regionalism" and foreign direct investment: the case of Mexico', *Journal of International Trade & Economic Development*, **12** (2), 151–84.

Waldkirch, A. (2003b), 'Vertical FDI? A host country perspective', Oregon State University working paper, Corvallis, OR.

Wei, S. (2000), 'How taxing is corruption on international investors?' *Review of Economics and Statistics*, **82**, 1–11.

Wells, Louis, Jr, Nancy Allen, Jacques Morisset and Neda Pirnia (2001), 'Using tax incentives to compete for foreign investment: are they worth the costs?', World Bank Foreign Investment Advisory Service occasional paper no 15, Washington.

World Bank (2003), *Global Economic Prospects and the Developing Countries 2003*, Washington: World Bank, Chapter 3.

Zee, H.H., J.G. Stotsky and E. Ley (2002), 'Tax incentives for business investment: a primer for policy makers in developing countries', *World Development*, **30** (9) September, 1497–516.

6. Proliferation of PTAs in East Asia: what does it mean for the Mekong countries?

David Robertson

For 40 years, export-led growth dominated development strategies in East Asia. The fall in world trade resulting from the current global recession raises doubts about this development paradigm. Nevertheless, for most small open economies of East and Southeast Asia trade is likely to remain a central focus of development.

This chapter briefly discusses the basis for the growth of manufacturing exports from the East Asian newly industrializing countries (EANICs), emphasizing the opportunities offered by OECD trade liberalization under GATT in the 1970s, and the pragmatic cooperation between governments and firms to exploit those opportunities.[1] It then traces the politico-economic forces resulting in the growth of bilateral trading agreements in the region during the 1990s and assesses the implications of this complex 'noodle bowl' of bilateral (preferential) trading agreements (PTAs) for the Mekong 4.

1 THE EAST ASIAN 'MIRACLE'

Export-led growth in East and Southeast Asia sprang from market-based enterprises and pragmatic cooperation between firms and governments. According to the World Bank (1993), the exceptional performance of these economies was not based on 1960s' received theory of development based on import substitution, financial aid and formal inter-government agreements. Rather, EANIC governments facilitated exports using fiscal and financial incentives and free trade zones to support local enterprises (Leipziger and Thomas, 1993; Gill and Kharas, 2007). Gradually, manu-facturers in OECD economies began to include these 'Asian tigers' in their production processes. New opportunities attracted foreign investment and generated employment in labour-abundant Asian economies.

'Factory Asia' was established by cooperation among East Asian governments, their entrepreneurs and OECD multinational enterprises (Baldwin, 2006) and depended on tariff reductions guaranteed by GATT bindings. Under contract to manufacturers and via wholesale or retail distributors in OECD economies, EANIC enterprises created supply chains for competitive components and consumer goods. Revolutionary improvements in transport and information technologies in the 1980s and 1990s stimulated specialization by process and enabled reliable supplies of labour-intensive products and components to reach markets 'just in time' on the other side of the world.

As advances in technologies created new opportunities and processing migrated to new locations in response to low wages, reliable labour, cheap land and tax concessions, 'free-trade zones' became less important and governments recognized that unilaterally dismantling tariffs in selected import categories also encouraged job-creating employment. Multinational enterprises (MNEs) established component and assembly plants in these low-cost locations and EANIC governments recognized the development opportunities provided by responsive customs' procedures. By the 1980s, rising labour costs in Japan encouraged its producers to out-source into Asia, particularly to Thailand and Malaysia.

The 'Asian miracle' did not depend on discriminatory trade agreements or new inter-government institutions but on entrepreneurs seeking cost savings to satisfy demands in global markets. Multinational enterprises were active in promoting trans-border links, while alert East Asian governments and entrepreneurs were eager to facilitate economic development with trade-promoting measures.

2 GLOBALIZATION BRINGS GOVERNMENT INTERVENTION

In the 1990s this East Asian model had to adapt to political changes in the region and new forces acting on East Asian economies. Hong Kong and Taiwan suffered changed status as China re-entered the global economy, while Korea's industrialization responded comprehensively to new market opportunities. For a variety of reasons, East Asian countries became less committed to trade liberalization, with the notable exception of Singapore, which chose an independent path.

From its beginnings in 1967, the Association of South-East Asian Nations (ASEAN) was a defensive alliance of 'non-aligned' states seeking to avoid outside influences (Brunei became the sixth member in 1984). Sensitive to each other's different circumstances and to past political and economic tensions, these governments avoided interfering in each other's affairs, made minimum commitments and met infrequently. Yet, in 1992, ASEAN members decided to establish bilateral trade agreements (in the form of the Asian Free Trade Agreement, AFTA). Probably a defensive strategy to facilitate coordination of policy positions in then current GATT and APEC negotiations, this clumsy bilateral construct maintained national independence but at the cost of third-rate trade regimes requiring a permutation of 15 bilateral preferential trade agreements to cover all six members. However, it secured their collective regional interest in international affairs, while protecting their national sovereignty.[2]

Developments in GATT in the 1990s caused concern to ASEAN and other authorities. Despite the diplomatic exhortations that opened the Uruguay Round of trade negotiations in 1986, its comprehensive agenda was daunting (Croome, 1995). When the GATT ministerial council meeting broke down over agricultural negotiations in Brussels in December 1990 leading players were flirting with bilateral trade alternatives. In 1989 the EU implemented its 'Single European Market Act' (1986) and shortly after, the United States opened bilateral negotiations with Canada and Mexico to form NAFTA, which took effect in 1992. US support for APEC in 1989 was another manifestation of interest in reciprocity and bilateral agreements.

Eventually the Uruguay Round trade negotiations were saved. The Final Act and the WTO Agreement were signed at Marrakech in April 1994 and the multilateral trading system seemed restored. Unfortunately, bilateralism and trade discrimination were abroad and important weaknesses in the Marrakech agreements were soon exposed: the crucial agreement on agriculture was ineffective and developing countries objected to 'the single undertaking' condition with respect to TRIPs (trade-related aspects of intellectual property rights) and TRIMs (trade-related investment measures) (Finger and Schuler, 2000). Anti-globalization NGOs attacked WTO decisions as impediments to the interests of developing countries. These tensions surfaced at the first WTO ministerial meeting in Singapore, December 1996 when OECD governments wanted to link trade policies to domestic policies on labour standards, competition policies, investment rules and government procurement policies. These proposals were vigorously opposed by developing countries. (Revival of these issues at the Cancun ministerial meeting in 2003, almost destroyed the WTO.)

Dissatisfaction with the WTO and Uruguay Round decisions were manifest again in the 'street theatre' at the Seattle ministerial meeting (1999). After the terrorist attacks on New York in September 2001, however, it became imperative that multilateralism should be emphasized at the

WTO ministerial meeting in Doha two months later. New comprehensive trade negotiations were declared. Unfortunately, the development agenda imposed on the new round became the bane of the negotiations, largely because OECD governments were unwilling to compromise on agricultural protection. Four subsequent ministerial meetings failed to show any progress towards agreement. The latest breakdown in Geneva in July 2008 was evidence that multilateral trade negotiations were a casualty of widening global diversity. GATT principles of reciprocity, non-discrimination and tariff binding are not suited to a disparate global economy with many conflicting goals. Trade preferences, tailor-made protection and bilateralism have become instruments of international diplomacy, regardless of the economic consequences.

ASEAN resentment at the Uruguay Round outcomes and the injustice of the 'single undertaking' in the final agreement were exacerbated by fallout from the 1996–97 financial crises in ASEAN economies. The IMF, the World Bank and Western banks are still blamed for the severity of that financial disruption and the ensuing economic recession in East Asia. Using the Bretton Woods institutions as a scapegoat is convenient for national authorities that were responsible for inadequate banking supervision, excessive offshore borrowing and inadequate legal infrastructures. A decade later the resentment is still tangible, and there is insistence that ASEAN must manage its own affairs, enhance its political independence and seek regional solutions.

3   INCORPORATING THE MEKONG 4

The ASEAN bilateral trade arrangements formed in 1992 were gradually extended to the four Mekong countries. Each ASEAN partner negotiated separate bilateral trade agreements with Vietnam (1995), Laos and Myanmar (1997) and Cambodia (1999). This expansion increased the extent of economic disparities among the ASEAN membership, as well as adding new political differences. The prospect of harmonizing 45 separate bilateral trade agreements among the ten ASEAN members was formidable.

Even among the original six ASEANs economic integration was impeded by political differences and economic disparities, which led to defensive trade policies. The two smallest economies in terms of population and physical size (Singapore and Brunei) have among the highest incomes per capita in the world. The former depends on the provision of services and its strategic location. The latter is blessed with oil reserves. At the other end of the scale, the population of Laos is slightly more than

Singapore, but its income per capita is only 2 percent of the Singapore level. Myanmar has the second largest landmass in ASEAN, after Indonesia, but it is one of the poorest countries in the world. Indonesia has the fourth largest population in the world and has the lowest income per capita among the original ASEAN members. Malaysia, Philippines, Indonesia and Thailand recorded strong economic growth until the 1997 Asian financial crisis. Growth recovered after 2000, but at less than earlier rates. Economic confidence was not fully restored in these countries when the 2008 global financial crisis struck. Foreign exchange reserves accumulated to guard against further financial disruption had withdrawn purchasing power from these growing economies, which diminished investment in vital infrastructure and slowed development.

The incorporation of the Mekong 4 into ASEAN was a political decision. Only minimal demands were asked of these fragile, non-democratic countries and their bilateral trade agreements contain long transition periods (up to 20 years). Even this has been too much for the military dictatorship in Myanmar, which keeps the economy stolidly closed and has yet to ratify its membership of ASEAN. In the closing years of the twentieth century, Myanmar was reporting substantial trade deficits, but since 2003 small surpluses have been recorded as natural gas and mineral exports have increased.

In 1997 the Mekong 4 traded little with each other according to available data. Vietnam, the most advanced of the four economies, is an enthusiastic member of ASEAN, although total trade with its partners has shown little response to ASEAN preferences (13 percent of total trade by value in 2006 compared with 12 percent in 1996). A small trade deficit with ASEAN was matched by a surplus with the rest of the world, which accounts for 86 percent of Vietnam's merchandise exports. Cambodia has a persistent trade deficit with ASEAN partners, but this is matched by a surplus with the rest of the world. Throughout the past decade Laos has reported trade deficits.

It is worth noting that the Mekong region is criss-crossed by historic trade routes between established settlements. The very low level of trade recorded between these Mekong neighbours suggests failure in data collection rather than a reflection of genuine economic links. It is not unusual in centralized developing economies for business statistics to be distorted.

The value of imports and exports increased for all the Mekong members in the period 1997–2006. Like the ASEAN six, Mekong 4 imports from China have increased strongly leading to large and growing bilateral trade deficits. Vietnam and Myanmar have shown most growth in trade with China.

Vietnam and Cambodia have achieved average annual GDP growth rates of 7–10 percent in the past decade. However, only Vietnam has recorded any substantial structural change, with an eight-fold increase in exports of manufactures to accompany smaller increases in exports of food and fuels. Vietnam's bilateral trade agreement with the United States has undoubtedly helped its economic development. US investment inflows have contributed to growth in industrial output and sustained Vietnam's trade with the rest of the world. An extension of the agreement with the United States is mooted but this will depend on the new US Administration. In 2008 Vietnam was combating severe inflationary pressures, which its complex ownership rules exacerbate and rudimentary banking laws complicate.

Cambodia and Laos have gradually increased their global trade. Both countries have a narrow range of exports, which causes export earnings to fluctuate and disrupts economic development. Cambodia exports logs and furniture, but extensive tree felling has caused environmental concerns, which are curtailing exports. There is little evidence that trade agreements with ASEAN partners have done much to increase growth prospects in Laos or Cambodia because they lack strong commercial links outside the Mekong region.

Myanmar remains a military-controlled dictatorship and, despite periodic announcements that controls will be relaxed, nothing changes. Myanmar has made no apparent effort to expand trade or political links with ASEAN partners, apart from taking its seat at ASEAN meetings. Import and export licensing, multiple exchange rates and widespread state ownership of production prevent integration with regional partners.

Myanmar's trade with its Mekong partners was, and remains, insignificant. Over the past decade, total exports and imports together accounted for around 25 percent of GDP. Myanmar's trade intensity is well below that of the other Mekong countries. Most recently, Myanmar's exports to ASEAN have marginally exceeded imports because of growing exports of mineral fuels – 90 percent of Myanmar's exports to ASEAN comprise gas exports to Thailand. Myanmar's mineral resources are attracting investment interest from China. A gas pipeline is planned from Ramree Island into southern China.

Myanmar's closed borders have become an issue with its ASEAN partners. Heavy-handed controls by the military that disrupted international aid after the recent cyclone that devastated southern Myanmar caused international dismay. Likewise, military confrontation on the Cambodian–Thai border has disturbed ASEAN core countries seeking to promote the ASEAN Economic Community (AEC).

4   ASEAN PLUS THREE

China's accession to the WTO in 2001 and remarkable export performance had immediate effects on its East Asian neighbours. China has absorbed raw materials, components and investment funds, as well as capturing overseas markets from its neighbours. Initially, the ASEAN defence was to seek links with Chinese industry by means of preferential trade agreements. However, by 2003–04 ASEAN countries recognized that more defensive action was necessary and took steps to consolidate their mutual trade by coordinating AFTA tariff liberalization.

In 2005 China reached an agreement with ASEAN whereby each member had a bilateral PTA with China covering merchandise trade, which was consistent with the ASEAN approach. These agreements were extended to include some service sectors in 2007, after Japan had invited ASEAN governments to negotiate bilateral trade negotiations. Japan had already negotiated 'new-age economic partnership' agreements (NEPs) with Singapore and Thailand, and wanted to generate interest in this instrument from other neighbours to satisfy Japan's unique trade interests.

These multiple agreements with China and Japan added to the complexity of administering ASEAN trade agreements. Cross-frontier transactions were subject to multiple 'rules of origin', which were expensive, time-consuming and difficult to administer. Administration increased transaction costs of regional economic integration and discouraged trade. APEC committees have been negotiating for many years to improve clearance times in ASEAN ports. A few years ago, it estimated that only around 10 percent of intra-ASEAN trade received tariff preferences. Most traders choose to pay full tariffs and taxes at the border to expedite clearance of cargoes.

The political tensions between the two potential outside 'hubs' for ASEAN trade – China and Japan – make a cohesive single trade agreement in East Asia unlikely. South Korea also has trade agreements with the ASEAN countries covering goods and services, but Seoul has its own problems with both Japan and China. Recent ministerial meetings of 'ASEAN plus three' may have eased tensions but a harmonious free trade agreement seems unlikely.

While governments on both sides of ASEAN bilateral agreements claim they bring benefits beyond trade creation (bypassing any mention of negative effects from trade diversion), the economic effects are uncertain, even after 15 years. These bilateral agreements usually included different tariff dismantling schedules, including 'honeymoon periods' for selected industries, to allow adjustment before protection began to be dismantled.

The latest ASEAN bilateral PTAs with Japan are even more selective. In the Doha Round negotiations Japan has tried to negotiate relaxation of conditions for 'free trade areas' contained in GATT article XXIV. This was intended to give legitimacy to Japan's 'new-age economic partnerships' (NEPs). These discriminatory devices include new timetables to reduce 'beyond-the-border' measures such as investment and competition policies, while pointedly excluding agricultural protection. This would reduce the commodity coverage of free trade areas (defined in GATT article XXIV as covering 'substantially all trade'), while including sensitive 'Singapore issues' that are anathema to developing countries. The stop–start Doha Round negotiations gave no consideration to GATT article XXIV.

Trade policy has shaped East Asian diplomacy in the past decade. Old suspicions and political tensions have submitted to commercial interests as preferential trade relations have spread, encouraged by the faltering Doha Round negotiations. However, while East Asia's total trade has increased strongly in the past decade, growth of intra-ASEAN trade has barely maintained its share at around 22 percent.

The strong growth of ASEAN exports to China indicate increasing dependence on providing intermediate inputs and components to Chinese factories, as well as the longstanding supplies to Japanese export industries. This reliance on Japanese and Chinese markets, however, is likely to compromise ASEANs economic freedom.

5   GLOBAL TRADE RELATIONS

The erratic record of WTO trade negotiations and repeated breakdowns in the Doha Round have exacerbated the shift towards preferential trade agreements (Sally, 2008). As long as major players in the WTO negotiations continue to protect their agricultural sectors, at the expense of multilateral trade in manufacturing and services, no agreement will be reached with non-OECD countries. Moreover, proposals that developing countries should be granted special treatment for a variety of reasons have confused negotiators. These 'special safeguard' concessions remove incentives for developing countries to seek efficiency, while providing the excuse for OECD governments to abrogate their obligations to liberalize.

The failure of OECD governments to maintain their commitment to multilateral trade liberalization since 1994 has exacerbated the shift to PTAs. (This worsened during the Doha Round negotiations with open support for PTAs because they focus on relaxing 'beyond-the-border' policies and reduced the need to undertake negotiations on politically sensitive tariffs.) Ultimately, OECD governments' unwillingness to commit fully to liberalization in the Doha Round encouraged the belief that bilateral trade agreements could substitute for multilateral trade (Robertson, 2006, ch. 6).

Unfortunately, so many PTAs have been established without scrutiny by the WTO/GATT that there is little prospect of assessing or modifying new PTAs (Baldwin et al., 2007). One positive result of increasingly complex bilateralism in East Asia has been to persuade ASEAN governments to accelerate their timetable to establish the ASEAN Economic Community (AEC). First proposed at the ASEAN Summit meeting in January 2007, this ambitious enterprise has become the focus of ministerial discussions.

6 ASIAN ECONOMIC COMMUNITY AND THE MEKONG 4

The invitation to the Mekong 4 to form PTAs with the ASEAN countries in the 1990s raised many questions. The AEC agreement raises many more. The focus in the 1990s was economic integration using trade liberalization. What were the prospects that these four underdeveloped, state-planned, Mekong countries would adapt? Even if their political regimes could respond to change, how long would adaptation take? The income gaps between the six original members of ASEAN have widened since 1992, but three of the Mekong countries are among the poorest economies in Asia. Only the Vietnam economy has recorded substantial economic growth since joining ASEAN. It has also become one of the most ardent supporters of economic integration among Asian economies.

A review of trade between the original ASEAN six and the Mekong 4 shows few discernible benefits from trade liberalization. One positive effect that could arise for the Mekong countries from associating with ASEAN would be benefits from 'learning-by-doing'. The 'Asian miracle' did not evolve from formal inter-government agreements or from domestic policy interference. The business enterprise demonstrated by the EANICs in the 1970s is scarce and stifled in state-planned economies.

Vietnam has taken advantage of market opportunities by relaxing many of its central planning and government controls. This has attracted foreign investment from the United States and neighbouring ASEAN countries (Thailand, Malaysia). Japanese and Chinese companies are also beginning to outsource component manufacture in Vietnam. Nevertheless, dismantling non-tariff barriers (technical standards, government regulations, laws, and so on) and especially overcoming state controls takes time.

Without substantial political reform, the other Mekong economies are unlikely to benefit much from trade liberalization.

7   ANOTHER STEP

The ASEAN's growing dependence on Chinese and Japanese markets encouraged their governments to seek stronger AFTA commitments with ministers to proposing a schedule for an ASEAN Economic Community (AEC) to be achieved by 2015. This will require a high level of regional integration among a group of very disparate economies. An action programme was agreed at the AEC Summit meeting in Singapore in November 2007. It is an ambitious programme and to achieve the targets ASEAN will have to go well beyond the PTAs established in 1992 (Hew, 2007).

Until recently, the concept of national sovereignty outweighed interest in regional institutions. If the AEC is to be operational by 2015, fundamental changes will be necessary among administrators, politicians and national leaders in countries with histories of suspicion and hostility. The 'ASEAN way' of consultation, consensus and non-interference will not build common institutions and common policies. Some progress might be feasible for the ASEAN six plus Vietnam, but a development gulf divides this group from the rest of the Mekong 4. AEC discussions have alerted ASEAN governments to difficulties facing the Mekong.

Non-interference in domestic affairs must be sacrificed if the AEC is to be achieved – or indeed, if an effective free trade area is to be achieved. Differences among the original ASEAN six economies have compromised their commitments to trade liberalization in the past.

Potential applicants for trade links with ASEAN, such as India and the EU, want open negotiations. The Australia–New Zealand 'free trade area' agreement with the ASEAN, signed in Bangkok in March 2009, is comprehensive and could provide a model for the AEC. US bilateral negotiations with Malaysia, Thailand and Vietnam have been temporarily suspended because of the change of administration in the United States. There is serious hostility to trade liberalization in the Democratic Congress and in the new Obama Administration. Even so, some new initiatives are under consideration (Bergsten, 2005).

8   CONCLUSION

Participating governments, the media and political commentators receive regional trade arrangements enthusiastically. Preferential trade agreements, which fall short of 'free trade agreements' as defined in GATT article XXIV, are regarded as alternatives to multilateral liberalization, or at least as a desirable 'second best'. Without analysing these divergences from liberal trade principles, it is evident that the pyramid of bilateral preferential trade arrangements formed by ASEAN and their extensions to China, Japan and Korea – and now Australia–New Zealand – create a complex structure for traders to deal with. Not only are they bilateral agreements that do not meet provisions of GATT article XXIV, they also violate the principle of non-discrimination (Anderson, 2005).

In the past 15 years global trade has experienced a disturbing increase in discrimination. With the growth of regional 'hubs', the number of 'spokes' has increased and a complex multi-layered pattern of discrimination has evolved (Wonnacott, 1996). The GATT/WTO rules relating to preferential trade (GATT article XXIV) have been ignored and there is little prospect that new rules can be devised (Lloyd and MacLaren, 2004).

The global financial crisis that struck in 2008 has seriously reduced global trade flows. The OECD has forecast a reduction in world merchandise trade of 13 percent in 2009. Several OECD governments have already taken putative steps to protect domestic industries, and the effects of recession have only just begun to take effect. Resort to trade discrimination is costly and politically dangerous for the global economy.

Unfortunately, many diplomats and politicians, and the media, regard any 'trade/commerce agreement' as beneficial, ignoring the evident benefits of non-discrimination and multilateral competition. Each country claims its preferential trade arrangements are comprehensive and genuinely liberalizing, but they discriminate against non-participants and cause inefficient trade diversion. The more bilateralism displaces multilateral trade negotiations, the more discrimination will occur. Any analysis of Asian bilateral trade agreements, with their many conditions, exceptions and escape clauses, and absence of disciplines, must have uncertain effects. Complex 'rules of origin' and exceptions clauses add to the uncertainties. Above all, negotiated regional agreements provide no legal protection for non-participants.

Any contribution from ASEAN PTAs to economic development in the Mekong countries will depend on collaboration between companies and government agencies similar to that behind 'the Asian Miracle' 40 years ago. Economic benefits from government-to-government trade agreements depend on private sector reactions and market enterprise. Quality public institutions need to be built in the Mekong economies for private sector firms (both domestic and international) to make the necessary investments and to take advantage of market liberalization. This is perhaps the next development challenge of the Mekong 4.

NOTES

1. EANICs initially comprise Hong Kong, Korea, Taiwan and Singapore. This group was later joined by Malaysia, Thailand, Indonesia and the Philippines. Their governments and firms took advantage of the generalized scheme of preferences established by UNCTAD in 1973, given GATT approval by the Tokyo Round 'Enabling Clause' in 1979.
2. This family of bilateral trade agreements is not a genuine 'free trade agreement' as defined by GATT article XXIV. Hence, AFTA is a misleading term.

REFERENCES

Anderson, K. (2005), 'Setting the trade policy agenda: what roles for economists', *Journal of World Trade*, **39** (2), 341–81.

Baldwin, R. (2006), 'Managing the "noodle bowl": the fragility of East Asian Regionalism', Centre for Economic Policy Research discussion paper no. 5561, London.

Baldwin, R., S. Evenett and P. Low (2007), 'Beyond tariffs: multilateralising deeper RTA commitments', WTO–HEI Conference, September 2007.

Bergsten, C.F. (2005), *The United States and the World Economy*, Washington DC: Institute for International Economics.

Croome, J. (1995), *Reshaping the World Trading System*, Geneva: World Trade Organization.

Finger, J.M. and P. Schuler (2000), 'Implementation of Uruguay Round commitments: the development challenge', *The World Economy*, **23** (4).

Gill, I.S. and Homi Kharas (2007), *An East Asian Renaissance; Ideas for Economic Growth*, Washington, DC: World Bank.

Hew, D. (ed.) (2007), *Brick by Brick: Building of an ASEAN Economic Community*, Singapore: Institute of Southeast Asian Studies.

Leipziger, D.M. and V.Thomas (1993), *The Lessons of East Asia*, Washington, DC: World Bank.

Lloyd, P.J. and D. MacLaren (2004), 'Gains and losses from regional trading agreements: a survey' *The Economic Record*, **80** (251), 445–67.

Robertson, D. (2006), *International Economics and Confusing Politics*, Cheltenham, UK and Northampton, MA, USA: Edward Elgar.

Sally, R. (2008), *New Frontiers in Free Trade*, Washington, DC: Cato Institute.

Wonnacott, R.J. (1996), 'Trade and investment in a "hub-and-spoke" system', *The World Economy*, **19** (3), 237–52.

World Bank (1993), *The East Asian Miracle*, New York: Oxford University Press.

PART II

Case studies of Mekong countries

7. Vietnam: country case study

Ben Bingham and Suiwah Leung[1]

1 INTRODUCTION

In the two decades since Vietnam launched its *Doi Moi* market reforms[2] the results have been widely hailed for sustaining economic growth, reducing poverty and increasing the standard of living. The transformation from a poor agrarian economy to an increasingly globally integrated market economy generated considerable optimism about the country's economic outlook. For example, the latest Socio-Economic Development Program (SEDP)[3] outlined Vietnam's ambition to become a middle-income country by the end of this decade and a modern industrial economy by 2020. This optimism was not confined to government circles; it reflected the consensus view, especially following Vietnam's accession to the WTO in January 2007.

In the wake of domestic turbulence and the severe downturn in the global economy in 2008 some of this optimism has waned. This chapter considers the challenges facing Vietnam in light of these recent developments. It reviews the two principal waves of economic reform over the past two decades and discusses the factors that made investors so optimistic about Vietnam's long-term outlook. It then discusses the deterioration in economic conditions over the past 12 months before addressing the broader reform challenges that Vietnam faces if it is to succeed in developing a modern market economy.

2 TWO DECADES OF REFORM

Doi moi, or economic renovation, began in 1986 but the effective opening of the country to international trade and investment did not start until 1989. Throughout the 1990s GDP grew at an average annual rate of 7–8 percent but from a very low base. Moreover, while *doi moi* resulted in significant integration of Vietnam's trade and capital flows with the Asian and the world economy, trade and investment policies tilted towards

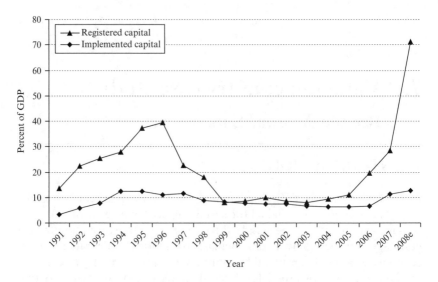

Source: GSO, Available at http://www.gso.gov.vn, accessed 19 September 2009.

Figure 7.1   FDI inflow into Vietnam

protecting the state sector limited prospects for continuing rapid economic growth. For example, most of the foreign direct investment (FDI) throughout the 1990s went into joint ventures with state-owned enterprises (SOEs).

Bias towards the state sector had a number of consequences. Firstly, the high concentration of FDI in capital-intensive projects in heavy industries and the oil and gas sector (Leung 2006) limited employment generation (Doanh 2002). Secondly, the bias reduced Vietnam's attractiveness as an investment destination, as the returns to foreign companies were being limited through partnerships with inefficient SOEs. As a result, FDI flows into Vietnam reached a peak in 1996 (well before the onset of the Asian financial crisis in July 1997) and did not pick up again until the deepening of domestic reforms took hold and Vietnam joined the WTO in 2007 (Figure 7.1). As multinational enterprises spearhead much of the spread of production networks in Asia, falling FDI in Vietnam suggested the country had yet to establish itself as a major competitor in this arena.

The Asian financial crisis was a wake-up call for Vietnam. Although less affected than other countries in the region, the sharp decline in Vietnam's FDI highlighted the limited prospects for sustaining rapid growth under the existing economic strategy. Politically, the country realized the need for a change in economic direction. To keep up with population growth and maintain social stability, the economy needed to generate 1.5 million jobs a year. The state sector could not generate job creation on this scale. The domestic private sector had to be unleashed and allowed to grow. Furthermore, it was evident that multinational enterprises looking to out-source their production processes were more interested in establishing 100 percent owned subsidiaries and mergers and acquisitions of private firms than joint ventures with SOEs.

In order to enhance competitiveness and generate employment Vietnam embarked on a second wave of reforms. The first step was the enactment of the Enterprises Law (2001). Previously, every private business, large or small, had to have a licence, which had to be renewed, sometimes monthly. The Enterprises Law abolished hundreds of different licences at one stroke. Further simplification of administrative procedures for busi-nesses, culminating in the Unified Enterprise Law (2006) and Common Investment Law (2006) equalized the treatment between state enterprises and the private sector and between domestic and foreign enterprises.

In the space of two years registered businesses more than doubled.[4] Private investment also responded, rising from 18 to 24 percent of GDP between 2000 and 2007. More importantly, there was a surge in non-agricultural employment, with preliminary data suggesting that private businesses gen-erated around 90 percent of the jobs created between 2000 and 2007. FDI firms alone generated 145 000 jobs per annum during this period.

GDP growth between 2000 and 2007 was second only to China's. In terms of socio-economic development, Vietnam is already approach-ing and, in some cases, exceeds that of ASEAN (5) – in particular, the Philippines and Indonesia. The surging demand for mobile telephones and internet connectivity also indicate an economy and society on the move.

As well as improving the regulatory environment, the government also sought to lower the costs of doing business. International phone charges fell sharply after 2001 and are now competitive with other cities in Asia. Container transportation and electricity costs also fell. These improve-ments combined with Vietnam's inherent strengths as an investment location – a large, low-cost, disciplined workforce; a young demographic structure; a strong work ethic and entrepreneurial spirit; and a location close to the major economic centres of the fastest growing region in the world – attracted attention in the global investment community. Vietnam's reputation for political stability and a forward-looking government also attracted investors.

Vietnam's accession to the WTO in January 2007 and commitment to continue opening up the economy to international competition further entrenched the domestic reforms and signalled the government's com-mitment to transforming the country into a fully-functioning market economy.[5] Being formally granted Permanent Normal Trade Relations status by the United States just prior to WTO accession also helped bring Vietnam to the notice of investors worldwide. As a result FDI surged to an estimated US$6.5 billion in 2007 and probably more in 2008.[6]

Foreign investors were not the only ones taking note of these changes – so were Vietnamese living abroad. Remittances into Vietnam through recognized channels of banks and other approved institutions rose steadily in the first five years of the new millennium (from around 4–6 percent of GDP).[7] Moreover, as with FDI, the data suggests that remittances accelerated sharply in 2006 and 2007 to around 9 percent of GDP (US$6 billion) and that remittances have remained robust in 2008.

Furthermore, there is some evidence that the portfolio (or profit) motive of remittances is significant (IMF 2006) and that a large proportion of remittances could well be capital inflows rather than a current account item. In addition, analysis shows remittances in Vietnam are positively correlated with the country's economic conditions (as proxied by its per capita GDP), with the general investment climate (proxied by FDI) and with the relaxation of the regulatory environment in the late 1990s (ibid.).

Previously, Vietnam had been out of the East Asian production networks. Even though its labour costs were relatively low, costs of transport, telecommunications, delays at customs and legal and regulatory risks made it unattractive to produce components or do assembly work in Vietnam.

Now, however, even the most cursory tour of the industrial zones surrounding Ho Chi Minh City and Hanoi, where familiar names (Canon, Panasonic, Samsung) are becoming increasingly evident, reveals change. A study of the nature of FDI projects over the past four to five years confirms this casual empiricism and supports the conclusion that foreign investors (principally Japanese and other Asian firms) are starting to locate assembly plants in Vietnam (see Appendix Table 7A.1). A sharp increase in imports in parts and components also indicates Vietnam's participation in production networks.

The buoyant mood surrounding Vietnam's prospects seemed encouraging but some commentators called for a reality check. Mallon (2007), for instance, highlighted the fact that the Vietnamese economy would become more vulnerable to the impact of international economic downturns, putting a premium on the need to maintain sound macroeconomic fundamentals. Constraints arising out of infrastructure and human capital bottlenecks and lagging institutional development in economic, social and legal spheres were also potential barriers to Vietnam's development goals.

Before addressing some of these longer-term challenges we turn to the macroeconomic turbulence that Vietnam encountered in 2008.

3 MACROECONOMIC TURBULENCE

Vietnam's success in attracting capital inflows paradoxically revealed some of the limitations of the past five years' reform. The accelerated pace of economic development that accompanied the surge in capital inflows in 2007 and its subsequent reversal in 2008 exposed the lack of reform of key economic institutions needed to manage a modern market economy, such as the State Bank of Vietnam (SBV) and Ministry of Finance. These have also complicated the response to the current global financial crisis.

The initial problems stemmed from the fact that the government was unprepared to manage the capital inflows of late 2006 to mid-2007. In excess of 20 percent of GDP, these large capital inflows came from multiple sources, including foreign direct investment, portfolio inflows and remittances. At the same time domestic residents invested their savings in the booming domestic economy. The resulting boost to demand proved inflationary and came on top of already rising global commodity prices. The increase in demand also fed into the balance of payments and rising imports put pressure on the trade deficit.

Slow to respond to signs that the economy was overheating, the government actually exacerbated the overheating. Monetary policy, hampered by the need to defend a rigid exchange rate peg,[8] was too loose for too long. Large-scale, unsterilized, intervention in the foreign exchange market fuelled rapid credit growth, which surged to over 50 percent in 2007. Aggressive expansion of investment by state-owned enterprises compounded an expansionary fiscal policy.[9] Weaknesses in bank supervision and especially the decision to grant 11 rural credit institutions full banking licences further complicated macroeconomic management. This not only added to the risk of banking vulnerabilities but may well have fuelled the credit boom itself, as credit expansion was most rapid among the newer smaller banks (credit growth in some of these banks exceeded 100 percent).

Rapid credit growth, combined with an expansionary fiscal policy, contributed to a sharp rise in inflation in 2007 (12.5 percent in December) and substantial widening of the current account deficit (from 0–10 percent of GDP). Economic conditions continued to deteriorate in the first half of 2008, with inflation rising further to 27–28 percent. The current account deficit reached 11.5 percent of GDP in the first half of 2008, as a result of a further surge in imports in the first quarter. Overstretched asset prices, especially in the property sector, and potential weaknesses in the banking sector added to the economy's vulnerabilities.

Weakening economic indicators began to weigh on investor sentiment as 2008 progressed. The stock market fell by close to 60 percent in the first half of 2008 and the property market, which had risen sharply in the second half of 2007, also went into reverse. More alarmingly, the Dong came under significant downward pressure in the second quarter. At one stage, the Dong was trading almost 10 percent outside of the official band and the offshore NDF rate, at the six-month horizon, was 25 percent more depreciated than the spot rate.[10] The emergence of a dual exchange rate regime raised doubts about the credibility of the exchange rate band and raised fears in some quarters about an imminent external crisis.

These fears retreated in the third quarter of 2008. More positive economic news, especially on inflation, trade and credit growth, provided reassurance that government efforts to stabilize the economy were working.[11] And, using a combination of tight liquidity, regulatory action and foreign exchange intervention the SBV took decisive steps to restore the credibility of the exchange rate band. This eased pressure on the Dong and helped reverse the slide in market sentiment.

No sooner had the government negotiated these challenges than the global economic crisis was upon them. The sharp deterioration in the global environment posed a significant challenge for macroeconomic management. On the one hand, with inflation decelerating rapidly on the back of falling commodity prices, the balance of risks, and consequently policy priority, had clearly shifted from containing inflation to supporting economic activity. As such, an easing of monetary policy and a more accommodative fiscal policy were clearly warranted. However, as with many emerging market economies, the task of policy makers has been complicated by the need to sustain external stability in the face of fragile financing flows and sentiment towards their currencies. Vietnam's less robust external position than its neighbours – Vietnam has a structural current account deficit and lower reserves (three months of imports) – constrained its ability to pursue expansionary policies.

The government responded quickly to the changing economic conditions and reversed the course of macroeconomic policies previously focused on restraining an overheating economy. The State Bank of Vietnam rapidly eased monetary policy, lowering its policy rates by seven percentage points to 7 percent and reducing reserve requirements sharply. The government also announced a broad economic stimulus plan to support economic growth. The plan, which covered a range of tax and expenditure measures, is likely to result in a significant easing of fiscal policy in 2009, although the exact extent of that easing remains the subject of some debate, as a result of the opacity of the government's fiscal operations.

The stimulus strategy has brought mixed results. On the one hand, it has succeeded in supporting economic activity, and all the evidence now suggests that the economic downturn in Vietnam will be much milder than other countries in the region. On the other hand, it has contributed to renewed pressures on the external position, albeit not as intense as in 2008. Thus, there has been a persistent shortage of dollars in the foreign exchange market throughout 2009, with the Dong trading outside of the official band by 2–3 percentage points, and access to foreign exchange in effect being rationed, imposing significant costs on enterprises.

While the challenges posed by the global financial crisis complicated economic management right around the world, in Vietnam they highlighted the importance of modernizing key economic institutions and endowing them with the capacity to respond effectively to the shifts in economic currents intrinsic to participating in a globalized economy. In particular, it has highlighted the fact that the management of a fixed exchange rate regime requires far greater finesse in the execution of monetary and fiscal policy, as well as financial sector supervision, than was necessary when Vietnam was still a relatively closed, state-dominated economy.

4 TOWARDS A MODERN MARKET ECONOMY: PHASE 3 OF REFORMS

As recent macroeconomic turbulence demonstrates, successful international integration requires the domestic institutions that enable a country to respond quickly and flexibly to domestic and international conditions. The new globalized environment places a premium on flexibility and innovativeness if countries are to avoid being trapped at the low-wage end of the value chain in production networks. Creating a truly competitive economy requires world-class government institutions fostering a dynamic and creative private sector. While Vietnam has the natural ingredients it lacks the institutions capable of realizing the potential of its highly entrepreneurial private sector.

Thus, while Vietnam faces many development challenges – infrastructure bottlenecks, scarcity of skilled labour, environmental challenges and so on – we focus here on the need for a third phase of reforms to give Vietnam the institutions needed to maintain economic transformation.

5 ROLE OF GOVERNMENT

As measured by the share of government expenditure in GDP, the size of government is actually much larger in advanced market economies than in most developing countries. But governments in advanced economies do different things. Rather than engaging directly in productive activities, they attend to market failures and equity, which they carry out through various forms of intervention and, in addition to providing basic public goods and services, they address externalities, engage in regulatory activities and provide social safety nets. Some also pursue more activist functions such as coordinating private sector activity and asset redistribution (World Bank 1997). Of course, the extent to which governments engage in these activities also depends on their capacity to do so. However, achieving adequate institutional capacity to deliver at least the intermediate functions of government would appear to be a minimum requirement for a modern market economy.

We now consider how Vietnam has adapted or not to the changes in government functions demanded by the transformation of its economy. The five-year socio-economic development plan (SEDP 2006–10) recognized the need to adapt and showed a much clearer acceptance of the private sector compared to its predecessors. With fewer production targets and more development objectives it suggests the government is moving out of the role of being a direct producer of goods and services and towards being a facilitator of private sector activity. However, shortcomings remain. The rest of this chapter considers some of the most significant.

6   STATE-OWNED ENTERPRISES (SOES)

Although a significant number of the 500 plus SOEs have been equitized (or privatized) in the past decade, there are still some very large state-owned business conglomerates (so-called General Corporations). This situation has been rationalized by the argument that size matters in world competition and Vietnam needs large SOEs to help it compete in the post-WTO world. The slogan of a 'market economy with socialist orientation' has, until late, prevented close scrutiny of these conglomerates.

The recent macroeconomic turbulence has turned the spotlight onto the operations of these General Corporations whose significantly increased investment activities (over 60 percent increase during 2007) helped overheat the economy. These investments were being financed by the domestic banking system as well as by foreign borrowings. A number of these General Corporations have very high debt–equity ratios and poor profitability, guaranteeing that at least a portion of recent investments will not be profitable. The prospect of a global recession will likely increase the already substantial stock of non-performing loans in the banking sector as well as cause loss of confidence on the part of international investors in Vietnam's government borrowings abroad.

So far, the government has successfully used administrative measures to reduce the large SOEs' public investments and their expansion in non-core activities, particularly banking and real estate. However, administrative measures are subject to arguments about definitions (is the building of storage facilities core or non-core business for the State Shipping Corporation?). And experience shows that administrative edicts are usually circumvented over time. Hence, in addition to strengthening SOEs' governance and advancing their equitization, Vietnam needs to take more decisive action against subsidizing capital going to the SOEs and make them compete with the private sector in the capital market. Not only would this reduce the future exposure of the domestic banking system to possibly increasing non-performing loans from the SOEs, it would also allow the flow of investment capital to the domestic private sector to aid, amongst others, in the making of 'economic discoveries' to move up the value chain of the regional production networks. Sustaining Vietnam's longer-term growth momentum requires continued reform of SOEs and the banking system.

Some positive steps have been taken in recent months. Under WTO commitments, the government has granted full banking licences to three foreign banks (HSBC, Standard and Chartered and the ANZ Banking Corporation). Experience in neighbouring countries shows that foreign banks provide competition for local banks in terms of gaining market shares (see Chapter 4 above). Such competition, together with improved prudential regulations from the SBV, could result in resistance towards further easy credit for the SOEs. However, steps need to be taken to advance the equitizing of the SOCBs. A move towards more realistic valuations of the state-owned commercial banks (and of some SOEs) would facilitate part acquisition of these entities by foreign strategic partners injecting new management techniques, personnel and improved business practices.

The partial sale of China's Industrial and Commercial Bank (ICBC) to foreign strategic investors provides an example.[12] The ICBC sold its 10 percent stake at a price equal only to around 25 to 30 percent of the then market price. Within one year, the contribution of the foreign strategic investors was such that the share price of ICBC more than doubled benefiting both the state owner and other domestic investors. This is in contrast to the recent failed equitization of the Vietcombank where the initial offering to foreign strategic investors was priced at unrealistically high levels.

Vietnam addressed the discrimination against the private sector in its trade and investment regimes in phase 2 of the reforms resulting in rapid growth and development between 2000 and 2007. Attention needs to be paid to developments in the capital market in phase 3 of reforms in order to advance the growth momentum and realize Vietnam's ambitions of being a modern industrial economy by 2020.

7   ECONOMIC POLICY MAKING

The development of institutions to manage a modern market economy has lagged behind reforms in other areas. The framework for economic policy making especially needs reform to meet the needs of a faster moving economic environment. Currently it is still relatively slow and cumbersome and over-focused on administration and regulation, rather than policy adjustments. Moreover, policy responses often lack the coherence and internal consistency needed to manage a modern market economy effectively. There also needs to be greater recognition of the importance of effective communication, as market economies operate inefficiently in the absence of timely and accurate economic data and information on government policies.

7.1   State Bank of Vietnam

One of the top priorities is to restructure the State Bank of Vietnam into a modern central bank. Prompted by the economic turbulence over the past year the government has recognized this priority and has asked the State Bank of Vietnam to accelerate the preparation of revisions to four key laws: the State Bank of Vietnam law, the law on credit institutions, the law on bank supervision and the law on deposit insurance. These laws were to be tabled for discussion with the National Assembly in 2009. The priority was to ensure these laws result in the State Bank of Vietnam gaining sufficient autonomy and powers to carry out the functions of a modern central bank.

Modernizing the State Bank of Vietnam is also important to foster the transformation of the financial sector in a safe and sound manner. As mentioned above, there are signs that the government is taking on board the generally positive experience of countries in the region, and has recently granted full subsidiary licences to three foreign banks.[13] Foreign banks (chiefly non-Japanese Asian banks) are taking minority stakes in the joint stock banks but these are still capped and serious foreign investment in the state-owned commercial banks (SOCBs) has yet to take place. Useful lessons could be learnt from China in this regard.

Increased foreign involvement in banking services requires much better coordination between the regulatory authorities of Vietnam and other banking regulators. With increased FDI in banking, an incident involving a bank's subsidiary may result in systemic risk in the host country but only relatively minor risk in the headquarter country. Whether the subsidiary should be rescued and by whom becomes an important issue. The SBV therefore needs to be given a clearly defined mandate as prudential regulator. This mandate needs to be made functional through resolving the conflict of interest inherent in being the owner and the regulator of the SOCBs. Accelerating the equitization of the SOCBs would help.

Bank finance cannot be relied upon to provide the financial resources needed for companies to develop an internationally competitive private sector. Access to securities markets is also important. The new Securities Law passed in 2006 requiring greater levels of disclosure on the part of companies is an important step. However, like other commercial laws, much depends on the enforcement ability of regulatory authorities, such as the State Securities Commission.

7.2 Ministry of Finance

Modernizing the Ministry of Finance to strengthen fiscal management is also a major priority. The extent of the challenge is illustrated by the fact that Vietnam only scored 2 out of a possible 100 percent in the *Open Budget Index (2006)* – a survey of fiscal transparency undertaken by the International Budget Project.[14] The low score reflects the fact that the government only provides limited information to the public on its budget and financial activities. While the government has taken steps to improve fiscal transparency – by making information available on budget plans and execution – the use of a non-standard classification system, incomplete coverage of fiscal transactions and a lack of realism in plan projections, evidenced by systematically large variations between plan targets and budget outturns, all make the stance of fiscal policy difficult to assess.

The problems at the Ministry of Finance go beyond making information public. There are weaknesses in internal management information systems that hamper the generation of reliable fiscal data as well as the formulation of robust fiscal plans. These problems are partly structural in origin – for example, a complicated budget structure with significant off-budget transactions – but also reflect internal management weakness, especially in the area of cash flow management stemming from a proliferation of different accounting and management systems operating across the government sector. A number of studies[15] have helped the government strengthen its Public Financial Management systems. However, progress has been gradual. Accelerated economic development accompanying Vietnam's increased integration into the global economy requires accelerated reform as Vietnam can ill afford to continue with a untransparent, ill-communicated fiscal policy. The planned revisions to the Budget law – presented to the National Assembly in 2009 – provide an important opportunity to expedite this process. Participating in a Fiscal Transparency ROSC may help achieve that objective.

8   LEGAL DEVELOPMENT

It has been said that the principles governing Vietnamese public institutions are the antithesis to those governing architecture. In architecture, form follows function: decide on what a building is to be used for, and then design the building accordingly. In Vietnam, the opposite is the case: function follows form. Nowhere is this truer than in the area of legal development. While a fairly complete set of commercial laws has been enacted, the courts and the judiciary systems are not yet up to the task of interpreting and enforcing them.

With respect to banking regulation, Vietnamese legislation is equal to or outperforms that of other countries in the region but the SBV lacks the autonomy and power to implement these laws promptly (Kovsted et al. 2005). With respect to public financial management, the State Audit of Vietnam is responsible to the National Assembly but actual auditing capacity is weak. More generally, there is little understanding that for these regulatory bodies to work effectively they need to be independent – not just in a legal or even in a financial sense but in the public perception that people with professional integrity run them.

9   PUBLIC ADMINISTRATION REFORM

Unlike developing countries such as India, the Vietnamese civil service is not very large – around half a million civil servants for 86 million people. In theory it is possible to improve the pay of civil servants while keeping the total payroll affordable. In reality, there are at least two main hurdles:

Historically, many civil servants had free housing as part of their remuneration. Two to three years ago there was a concerted effort to find a monetary equivalent for this and incorporate this component into the salary package. The idea was that civil servants could then rent their apartments back from the government. One problem has been the lack of strata titles to those apartments occupied by civil servants. To date, the government is still working through this issue.

The second problem is more related to culture than to law. Civil service pay in Vietnam is considered as a 'retainer'. Civil servants are expected to earn additional salaries through working on projects – whether foreign aid projects or domestically-funded development projects. This might be viewed as a rather extreme form of performance pay. The well-trained specialist gets plenty of projects and hence lots of extra pay but the ordinary civil servant working at the counter is likely to have to survive on the bare minimum. Until this culture changes it is hard to make headway in rationalizing civil service remuneration and hence reduce the temptation to take bribes at the lower end of the civil service spectrum.

10 CONCLUSIONS

This chapter briefly surveys the economic reforms that led to a remarkable transformation of the Vietnam economy over the past two decades and generated the optimism that fuelled the government's avowed ambition of joining the ranks of middle-income countries by the end of the decade and becoming a modern industrial economy by 2020. The chapter points out, however, that there are some significant near-term challenges around which the authorities need to navigate. A third phase of reforms needs to focus on transforming the role of government if Vietnam is to achieve its long-term goals. In the medium term Vietnam should aim at a private sector that is innovative and nimble, capable of developing international brand name products and responding proactively to changes in the world and the regional environment. This means freeing investment capital in order to finance private sector activities. This hi-tech private sector would need to be supported by world-class public institutions staffed by well-trained professional civil servants. Hence, a medium-term programme of capital market plus targeted public sector reform would seem to be the next challenge.

NOTES

1. Capable research assistance by Ha Trong Nguyen is gratefully acknowledged. The views in this chapter are those of the authors and should not be attributed to the IMF, its Executive Board or its Management.
2. Doanh (1996), Leung and Vo (1996), World Bank country reports (various years).
3. The Five-year Socio-Economic Development Plan, 2006–2010.
4. Admittedly, some businesses were already in existence but failed to be registered before 2001.
5. The impact of Vietnam's WTO accession has been well-analysed in a number of publications, including the IMF Vietnam country report 2007.
6. The latest IMF estimates project FDI inflows at US$8 billion in 2008.
7. Remittances were also boosted by a number measures taken in the wake of the Asian

financial crisis to encourage remittance flows through official channels (see Appendix Box 7A.1).

8. Pegging the Dong to a depreciating US dollar exacerbated the easing of monetary conditions.
9. Bank borrowing by the SOEs increased two-and-a-half-fold to 10 percent of GDP in 2007.
10. The offshore NDF market for the Dong is very thin and is not a good predictor of the future path of the exchange rate. However, it is a useful gauge of sentiment towards the Dong.
11. In March 2008 the government announced an eight-point plan to restore macroeconomic stability, which featured a combination of tighter monetary and fiscal policies, as well as restraint on SOE investment.
12. See Policy Discussion Paper no. 2, Fullbright Economics Teaching Program and Kennedy School of Government, Ho Chi Minh City, May 2008.
13. ANZ, HSBC and Standard Chartered.
14. The International Budget Project, Open Budget initiative http://www.openbudgetindex.org/.
15. These include the IMF–World Bank study, 'Towards Fiscal Transparency' (1999); the 2001 Country Financial Accountability Assessment; and the 2004 Public Expenditure Review.

REFERENCES

Doanh, Le Dang (1996), 'Economic developments and prospects', in Suiwah Leung (ed.), *Vietnam Assessment: Creating a Sound Investment Climate*, Singapore: Institute of Southeast Asian Studies.

Doanh, Le Dang (2002), 'Foreign direct investment in Vietnam: results, achievements, challenges and prospect', paper presented at the conference on 'Foreign Direct Investment: Opportunities and Challenges for Cambodia, Laos and Vietnam', International Monetary Fund and the State Bank of Vietnam, Hanoi, 16–17 August.

Dollar, David and Jennie Litvack (1998), 'Macroeconomic performance and poverty reduction', in David Dollar, Paul Glewwe and Jennie Ilene Litvack (eds), *Household Welfare and Vietnam's Transition to a Market Economy*, Washington, DC: World Bank, pp. 1–26.

The International Budget Project (n.d.), *Open Budget Initiative*, accessed 22 December 2009 at www.openbudgetindex.org.

International Monetary Fund (IMF) and World Bank (1999), *Vietnam: Toward Fiscal Transparency*, joint IMF-World Bank report, Washington, DC: IMF and World Bank.

International Monetary Fund (IMF) (2006), 'Vietnam: selected issues', *IMF Country Report No 06/20*.

IMF (2007), 'Vietnam: selected issues', *IMF Country Report No 07/385*.

Kovsted, Jens, John Rand and Finn Tarp (2005), *From Monobank to Commercial Banking: Financial Sector Reforms in Vietnam*, Copenhagen: Nordic Institute of Asian Studies.

Leung, Suiwah E. (2006), 'Integration and transition – Vietnam, Cambodia and Lao PDR', paper presented at the conference 'Accelerating Development in the Mekong Region – the Role of Economic Integration', 26–27 June, Siem Reap, Cambodia.

Leung, Suiwah E. and Tri Thanh Vo (1996), 'Vietnam in the 1980s: price reform and stabilization', *Banca Nazionale Del Lavoro*, **19** (7), 187–208.

Mallon, Raymond (2007), 'Vietnam: recent economic development and key challenges', paper presented at Vietnam Update Conference, The Australian National University.

World Bank (1997), 'The state in a changing world', in *World Development Report*, Oxford: Oxford University Press.

World Bank (2001), *Vietnam: Country Financial Accountability Assessment*, Washington, DC: World Bank.

World Bank (2004), *Vietnam: Public Expenditure Review and Integrated Fiduciary Assessment*, Washington, DC: World Bank.

World Bank (2006), 'Vietnam: aiming high', in *Vietnam Development Report 2007*, Hanoi: World Bank.

APPENDIX

BOX 7A.1: GOVERNMENT POLICIES AND DECISIONS AFFECTING REMITTANCES

The factors that have encouraged the flow of remittances through official channels in recent years have been as follows:

- Arbitrary treatment of formal transfers, which in the past included possible seizure, has been discontinued, and the process of monitoring has been relaxed.
- Migration and remittances have been encouraged by a number of labour and immigration regulations implemented since the mid-1990s. These have included Government Decree No. 12/1995/ND-CP on social security registration, Government Decree No. 152/1999/ND-CP and Circular No. 28/1999/TT-BLDTBXH on the implementation of the Labor Code with regard to temporary workers abroad, and Decree No. 05/2000 on the exit and entry of Vietnamese citizens. Aside from facilitating migration, these decisions are likely to have affected remittances through their positive impact on market confidence.
- A 5 percent tax on remittances was removed in 1997, and the personal income tax on them was removed in August 1999 (Government Decision No. 170-1999-QD-TTg).
- Regulations mandating that transfers can be withdrawn only in local currency were removed in August 1999 (Decision No. 170 above). At present, transfers can be withdrawn in foreign currencies or maintained in bank accounts in these currencies.
- Large transfer companies, such as Western Union and Moneygram, have been allowed to operate in the market and to form alliances with local banks. This has given migrants access to a large distribution network that covers Vietnam's most important urban and rural areas.
- Government Decree No. 81-2001-ND-CP allowed *Viet Kieu* to purchase residential housing in Vietnam. This right was reasserted by a recent Joint Ministerial Circular (02-2005-TTLT-BKH-BTP-BNG-BCA), which also further

---

liberalized regulations governing investments by foreigners and *Viet Kieu* (for example, by removing the 30 percent cap on ownership of a single company if that company is not governed by the Law on State-Owned Enterprises).

Source: IMF (2006).

Table 7A.1 FDI inflow into Vietnam: parts and components

Approved date	Project name	Investor	Register capital (USD)	Industry
02/01/2001	Wooree Vina Ltd. Co.	Wooree Lighting Co., Ltd	11 850 000	Electronic products manufacturing
10/08/2001	Sumitomo Bakelite Ltd. Co.	Sumitomo Bakelite – Japan	60 000 000	Computer and electronic parts
04/10/2001	Denso Vietnam Ltd. Co.	Denso International Asia and Sumitomo Corporation, Japan	21 700 000	Automobile part production and assembly
29/04/2002	Sakurai Vietnam Ltd. Co.	Sakurai Ltd. Co. – Japan	13 300 000	Laser machine and other manufacturing
13/06/2002	Matsuo Industries Vietnam Ltd. Co.	Matsuo Industries – Japan	15 000 000	Plastic and steel parts for automobile
13/06/2002	New Vietnam Ltd. Co.	Nagakura Manufacturing Co., Ltd. – Japan	13 002 940	Steel parts for automobile
02/07/2002	Fujikin Vietnam Ltd. Co.	Fujikin Ltd. Co. – Japan	20 000 000	Super precious parts in capacity controlling system manufacturing
04/07/2002	Vietnam Semiconductor Ltd. Co.	Saigon Investment Group Ltd., the US	30 000 000	Wafer transistor manufacturing
22/10/2002	Kayaba Vietnam Ltd. Co.	Kayaba Industry Co., Ltd – Japan	16 440 000	Automobile and motorbike part production and assembly
17/12/2002	Hal Vietnam Ltd. Co.	Hiroshima Aluminium Industry; Sumitomo Corp. – Japan	14 980 000	Automobile and motorbike part production

Date	Company	Partner	Capital	Business
16/06/2003	Panasonic Home Appliances Vietnam Ltd. Co.	Matsushita Electric & Sumitomo Corp. – Japan	23 267 000	Domestic electronic manufacturing and assembly
20/11/2003	Việt Hoa Electronic Ltd. Co.	Huacheng Toko Electronics Co., Ltd. – Taiwan	15 300 000	Electric manufacturing and assembly
09/06/2004	SATO Vietnam Ltd. Co.	SATO – Japan	11 666 000	Electronic printer manufacturing and assembly
12/08/2004	Sanyo Di Solutions Vietnam Ltd. Co.	Sanyo Asia Pte. Ltd. – Singapore; Sanyo Sales & Marketing Corp. – Japan	30 000 000	Camera and other parts manufacturing
09/09/2004	Toyoda Gosei Haiphong Ltd. Co.	Toyoda Gosei Company – Japan	44 955 000	Air bag for automobile
05/10/2004	RENESAS Vietnam Design Ltd. Co.	Renesas Technology Corp. – Japan	13 000 000	IC transistor hardware and software R&D
04/01/2005	YAMAHA Motor Vietnam Ltd. Co.	Yamaha Motor Co., Ltd. – Japan	47 619 000	Engine parts manufacturing
12/03/2005	Mabuchi Motor Danang Ltd. Co.	Mabuchi Motor Co., Ltd. – Japan	39 900 000	Small engine manufacturing and assembly
12/05/2005	TATUNG Vietnam Ltd. Co.	TATUNG Co., Ltd. – Japan	35 000 000	Domestic electronic product manufacturing and assembly
02/06/2005	Atsumitech Vietnam Ltd. Co.	Atsumitech Co., Ltd. – Japan	15 236 000	Precision mechanical product manufacturing and assembly

8. The Lao People's Democratic Republic: growth, reform and prospects

Kotaro Ishi

1 INTRODUCTION

A landlocked location, a mountainous geography, a rough topology and poor transport infrastructure largely disconnected the Lao PDR from regional and global economies until the middle of the 1980s.

Over the last two decades, however, the country has made remarkable progress in transforming a centrally planned economy into a market-oriented system. Introduced in 1985, the New Economic Mechanism (NEM) marked the cornerstone of the shift in the government's economic policy. Objectives included breaking up the elements of the command economy inherited from the decade of socialist rule and introducing an integrated market economy. Reform covered every aspect of the economy, including pricing, domestic and external trade, exchange rate, state-owned enterprises (SOEs), banking and finance. They yielded progress in both system transformation and macroeconomic management. Nowadays, prices are mostly market-determined and private enterprise plays a more important role than SOEs. Notably, trade has become relatively open with Lao PDR's economy integrating into the global economy, especially with its neighboring ASEAN economies. Moreover, quite recently, Lao PDR has been emerging as a resource-rich country, with large-scale foreign investment in minerals and hydro-power.

However, daunting challenges face Lao PDR. The priority is how to entrench gains, improve growth and reduce poverty. In particular, with the prospect of further trade liberalization (including entry to WTO), advancing necessary structural reform remains crucial to reap the benefits from deeper integration into the global economy. Besides, the country's ability to cope with shocks attendant upon these increased linkages will become increasingly important. The emerging natural resource sector would also pose a new challenge to the government, as experience shows that resource richness brings benefits only if resources are well managed. Accordingly, this chapter argues that the present poor quality of institutions might become a bottleneck for sustainable and faster growth. The next section examines economic reforms under NEM. Section 3 provides quantitative assessment of macroeconomic performance. Section 4 discusses microeconomic issues related to trade policy and institutions, and Section 5 concludes.

2 FROM A CENTRALLY PLANNED ECONOMY TO A MARKET-ORIENTED SYSTEM

2.1 Setting for Reform

Following the foundation of Lao PDR in 1975, the government adopted the model of a socialist state, similar to China and Vietnam, with a high degree of centralization of economic decision-making and little reliance on market pricing. What was produced, by whom, and for what uses were mainly subject to administrative decisions (Saignasith, 1997). Prices were controlled most often at or below market clearing levels, domestic and external trade was strictly regulated, and multiple exchange rates were administered for official transactions. SOEs played a major role in providing goods and services but were strictly controlled by the state with no room for managerial flexibility of autonomy. In the banking sector, the State Bank of the LDR carried out both central bank and commercial banking functions, as a *mono* bank.

The failure of the command economy model became increasingly apparent by the middle of the 1980s. The level of per capita GDP lagged behind other low-income economies, while inflation remained much higher (Table 8.1). The fiscal situation deteriorated with the overall deficit widening to 15–20 percent of GDP, while external positions remained weak with the ratio of international reserves to imports amounting to only 3–6 weeks in the first half of the 1980s. During these periods there was increasing recognition that detailed centralized planning and artificially low prices reduced incentives in economic activity. The government took some initial measures to remove various restrictions on internal and external trade and adjusted official prices drastically, with the aim of bringing unauthorized activities back into official channels and revitalizing the economy. Nevertheless the central planning mechanism remained virtually intact.

2.2 Embarking on NEM

In 1985, the government launched NEM, covering all economic sectors (see Box 8.1 for more details).[1] Private initiatives immediately revived,

Table 8.1   Key economic and social indicators in the middle of the 1980s (1983–85 average)

	Per capita GDP (Constant 2000 USD)	Inflation (percent)	Life expectancy at birth (years)	Infant mortality (per 1000)
Lao PDR	215	68.1	52	129
Cambodia	...	5.7	53	85
Vietnam	200	68.7	63	40
Low-income countries[1]	268	13.5	54	103
ASEAN 4	1101	9.9	64	44

Note: 1   Economies with per capita GNI equal to or less than $905 in 2006.

Source: World Bank, World Development Indicators database.

with a significant impact on the supply and range of goods available in markets. In particular, the services sector was the quickest to respond to change in the incentive mechanism: private and public transport operators took advantage of the removal of internal trade restrictions, while businesses involving handicrafts and consumer services (for example, repair shops, tailors, and restaurants) rapidly emerged.

However, economic performance in the late 1980s was disappointing. Reform in the SOE sector led to a drop in budgetary transfers, while the new tax system remained rudimentary. Increases in civil service wages, in part to monetize fringe benefits, contributed to a rising wages bill, leading to a widening fiscal deficit. Money growth was also high, reaching nearly 90 percent by 1989, reflecting monetization of the budget deficit and rapid credit expansion of SOEs. Expansionary fiscal and monetary policy, together with a severe contraction in agriculture output due to a protracted drought, triggered reacceleration in inflation in the late 1980s.

2.3   Macroeconomic Stabilization and Structural Reform in the 1990s and into the Early 2000s

Facing macroeconomic destabilization, the government reinvigorated its efforts in economic reform in 1989 and has since launched a series of economic reform programs supported by many donors.[2]

At the onset, the immediate policy focus was to restore macroeconomic stability, while maintaining the momentum of reform. To this end, the authorities sought to tighten monetary policy, including credit aimed at

BOX 8.1   LAO PDR: KEY REFORM MEASURES UNDER NEM IN THE LATE 1980s

At the onset, the main focus of the program was an improvement of efficiency of SOEs, starting with a limited number of enterprises and later on including virtually all enterprises by the end of 1988, except for utilities and nonviable ones. The government granted operating autonomy to enterprises, allowing them to determine production levels and mix investment employment and wages, and at the same time abolished the system of economy-wide production targeting.

During 1987–88, substantial progress was achieved in liberalizing internal and external trade. In early 1987, trading companies were consolidated, and provincial trade restrictions, most notably those related to the rice trade, were eliminated.[1] Transport, which was a monopoly of state and provincial enterprises, was opened to the private sector. Joint public companies and private companies were permitted to trade domestically and abroad in most goods.[2]

In June 1987, the government decided to free the administrative price setting mechanism, allowing all prices, except those of utilities, public services, and several key industrial products, to be negotiated freely between the parties to a transaction without interference from the authorities.

During 1986–87, an increasing share of transactions was allowed to take place at exchange rates closer to the prevailing parallel market rate. In September 1987, the government started rationalizing the exchange rate system, by reducing the number of exchange rates to four,[3] and subsequently decided to unify all rates, effective 1 January 1988.

As the domestic revenue base shrank as a result of an increased financial autonomy granted to SOEs, the government introduced a new tax system in the 1988 budget, including the replacement of SOEs' transfer to the budget with profit and turnover taxes. Efforts were made in 1988 to reorder expenditure priorities. Subsidies to civil servants and other consumer subsidies were gradually phased out, while civil service wages were raised. At the same time, a substantial retrenchment of central government staff began.

Reform of the financial system began in October 1988. The process of separating central and commercial banking functions of the State Bank of the Lao PDR (a mono bank) commenced.

Notes
1. Before 1987, trade between provinces was restricted to encourage regional rice self-sufficiency.
2. Exports of substantial goods, mainly those required to comply with trade contracts with the nonconvertible currency area (such as coffee, tobacco, logs, and process wood), continued to be reserved for state trading companies.
3. Before the implementation of this measure, there existed seven different exchange rates

SOEs and raising interest rates to positive levels on a real basis. They also strengthened the fiscal balance through tax reform and expenditure containment. Subsequently inflation fell to about 10 percent in 1991, to 6 percent in 1992 and stayed mostly in the single digit range through the middle of the 1990s. The external position also strengthened, with higher exports growth and larger aid inflows offsetting the sudden loss of financial assistance from the former Soviet Union in 1991.

During the first half of the 1990s, with the initial objective of stabilization broadly achieved, the government focused on deepening structural reform. A two-tier banking system and central bank were established under a new Central Bank Law. Most interest rates were liberalized by the middle of the 1990s and a modern tax structure was established. The government also centralized fiscal management, consolidating central and provincial budgets into a single budget document and establishing the National Treasury in August 1991. An SOE privatization program reduced the number of SOEs from over 600 in 1988 to about 30 by the end of 1997. In the external sector, the authorities further advanced trade liberalization: all exports and imports other than those on specified lists were freed from quantitative restrictions. Tariff rates were also reduced substantially, placing the Lao PDR as one of the lowest tariff rate countries relative to its neighbors by the middle of the 1990s.[3] The authorities allowed private entry into the banking sector to enhance competition, while recapitalizing state-owned commercial banks (SOCBs) to clean up non-performing loans.

However, during the Asian crisis macroeconomic performance deteriorated, reflecting not only external shocks but also a lax macroeconomic policy stance (IMF, 2002 and 2005a). On the eve of the outbreak of the crisis, the government, anxious to accelerate the pace of development, launched a series of large investments in irrigation to enhance food sufficiency. The investment plans were pushed through without due consideration about macroeconomic considerations and financed largely through borrowing from the central bank, which resulted in an increase in liquidity and fed into triple-digit inflation rates, large exchange rate depreciations of the local currency, the kip, and a loss in international reserves in early 1999. The deterioration in macroeconomic conditions weakened the banking system. In the external sector, the authorities partially reversed early progress made in trade liberalization and imposed trade bans, quotas, and other restrictions to contain exchange rate pressures.

Against this backdrop, the authorities launched stabilization measures in the middle of 1999. The Bank of Lao PDR imposed a strict limit on credit to the government, and issued central bank securities to mop up excess liquidity. The government tightened fiscal policy with stronger efforts in revenue mobilization and expenditure constraints, resulting in a sharp reduction in the overall deficit. By the end of 2000, these measures reduced inflation to about 10 percent, stabilized the kip exchange rate and recovered international reserves.

Since then, macroeconomic stability has broadly been maintained, but the reform agenda remains unfinished. Growth has been robust, inflation has lowered, international reserves have increased and poverty has reduced. The government has taken major steps to advance trade reform under AFTA commitments and initiated formal negotiations for WTO accession, while the financial positions of SOEs have improved. However, progress in structural reform in other areas has been weak. In particular, private sector developments have not advanced as rapidly and deeply as envisaged, a reflection of insufficient progress in improving the investment climate (see IMF 2006b).

3 ASSESSING MACROECONOMIC PERFORMANCE

During the overall period of economic reforms Lao PDR has experienced relatively favorable growth. Real GDP growth jumped 6.5 percent a year in the first half of the 1990s, up from less than 4.5 percent in the late 1980s and has thereafter been sustained at a reasonably high level (Figure 8.1). With GDP growth higher and population growth lower, per capita GDP growth has expanded at an increasingly faster pace over the last two decades. Moreover, poverty has fallen; the poverty headcount had declined to one third of the population by the early 2000s from nearly half a decade previously.

Cross-economy comparisons confirm that Lao PDR has been one of the fastest growing low-income economies. However, Lao PDR's growth lagged behind neighboring Cambodia and Vietnam (Figure 8.2). Of note is Lao PDR's outstanding growth record compared to other geographically-disadvantageous economies. Radelet et al. (1997) and Gallup et al. (1999) argued that geography matters for economic development. Landlocked economies in particular are disadvantaged when competing in global markets due to their lack of access to the sea. For developing economies,

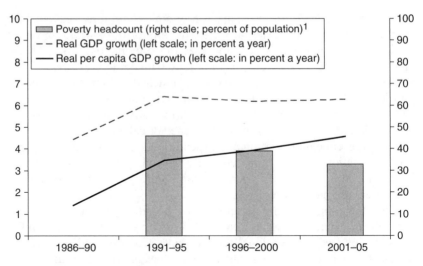

Note: 1. Data are not available for 1986–90 periods.

Source: World Bank, World Development Indicators database.

Figure 8.1   Lao PDR: real GDP growth and poverty headcount

where transport infrastructure is poor and institutions and governance are weak, the costs of trade and investment are much higher than those for advanced countries. Gallup et al. (1999) also demonstrated that low population density in coastal regions would be unfavorable for growth.[4] Lao PDR satisfies all these unfavorable conditions (Table 8.2): it is landlocked, with scarce population density along the Mekong river (which is navigable to the sea but vessels that can travel are limited to small ones especially during the dry season). However, despite these disadvantages, Lao PDR has recorded relatively fast growth compared to other low-income economies – and the fastest growth among other landlocked economies – over the last decade.

Evidence indicates that Lao PDR's growth has been driven by higher investment. As widely recognized, promoting capital accumulation plays a critical role in development, which often poses a challenge to developing economies where domestic savings is inadequate. During 1996–2006, the investment rate in Lao PDR averaged 27 percent of GDP, only slightly below Vietnam but above Cambodia and even ASEAN 4 (Table 8.3) and should be considered high by standards of developing economies. Conversely, savings, which averaged around 17 percent during the same period for Lao PDR was clearly insufficient to meet investment needs.

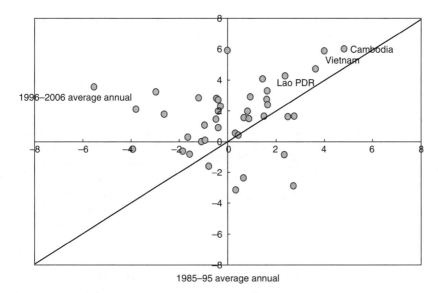

1985–95 average annual

Note: 1.   The definition of low-income countries is due to the World Bank.

Source: World Bank, World Development Indicators database.

Figure 8.2   Low-income countries: per capita real GDP growth (year-on-year percent change)[1]

Table 8.2   Geography

	Lao PDR	Cambodia	Vietnam	All developing countries[1]
Proportion of the region's population within 100 km of the coastline or ocean-navigable river	0.1	0.2	0.8	0.5
Density of human settlement (population per squared km) in the coastal region (within 100 km of the coastline	27.2	62.7	323.7	144.6
Landlocked (Yes = 1, No = 0)	1.0	0.0	0.0	0.2

Note: 1.   59 developing countries in the world available in the dataset of Gallup et al. (1999).

Source: Gallup, Sachs, and Mellinger (1999).

Table 8.3   *Investment and saving balance (in percent of GDP; 1996–2006*
            average)

	Lao PDR	Cambodia	Vietnam	ASEAN 4
Gross national saving	16.6	14.4	29.7	28.1
Gross capital formation	27.4	17.7	31.0	24.8
Current account balance	−10.3	−3.2	−2.1	3.3

Source: IMF, World Economic Outlook database.

The gap was financed by external sources of savings, as reflected in a large current account deficit.

Some other data suggest that caution would be required in assessing the Lao PDRs' growth performance.

● Growth has been increasingly driven by large natural resource projects (Figure 8.3). Lao PDR's vast mineral and hydro resources (Box 8.2) had long been underdeveloped and large-scale investment and operations only began in recent years. The natural resource sector does not have significant productive linkages to the rest of the economy (non-large natural resource sector), in which growth had remained moderate.

● Despite the government's efforts to liberalize the trade system, the pattern of growth seems to have been less driven by exports compared to other peer economies. The simple average tariff in Lao PDR is below 10 percent, lower than the average of developing countries in Asia (Figure 8.4). The weighted average rate is similar to Vietnam and the regional average. Tariff rate dispersion, measured by the standard deviation, is also very low. However, while exports appear to have been a leading growth sector in the first half of the 1990s, they leveled off thereafter. Exports have again picked up in recent years, but mostly reflected natural resource exports that have just come on stream. Besides, imports growth has also been sluggish, raising concerns about to what extent domestic production has benefited from the trade liberalization efforts to date. These trends in trade indicators mark a sharp contrast to the cases in other neighboring developing countries in which both exports and imports have progressively expanded over the last decade.

To more formally examine Lao PDR's growth pattern, the sources of growth can be decomposed using standard growth accounting. Production

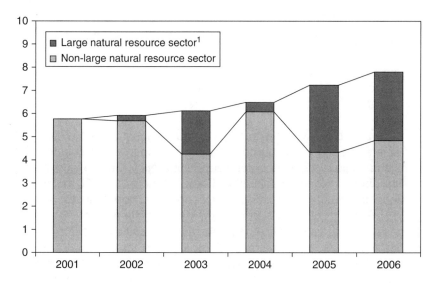

Note: 1. Large mining and hydropower projects.

Source: IMF (2007b).

Figure 8.3 *Real GDP growth by sector (percentage contributions to overall growth rate)*

(*Y*) process is assumed to be conventional Cobb–Douglas technology, which utilizes physical capital (*K*), worker (*L*), and total factor productivity (*A*) as inputs:

$$Y_t = A_t K_t^\alpha L_t^{1-\alpha}$$

where α represents the elasticity of output with respect to physical capital, and *t* represents year. Expressing all variables in per worker terms (denoted by small caps), taking log and derivative with respect to time, we can obtain (omitting time indices),

$$\frac{\dot{y}}{y} = \frac{\dot{A}}{A} + \alpha\frac{\dot{k}}{k}$$

where $\dot{x}$ represents growth of a variable *x*. Growth in output per worker can be decomposed into that in total factor productivity and physical capital per worker.[5]

Growth accounting suggests that much of the Lao PDR's strong growth resulted mainly from capital formation and less from total factor

BOX 8.2   LAO PDR: THE RESOURCE SECTOR[4]

Lao PDR has vast mineral and hydro resources. These sectors had long been underdeveloped, and large-scale investment and operations only began in recent years.

Mineral sector. Available geological data suggest that Lao PDR's mineral wealth could be comparable to resource-rich countries in the region, such as Indonesia, Papua New Guinea and the Philippines (World Bank 2006b). There are more than 570 mineral deposits identified, including gold, copper, zinc and lead, tin, and iron. Proven gold and copper reserves are estimated at 72 tons and 1.7 million tons, while probable reserves could be as large as 500–600 tons for gold and 8–10 million tons for copper. Large-scale gold and copper mines have been developed by Australian investors – Lang Xang Minerals, Ltd. (Oxiana) starting in 2003 and Phu Bia Mining, Ltd. (Pan Australian) starting in 2005.

Hydropower sector. The existing installed capacity – developed in the late 1990s to meet Thailand's demand for electricity – will be almost quadrupled when seven additional power plants enter into operation by mid-2010. The increased capacity will be sufficient to cover the export agreements already signed with Thailand and Vietnam for the delivery of 5000 MW over the next decade. Several additional sites have been identified for possible future development, which if fully implemented could almost double the generation capacity levels projected for 2010.

Against this backdrop, the sizable foreign direct investments for the production of gold and copper and export-oriented hydro-power have taken place in recent years. These activities are beginning to have a visible direct impact on the balance of payments, fiscal revenues and growth, increasingly dominating Lao PDR's overall economic performance. A potential concern is that the resource sector does not have significant productive linkages to the rest of the economy (the non-resource sector), but it does have the potential to adversely affect it through its impact on inflation and exchange rate appreciation.

So far, the economic impact has been moderate. However, the full impact of the resource sector is yet to be fully felt and whether it becomes a blessing or a curse will depend on the government's policy response, namely, whether it can ensure that any adverse effects are mitigated and that the conditions for promoting a higher growth of the non-resource sector are in place.

Note:
1. This box drew from IMF (2007a and 2007b).

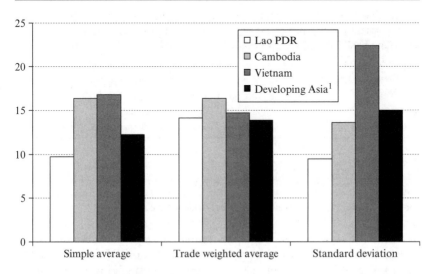

Note: 1. The simple average of selected Asian developing countries: Bangladesh, Bhutan, Cambodia, China, India, Indonesia, Lao PDR, Mongolia, Nepal, Papua New Guinea, Philippines, Sri Lanka, Thailand and Vietnam.

Source: World Bank, *World Trade Indicators* database.

Figure 8.4   Tariff (percent)

productivity.[6] Growth of output per worker in Lao PDR was one of the fastest during the 1990s, even outpacing emerging East Asian economies. However, in Lao PDR, more than 80 percent of the increase was accounted for by physical capital accumulation during this period, as opposed to the case of the emerging East Asia in which the contribution of productivity growth was much larger. This same trend has continued in more recent years. Over the period 2000–04, output per worker grew 2.9 percent a year in Lao PDR, to which total factor productivity growth contributed only 0.4 percentage points.

Altogether, the above-stylized facts suggest several unique patterns

Table 8.4   Growth accounting (annual percentage changes)[1]

	Output per worker	Contributions to output per worker growth	
		Physical capital per worker	Total factor productivity
		1990–99 average	
Lao PDR	3.6	3.0	0.6
Developing economies	1.4	0.7	0.7
Emerging East Asia[2]	3.1	2.1	1.0
Sub-Saharan Africa	−0.1	−0.02	0.1
Industrial economies	1.5	0.6	0.9
All economies	1.2	0.5	0.7
		2000–04 average	
Lao PDR	2.9	2.5	0.4

Notes
1. Regional averages are simple average.
2. Indonesia, Korea, Malaysia, Philippines, Singapore and Thailand.

Sources: Bosworth and Collins (2003); authors' calculations.

in Lao PDR's growth over the past years. One would expect that trade liberalization would open the economy, but for Lao PDR this appears to be negative. While the level of tariff rates is now much lower than in the early days and comparable with other neighboring countries, trade has not grown in Lao PDR as fast as in other developing countries. One would also expect that trade liberalization would increase competition and thus contribute to raise productivity and growth, an important growth channel stressed by Dollar and Kraay (2002), Bolaky and Freud (2004) and Chang (2005).[7] Again, in Lao PDR, this was negative. What has gone wrong in Lao PDR, or are we missing anything?

The next section examines this question.

4   TRADE POLICY, INSTITUTIONS AND BUSINESS ENVIRONMENT

4.1   Trade Policy[8]

As noted, Lao PDR has already made significant progress in trade liberalization, resulting in a lower and less disperse tariff structure. While in the past the liberalization was taken unilaterally, more recently authorities have pursued bilateral and regional agreements. In 1998, Lao PDR joined the ASEAN Free Trade Area (AFTA), and is committed to reduce tariffs on imports from ASEAN countries in the 0–5 percent range by the end of 2008. Subsequently, in 2003, the Early Harvest Program of the ASEAN China Free Trade Agreement entered into force, while in 2005, the US–Laos Bilateral Trade Agreement became effective, under which the US granted normal trade relations treatment to products of Lao PDR. On the multilateral front, the government has been stepping up its WTO negotiations, with the intention of joining the WTO by 2010. A third working party took place in November 2007.[9]

However, non-tariff barriers to imports remain.[10] The IMF Non-tariff Barriers rating for Lao PDR scores three (worst), in comparison with most other Asian countries scoring two. Similarly, the World Bank Non-tariff Measures Frequency ratio reaches 37 percent, the second highest in Asia after India. Although exchange rate controls have largely been eliminated and the foreign exchange system no longer presents a significant barrier to trade, the less favorable rating for Lao PDR most likely reflects cumbersome import procedures. For many years the government required importers to submit an annual importation plan to the Ministry of Industry and Commerce or to relevant provincial authorities,[11] while imposing license requirements for several products as listed in Notification of the Ministry of Commerce No. 285 (issued March 17, 2004).[12] Although the protective nature of import licensing is reportedly now much less than in the past (World Bank, 2006b) and most licensing requirements are merely technical measures to ensure quality control, safety, or animal quarantine, licensing for imports is often implemented in a non-transparent manner, particularly in the provinces. This raises concerns about governance, thereby negatively affecting the business and investment environment.

The actual use of trade preferences available for Lao PDR has increased in recent years but scope for further utilization exists. In 2001 the preferential utilization rate – defined as the ratio of preferences claimed to total potential preferences – in the EU market was below 60 percent (World Bank, 2006b). However, recent data suggest that the preferential utilization rate increased to 74 percent for Lao PDR, higher than Cambodia and Vietnam and comparable to the average of low and middle–low income countries (Table 8.5). Nevertheless, the utilization rate in Lao PDR is still lower than some of other Asian developing countries, such as Indonesia, Nepal, the Philippines and Thailand, suggesting that there is room to further raise the use of preferences.[13] The underutilization of preferences could be due to complexity in rules of origin and difficulty in managing them. But it could also reflect the weak ability

Table 8.5   Lao PDR's preferential exports to EU: utilization rate[1] (in percent, the latest available year, 2005 or 2006)

Lao PDR	73.7
Cambodia	68.9
Vietnam	68.7
Selected Asia	
Bangladesh	64.4
India	73.9
Indonesia	82.6
Mongolia	45.9
Nepal	91.3
Philippines	86.2
Thailand	88.7
Low and lower–middle income countries average[2]	77.6

Notes
1. The ratio of the value of claimed preferences to the value of potential preferences. The value of claimed preferences is defined as the difference between the MFN duty and the actual preferential duty. The value of potential preferences is defined as the difference between the MFN duty and the potential preferential duty.
2. Low and lower–middle income countries are those with per capita GNI $905 and less, and $906–$3595, respectively.

Source: World Bank, *World Trade Indicators* database.

of the country to take the preferential opportunities due to inadequate supply response.

In sum, there remains room to enhance trade policy effectiveness. Vigorously advancing trade liberalization, especially in areas of non-tariff barriers, is still an important policy priority. Here the government can use opportunities presented by WTO accession, which challenges a developing country where capacity is weak. Nevertheless, gains of additional market access following WTO entry may be limited given that Lao exporters have already received Most Favored Nation treatment or even better ones. However, WTO accession can be considered a guide for Lao PDR's own reforms, in particular, through strengthening the legal framework and institutions for a support of a market economy.

4.2   Institutions and Business Environment

Trade liberalization alone is unlikely to promote growth. Recent growth literature emphasizes the role of institutions, which can facilitate trade and enhance investment, productivity and eventually growth.[14] The resulting higher incomes and greater openness in turn leads to further improvement in the quality of institutions, creating a virtuous cycle.[15]

This chapter focuses on the following three measures of institutions, all widely used in the recent growth and trade literature.

1. The quality of governance matters for overall economic development as it determines government effectiveness and efficiency not only in utilizing public resources but also in promoting a business-supportive environment and protecting investors' property. According to governance indicators, compiled by Kaufmann (2007), Lao PDR fares poorly compared to the average of developing economies in Asia on all indicators but political stability.[16]
2. The quality of business regulation and property rights affects various aspects of business decisions, particularly incentives to invest, start or expand a business, and innovate because investors are concerned about business costs and the protection of investment returns. The World Bank (2008) *Doing Business* survey shows that Lao PDR is ranked 164th out of 178 countries in the overall 'ease of doing business' indicator. While 'starting a business' fares better than the average of Asian developing countries, all other indicators, particularly 'registering property' and 'protecting investors', score very poorly.
3. The quality of trade logistics directly affects the ability of firms to quickly move goods across borders.[17] The Logistics Performance Index[18] – newly developed indicators by the World Bank in 2007 – sheds light on how Lao PDR's quality of logistics, such as efficiency of the customs clearance process and competence in the local logistics industry, compares with other neighboring countries. Similar to the other two indicators discussed above, the logistic index ranks Lao PDR worse than any other countries in all areas of performance.

Overall, available indicators suggest that institutions and the business environment in Lao PDR are seriously unfavorable. One could argue that if other business costs, such as wages and rent, are sufficiently low, it could compensate for poor institutions and business climate. However, this does not appear the case. The latest survey by the Japan Export Trade Organization shows that while wages, rent and electricity prices in Vientiane (Lao PDR) are much lower than cities in more advanced countries, such as Hanoi (Vietnam), Batam (Indonesia) and Bangkok (Thailand), they are not significantly cheap compared to other low-income countries (Table 8.6). For example, wages for workers in Vientiane are the second-lowest after Dhaka (Bangladesh), but those for engineers and

Table 8.6   Investment-related costs comparison in major cities in Asia (2007, in USD)[1]

	Laos[2] Vientiane	Cambodia Phnom Penh	Vietnam Hanoi	Other Asian countries					Average of 8 cities
				Bangladesh Dhaka	China Qingdao	Indonesia Batam	Sri Lanka Colombo	Thailand Bangkok	
Wages (monthly)									
Workers	69 (2)	100.0	142.5	**57.2**	111.0	112.7	96.0	164.0	111.9
Engineers	217 (4)	170.0	362.5	**126.1**	214.5	298.5	184.2	383.0	248.4
Managers	417 (4)	**300.0**	1026.5	309.7	333.5	752.9	453.2	684.0	551.4
Rent (per square meter)									
Industrial estate	1.0 (4)	1.8	0.2	**0.1**	1.5	5.5	0.9	5.4	2.2
Office	7.5 (2)	8.0	22.0	**7.1**	32.0	10.9	9.5	13.7	14.7
Electricity (business use, kWh)	0.07 (3)	0.16	0.08	0.18	0.10	0.09	0.18	**0.05**	0.12
Memorandum item									
Per capita GDP	656.0	600.0	818.1	447.0	2466.9	1839.6	1506.0	3627.5	1495

Notes:
1. The figures in bold indicate the least cost for each category.
2. The figure in the parentheses is a ranking (from lower to higher cost city) among the eight cities in the table.

Source: Japan External Trade Organization, 'The 17th Survey of Investment-Related Cost Comparison'.

managers in Vientiane are higher than in Dhaka, Phnom Penh (Cambodia) and Quigdao (China). The level of rent in industrial estates in Vientiane is also higher than in Hanoi, Dhaka and Colombo (Sri Lanka).

4.3 Openness Regressions

A cross-country regression analysis is employed to verify the association between trade openness and the other explanatory variables discussed above. A main question to be considered is whether tariff levels alone are correlated with trade openness or other variables, such as institutions. In a sample of 62 low and middle–low income countries, the following cross-sectional equation has been estimated by ordinary least squares (OLS):

$$Y_i = \mu_i + \beta\,[population]_i + \gamma\,[trade\,policy\,\text{variables}]_i$$
$$+ \varphi\,[Lao\,P.D.R.\,dummy]_i + \varepsilon_i$$

where i denotes an economy and $\varepsilon_i \sim IID(o, \sigma_i^2)$.

The dependent variable, Y_i, is trade openness, defined as a total of exports and imports of goods and services as a percentage of GDP. The logarithm of population is included to control the size of domestic market: that is, a country with larger domestic markets tends to trade less. Trade policy variables include tariff rates (in percent) and non-tariff barrier ratings calibrated by the IMF. They also include other explanatory variables, such as institutions (ease of doing business ranking) and logistic performance index. Finally, the Lao PDR dummy (value 1, otherwise, 0) is included to examine if Lao PDR is unusual compared to the average across sample countries.

The estimation results confirm the close relationship between openness and trade policy variables (Table 8.7). As expected, population and tariff rates are negatively correlated with openness. The precisions of the estimates increase with the use of cross terms with institutional variables (tariff rates × institutions in model 4). Coefficients of non-tariff barriers are all positive, which is counterintuitive and could reflect data deficiency (lack of variations in variables). However, the logistic performance index is negative and significant when combined in cross terms with tariffs and institutional variables ('tariff rates × institutions × logistic performance' in model 5). The estimated model has become more precise, suggesting the important role that these institutional variables play in linking openness and tariff rates. The Lao PDR's dummy is not significant for all models: thus the Lao PDR's openness is just what one would expect for a country with the Lao PDR's trade policy and the other explanatory variables.

Table 8.7   *Cross-section regression[1] dependent variable: total trade as a percentage of GDP*

Model number	1	2	3	4	5
Constant	121.78	81.16	98.21	101.44	104.72
	(10.00)**	(6.34)**	(6.52)**	6.80**	6.92**
Population (log)	−9.08	−11.54	−11.57	−11.86	−12.33
	(−3.33)**	(−4.02)**	(−4.14)**	(−4.29)**	(−4.48)**
Tariff rates	−1.82	–	−1.73	–	–
	(−2.05)*		(−2.03)*		
Non-tariff barrier rating	–	19.71	19.05	16.39	15.43
		(2.50)*	(2.48)*	(2.13)*	2.01*
Tariff rates × Ease of Doing Business	–	–	–	−0.01	–
				(−2.40)*	
Tariff rates × Ease of Doing Business Ranking × Logistic Performance Index	–	–	–	–	−0.005
					(−2.63)*
Lao PDR dummy	−13.38	−46.61	−43.44	−34.67	−32.41
	(−0.43)	(−1.41)	(−1.34)	(−1.08)	(−1.01)
Memorandum items					
Number of observations	62	62	62	62	62
Adjusted R-squared	0.16	0.19	0.23	0.25	0.27

Note: 1. T-statistics in parentheses (** and * indicate significant at 1 and 5 percent, respectively).

Source: Fund staff estimates.

5   CONCLUSIONS

As envisaged in the National Socio-Economic Development Plan 2006–10, the government is committed to further integrating the economy with the rest of the world to enhance growth and reduce poverty. Over the past one-and-a-half decades, Lao PDR has taken significant steps to introduce and develop a market-oriented economy. However, major challenges lie ahead. Notably, tariff reductions alone will not be enough to capture larger benefits from further integration. Building sound institutions and fostering a good business environment will be critical. Empirical results indicate that these variables play a significant role in connecting openness and trade liberalization.

Today's economic landscape is quite different than it used to be. In Asia, intra-regional trade has deepened, leading to quite sophisticated regional production network (World Bank, 2007). Regional trade of goods and services, including technology transfer, is expected to grow further, bringing the benefits of economies of scale to even a smaller country in Asia. Whether and how much Lao PDR will be able to grab such benefits rest on its efforts to advance needed economic reforms.

NOTES

1. Otani and Do Pham (1996) discuss the main elements of reform programs under NEM.
2. The main donors that have been actively engaged in Lao PDR since the early 1990s include: among multilateral donors, Asian Development Bank, IMF and World Bank; and among bilateral donors, China, France, Germany, Japan, Sweden, Thailand and Vietnam.
3. Before 1988, tariff rates ranged from 5 to 200 percent with numerous exemptions. During the first half of the 1990s, the government reviewed the tariff structure several times. In 1995, the simple average of import tariff rates was 14 percent in the Lao PDR, compared to 44 percent in Thailand, 20 percent in Cambodia and 12 percent in Vietnam. At that time, only timber exports remained subject to quantitative restrictions.
4. They showed evidence that high growth in developing economies has often been achieved through labor-intensive manufacturing exports that require good access to internal and external trade.
5. Note that total factor productivity is measured as a residual, and a change in the measured productivity might reflect not only technological innovation but also human capital quality, political and external shocks, changes in government policies and institutions, and a measurement error. Other shortcomings of growth accounting include the need to make a fairly arbitrary assumption about the production function form. There is an extensive discussion on growth accounting issues in Bosworth and Collins (2003).
6. Except for the Lao PDR, data are due to Bosworth and Collins (2003). For the Lao PDR, output per worker was calculated as real GDP divided by labor force, and capital stock was estimated using a perpetual inventory model, where the depreciation rate equals 0.05. The underling data are from IMF, *World Economic Outlook* database and World Bank *World Development Indicators* database.
7. In addition, see for example, Sachs and Warner (1995), Ades and Glaeser (1999) and Frankel and Romer (1999) for broad studies about growth and trade. Studies focusing on trade and productivity include Coe et al. (1997), Hay (2001) and Jonsson and Subramanian (2000). Note that the positive linkage between trade openness and growth is still under debate: for example, Rodríguez and Rodrik (2000) doubted the robustness of a finding of a link between openness and growth.
8. Discussions in this section partly drew from Diagnostic Trade Integration Study for Lao PDR. See the World Bank (2006b).

9.　The negotiations are still in the early stages (WTO press statement, 2007).
10.　Non-tariff barriers include price control measures, variable charges, quantitative restrictions and non-automatic licensing.
11.　This policy was annulled recently in March 2007 (Ministry of Industry and Commerce Order No. 0453).
12.　Products that require import licenses include: (1) petrol and gas, (2) vehicles and parts, (3) diamonds, (4) cement, (5) steel, (6) fresh or frozen meat and fish, (7) canned fruit, (8) milk products, (9) prepared food including canned foods, (10) coloring and preserving products for foods, (11) sugar substitutes, (12) beverages, (13) food seasoning products, (14) human medicines, (15) animal medicines, (16) animals, (17) raw and semi-manufactured products used in manufacturing, (18) fertilizers and pesticides, (19) video cassettes, CDs, etc., (20) computer games, (21) sculptures and paintings, (22) sporting guns, (23) chemicals, (24) gold and silver ingots and (25) telephones, fax and telecommunications equipment. In addition to import licensing, Notification of Ministry of Commerce No. 284 (issued March 17, 2004) prohibits the importation of weapons, illegal drugs, toxic chemicals, hazardous materials and pornographic materials.
13.　Evidence available also suggests that trade preferences remain under-utilized in US and Japanese markets.
14.　North (1990), who is widely cited in the literature, defined institutions as the set of formal rules and informal conventions that provide the framework for human interaction and shape the incentives of members of society. See International Monetary Fund, *World Economic Outlook* (2003 and 2005a) for more discussion about the role of institutions.
15.　The causality among trade liberalization, openness, growth and institutions is an important issue in the growth literature but beyond the scope of this chapter. While a heated debate on the causality issue continues – see for example, Rodrik et al. (2002) – there seems to be a general consensus in the literature that these variables tend to improve or grow hand in hand.
16.　Other indicators include control of corruption, rule of law, regulatory quality and government effectiveness.
17.　For example, Hausman et al. (2005) found that logistics performance had a statistically significant relationship with the level of bilateral trade.

REFERENCES

Ades, Alberto F. and Edward L. Glaeser (1999), 'Evidence on growth, increasing returns and the extent of the market', *Quarterly Journal of Economics*, **114** (3), 1025–45.
Bolaky, B. and C. Freund (2004), 'Trade, regulations and growth', World Bank Development Research Group working paper no 2049.
Bosworth, Barry P. and Susan M. Collins (2003), 'The empirics of growth: an update', *Brookings Papers on Economic Activity*, **34** (2003–2).
Chang, R., L. Kaltani and N. Loayza (2005), 'Openness can be good for growth: the role of policy complementarities', World Bank policy research working paper no 3763.
Coe, David T., Elhanan Helpman and Alexander W. Hoffmaister (1997), 'North–South R&D spillovers', *Economic Journal*, **107**, 134–49.
Dollar, David and Aart Kraay (2002), 'Institutions, trade, and growth', *Journal of Monetary Economics*, **50**, 133–62.
Frankel, Jeffrey A. and David Romer (1999), 'Does trade cause growth?', *American Economic Review*, **89** (3), 379–99.

Gallup, John Luke, Jeffery D. Sachs and Andrew Mellinger (1999), 'Geography and economic development', Center for International Development at Harvard University working paper no 1, March.

Hausman, Warren H., Hau L. Lee and Uma Subramanian (2005), 'Global logistics indicators, supply chain metrics, and bilateral trade patterns', World Bank policy research working paper no 3773.

Hay, Donald A. (2001), 'The post-1990 Brazilian trade liberalization and the performance of large manufacturing firms: productivity, market share and profits', *Economic Journal*, **111** (473), 620–41.

International Monetary Fund (IMF) (2002), 'Lao People's Democratic Republic: staff report for the 2002 Article IV Consultation and second review under the Poverty Reduction and Growth Facility, and request for waiver of performance criteria', IMF country report no 02/221.

IMF (2003), *World Economic Outlook*, September, Washington, DC: IMF.

IMF (2005a), 'World Economic Outlook', September, Washington, DC: IMF.

IMF (2005b), 'Lao People's Democratic Republic: 2004 Article IV consultation – staff report; public information notice on the Executive Board discussion; and statement by the Executive Director for the Lao People's Democratic Republic', IMF country report no 05/8.

IMF (2007a), 'Lao People's Democratic Republic: 2007 Article IV consultation – staff report; public information notice on the Executive Board discussion; and statement by the Executive Director for the Lao People's Democratic Republic', IMF country report no 07/360.

IMF (2007b), 'Lao People's Democratic Republic: selected issues and statistical appendix', IMF country report no 07/359.

Jonsson, Gunnar and Arvind Subramanian (2000), 'Dynamic gains from trade: evidence from South Africa', International Monetary Fund working paper no 00/45.

Kaufmann, Daniel, Aart Kraay and Massimo Mastruzzi (2007), 'Governance matters VI: governance indicators for 1996–2006', World Bank policy research working paper series no 4280.

North, Douglass G. (1990), *Institutions, Institutional Change and Economic Performance*, New York: Cambridge University Press.

Otani, Ichiro and Chi Do Pham (1996), 'The Lao People's Democratic Republic: systemic transformation and adjustment', International Monetary Fund occasional paper 137.

Radelet, Steven, Jeffrey Sachs and Jong-Wah Lee (1997), 'Economic growth in Asia', background paper for the Asian Development Bank's 'Emerging Asia' study, Harvard Institute for International Development discussion paper no 609.

Rodríguez, Francisco and Dani Rodrik (2001), 'Trade policy and economic growth: a skeptics guide to the cross-national evidence', in B. Bernanke and K. Rogoff (eds), *NBER Macroeconomics Annual 2000*, Cambridge, MA: MIT Press.

Rodrik, Dani, Arvind Subramanian and Francesco Trebbi (2002), 'Institutions rule: the primacy of institutions over geography and integration in economic development', National Bureau of Economic Research working paper 9305.

Sachs, Jeffrey D. and Andrew Warner (1995), 'Economic reform and the process of global integration', *Brookings Papers on Economic Activity*, 26 (1995–1), 1–118.

Saignasith, Chanthavong (1997), 'Lao-style new economic mechanism', in Mya

Than and Joseph L.H. Tan (eds), *Laos' Dilemmas and Options: The Challenge of Economic Transition in the 1990s*, New York: St Martin's Press, Chapter 2.

World Bank (2006a), 'Building Export Competitiveness in Laos', accessed at www. integratedframework.org/countries/laopdr.htm.

World Bank (2006b), 'Sector plan for sustainable development of the mining sector in Lao P.D.R', World Bank Economic Geology DFR2.

World Bank (2007), *An East Asian Renaissance: Ideas for Growth*, Washington, DC: World Bank.

World Bank (2008), 'Doing Business' database, accessed at www.doingbusiness. org.

World Trade Organization (2007), 'Laos looks to accelerate membership negotiations', accessed at www.wto.org/english/theWTO_e/acc_e/a1_laos_e.htm.

9. The impact of globalization on economic development in Myanmar

Trevor Wilson, Leslie Teo and Masahiro Hori

1 INTRODUCTION

This study demonstrates that while improved communications, increased regional trade links and migration have strengthened Myanmar's integration into the global economy, the benefits of globalization are not pervasive and have not brought significant improvements in general social economic conditions. Despite historically strong global ties and attempts at opening up, Myanmar remains a comparatively closed economy. Lack of reinforcing institutions and policies and pervasive government controls render ineffective efforts by the military authorities to open the country economically after 1988.

Indicators of economic development and globalization[1] leave little doubt about Myanmar's decades of poor economic performance and isolation. This includes: (i) GDP growth that has been lower than its potential, despite rich resources; (ii) high inflation, caused primarily by large fiscal deficits financed through money creation; (iii) exchange rate[2] and trading systems that discourage international transactions and distort economic activity; and (iv) a weak investment climate (poor infrastructure, pervasive controls on economic activity, even after 1988, and nontransparent rules and regulations). The single most important reason for such poor economic performance is poor economic policies that place more weight on control and security than the development of a vibrant private sector-led economy. One consequence is that over the last five decades real per capita GDP has only doubled in Myanmar compared to an average increase of about twelve times for East Asia and Pacific economies.

More specifically, such policies not only dilute the effects of globalization but they leave Myanmar one of the world's most isolated nations. For example, according to the comprehensive KOF Index of Globalization, Myanmar ranks 120th out of 122 countries in its annual survey of globalization for 2007.[3] Myanmar is also listed second last in Transparency International's global openness index. This means Myanmar is not well

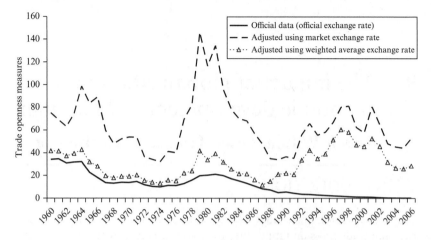

Sources: Central Statistical Organization, Statistical Yearbook, Review of the Financial Economic and Social Conditions (various issues); and authors' estimates.

Figure 9.1   Trade openness measures for Myanmar: official statistics vs. adjusted estimates

placed in the international competition for FDI, or in participation in international supply chains where reliability and timeliness are critical. Another measure of openness, trade as a percentage of GDP, shows that trade – buttressed by exports of gas – has only recently returned to levels comparable to the 1960s when isolationist policies were imposed in earnest (Figure 9.1).[4]

Nevertheless, there have been attempts, especially since 1988, to open up the economy and undertake reforms, even if these have been inconsistent and patchy. While this process has slowed considerably since 2000, the economic impact of globalization in Myanmar is most likely underestimated in the KOF and Transparency International indices and conventional economic measures of globalization. At the same time, regional and global linkages exist but, unlike the rest of ASEAN, have remained rather basic.

2   POST-WORLD WAR II ECONOMIC CONDITIONS IN BURMA: WEAK FOUNDATIONS FOR THE FUTURE?

Although devastated by World War II, Burma possessed certain advantages compared to its Asian neighbours at the time of independence in 1948. The

British left physical infrastructure (road, rail, shipping, and so on), many Burmese were well educated in English (an advantage later in the globalized world of the twenty-first century) and the country boasted some of the leading educational institutions in the region. By 1930 Burma was already a significant producer and exporter of oil and minerals as well as forestry and agricultural products, where Burma enjoyed comparative advantage.

To a great degree the impact of colonization was superficial: the large cities were developed with some links between them, but much of the country was untouched by development. Road, rail and shipping (river and marine) links, on largely north–south lines, facilitated the export of Burmese products, but did little to improve local supply networks. Remote rural areas, in particular those where the population was non-Burman, did not share in the benefits of economic development. Indeed, one of the main British legacies was political fragmentation of the colony (along divide and rule principles) leaving economic development that was not as integrated as it might have been. Yet growth achieved respectable levels and communication hubs in shipping and later aviation contributed to some intra-regional trade but did little to promote local entrepreneurship. More generally, outside of agriculture, participation by the indigenous population was limited: Chettiars from India, for instance, dominated commerce.

World War II destroyed these developmental achievements. The protracted internal insurgency that followed independence and was not terminated until the military regime negotiated ceasefire agreements in 1989–94 did not help. The deliberate shift to quasi-socialist[5] economic policies after independence, aimed at establishing indigenous control over the colonial-controlled economy and its resources, had the unintended effect of slowing modernization of the economy after the war. It was not until 1957 that GDP recovered to 1938 levels. The pursuit of national unity and consolidation exacted an economic cost.

3 ECONOMIC DEVELOPMENT UNDER NATIONALIST POLICIES: ISOLATION AND ITS COSTS

All post-independence governments were obsessed with consolidating local ownership. The 'Burmese Way of Socialism' initiated by General Ne Win after 1962 significantly reversed market-oriented economic development. Economically, the Ne Win government was committed to autarkical economic development based on exaggerated fears about outside threats to Burma's national integrity and unity. The nationalization of most businesses and the imposition of state ownership destroyed local entrepreneurial skills and many had not recovered even decades later. Furthermore, strong police-state controls exercised by the army under Ne Win's direct authority reinforced Burma's comprehensive isolation.

Under Ne Win the economy consisted of centrally directed economic planning at the high policy level and a multitude of state-owned enterprises (SOEs) at the operational level. As economic mismanagement worsened in the 1970s and 1980s no checks and balances existed that could halt the drift into political and economic chaos. SOEs operated highly inflexibly, without any incentive to undertake reform or change, unlike their counterparts in China, or later Vietnam. Almost always unprofitable, they drained state revenues while offering rent-seeking opportunities and perks and appointments for an expanding military officer corps. Government price controls acted as a disincentive to expanding production. With control of the banking system the state prohibited foreign banking operations, thus exacerbating economic isolation.[6]

Opposition to foreign investment and joint ventures further retarded economic development. A seven-day visa system actively discouraged tourism up until 1988. Consequently Burma hosted fewer multinational corporations than most developing countries and gained little from the transfer of technology and business skills that generally accompanies multinational investment.

Given these policies, it is not surprising that economic performance during this period was weak. Average GDP growth – at around 3 percent – was much lower than regional neighbours and inflation remained a constant problem. Real per capita income grew, on average, less than 1 percent per year from 1962 to 1988, while exports and imports also saw little growth. Indeed, rice exports fell from about US$200 million in 1962 to nearly zero in 1988.

Yet Burma was not entirely isolated economically. It received various forms of foreign assistance, including $2 billion under the Colombo Plan from 1952–1975, $530 million in loans from the World Bank between 1973 and 1988 and $540 million in loans from the ADB between 1973 and 1988. Burma even encouraged the organization of a Consultative Group under the auspices of the World Bank from 1976. But World Bank and ADB loans were mainly used for physical infrastructure or commodity loans and the technical assistance was mainly for technocratic training. Many Burmese studied abroad during this period, mainly in the professions, and many returned to work as civil servants, but there was relatively little spillover of know-how to local enterprises. Few Burmese gained qualifications that could be applied in the under-developed business sector. International assistance was not designed to promote the market economy or to encourage regional economic integration.

4   THE POST-1988 DRIVE FOR ECONOMIC REFORM: OPENING UP BUT NOT CATCHING UP

The causes of the 1988 demonstrations and subsequent military crackdown were as much economic as they were political. It is no accident that the first actions by the new military regime in 1988–89 were economic in character and designed explicitly to reverse the disastrous course of socialism and isolation. Subsequently, the military regime actively encouraged the business sector and military leaders were frequently strongly critical of past socialist practices, although they did not always meet their stated economic policy goals and stopped short of dismantling the instruments of state-owned controls over the economy.

Key legal reforms during the SLORC/SPDC[7] period, which began a transformation of the economy and opened the doors to globalization, included the Foreign Investment Law (1988), the Central Bank of Myanmar Law (1990), the Financial Institutions of Myanmar Law (1990), the Tourism Law (1990), the Mines Law (1994) and the Myanmar Citizens Investment Law (1994). Ostensibly committed to what it called 'market-oriented development', the new military leadership permitted private entrepreneurship, introduced private banks in 1990 and in 1995 instituted a privatization programme. Industrial zones appeared in some 18 strategic locations, including in some border areas. Committed to transforming Myanmar into a 'modern developed economy', the government also introduced a computer law, permitted the Internet and promoted education in business studies and computer sciences. It adopted a positive approach to tourism (including new forms such as eco-tourism) and, as peace was restored through ceasefire agreements, opened many areas to tourism and related development.

As a result, economic performance improved. Average GDP growth and real per capita growth rose to about 5 percent while exports grew, on average, more than 10 percent per year. Inflation, however, increased significantly, fuelled by the government's inability to keep its finances in order (Table 9.1). Economic performance subsequently stagnated, despite significant improvement in the country's exports after 2000 as the Gulf of Martaban gas fields began producing, adding about US$1.5 billion worth of exports a year to Thailand. By 2006 Myanmar was the world's largest producer of pulses and beans by volume. Nevertheless, macroeconomic stability proved elusive with high inflation exacerbated by the 2003–04 banking crisis.

A boom in FDI followed the initial decisions to open up to foreign investment but slowed down significantly after 1999 (Figure 9.2), except for the gas and hydroelectric sectors. Myanmar's willingness to conclude

Table 9.1   Selected macroeconomic indicators (in percent)

	Official statistics				Authors' estimates	
	1962–2006	1962–1988	1989–1998	1999–2006	1962–1988	1999–2006
Real GDP annual growth rate	5.3	3.1	5.4	12.7	3.9	4.8
Annual inflation rate	15.0	8.4	27.8	21.0	16.4	28.9
Rate of depreciation in market exchange rate	12.9	7.2	22.2	20.6	n/a	n/a
Annual growth in exports, real	5.6	0.2	10.8	17.3	n/a	n/a
Annual growth in imports, real	1.6	−0.7	9.9	−0.9	n/a	n/a
Annual growth in real per capita GDP	3.4	0.9	3.6	11.4	2.0	3.6
Real GDP per capita (1962=100, end period)	405.2	119.5	170.4	405.2	226.6	226.6

Sources: IMF, International Financial Statistics; World Bank, World Development Indicators; and authors' estimates.

bilateral investment protection agreements also signified a certain acceptance of global norms, but it has so far only concluded a small number of such agreements – with China, Laos, Philippines and Vietnam – fewer than either Laos or Cambodia. It has double taxation avoidance agreements with only the UK, Malaysia, Singapore, Vietnam, Thailand, Korea, India and Indonesia.

5   THE 'MYANMAR ROAD TO GLOBALIZATION': NATIONAL COHESION THE DEFAULT POSITION

Around 2000, Myanmar's leadership acknowledged the phenomenon of globalization and urged a principled approach to its adoption. SPDC spokesman General Khin Nyunt described globalization as 'an undeniable fact of life. Nations were more now more integrated and more interdependent than ever before'. He recommended the acquisition of 'competencies and skills to meet these challenges posed by globalization' and to

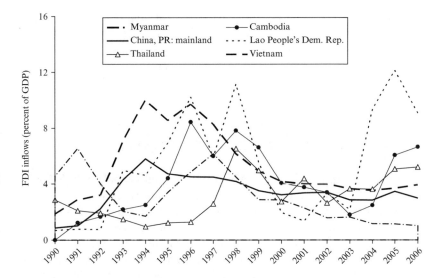

Sources: IMF, *International Financial Statistics, World Economic Outlook*, and authors' estimates.

Figure 9.2   *Foreign direct investment inflows (percent, relative to nominal GDP)*

avoid Myanmar being 'marginalized' by globalization.[8] Later, Khin Nyunt described globalization as bringing 'new opportunities as well as new challenges' and insisted that 'no nation can stay aloof and in isolation' from globalization.[9] This shift away from caution and hesitation about exposure to international economic forces was formally followed through at technical and administrative levels, even if underlying policies remained unchanged.

Myanmar's cautious acceptance of global convergence after 1988 included internet access, although under very tight control and with certain websites and information proscribed. Individuals and companies adapted to the internet's commercial advantages but unreliability caused by frequent officially-initiated disruptions to internet services left Myanmar behind its neighbours in this area. Satellite television broadcasts were also accepted, and in time, satellite dishes appeared throughout the country and became a major means by which the public were kept informed of international developments, as well as entertained by foreign films and sporting events. Mobile telephones were quickly adopted after the late 1990s, although they remained expensive and the penetration rate was low compared to most other countries.

Generally, the cultural and social impacts of globalization remained a cause for official concern and by 2004 provoked official measures aimed at countering the worst influences by promoting traditional values and behaviour, including conformity with the traditional dress code[10] but this did not extend to a systematic campaign to stamp out foreign fashions or practices.

6   THE ROLE OF REGIONAL INTEGRATION IN GLOBALIZING MYANMAR ECONOMICALLY

Myanmar's decision to join ASEAN in 1997 not only signalled the SPDC's commitment to internationalization and to bringing Myanmar into greater conformity with its neighbours, it also aimed to integrate Myanmar into the regional economy, including ultimately the system of trans-Asian transport links, customs and quarantine harmonization and trade liberalization through the ASEAN Free Trade Agreement to which Myanmar duly signed (with a concessional implementation schedule). Myanmar's leaders have never really questioned this commitment, even when forced to give up chairing ASEAN in 2005 over their lack of political reform.

Myanmar endeavoured to implement ASEAN commitments, potentially shortening the time and effort required to bring its economy into line with regional benchmarks. ASEAN membership highlighted comparisons between Myanmar's performance and its neighbours, but also allowed for some positive 'demonstration effects'. Myanmar has been a signatory to most formal ASEAN agreements, including those relating to trade and industrial cooperation such as the 2004 protocol on sectoral integration in the electronics industry. It increased the number of items included in ASEAN's Common Effective Preferential Tariff (CEPT) scheme from 5472 to 8229 and reduced items on the general exclusion and sensitive lists by about 50 percent between 1998 and 2007.

Since tariffs were not the main impediment to trade, Myanmar's participation in most AFTA liberalization and integration programmes did not have a significant impact on Myanmar's economic integration into ASEAN, even though trade with ASEAN rose to above 50 percent of Myanmar's total trade by 2005.[11] Although the government began phasing out priority lists in 2007 and import and export licenses – the main obstacles to trade – were to be granted more expeditiously and predictably, the impact of these changes remains to be seen. Myanmar still lags behind its ASEAN neighbours in developing the underpinning institutions for a market economy and its weaknesses in governance probably mean that the Myanmar economy is not well placed to avoid the negative consequences of globalization when they appear.

Equally, Myanmar's trade regime has not been substantively influenced by WTO disciplines promoting openness, transparency and fairness. As a Least Developed Country it has been granted additional time to implement most of its Uruguay Round obligations. No case against Myanmar has ever been brought in the WTO[12] because it is not a significant market for imports and competition in its internal market is weak. Although Myanmar attends WTO meetings and participates in WTO training programmes, it is not active in the organization, and makes only some of the notifications expected of it under the Uruguay Round agreements.

Intellectual property protection in Myanmar is not very effective and pirated products are widely and openly available across the country, as admitted in the government-controlled media in 2007. Although Myanmar joined the TRIPS agreement and the World Intellectual Property Organization in 2001, it is not required to conform with WIPO rules until 2013 and does not have to introduce IP protection measures under TRIPS until 2015. Nevertheless, the government has started a process of improving IP protection and lawyers with experience of Myanmar report that adequate arrangements can, with some effort, be found.[13] However, lack of adequate other legal protection is also a negative factor. As the Asia Law brief stated in 2003: 'significant change is necessary if Myanmar is to match the legislative standards of many other nations in Asia'.[14]

7 MYANMAR'S LIMITED PARTICIPATION IN REGIONAL PRODUCTION CHAINS

In contrast to other ASEAN members, Myanmar's economic reforms have not resulted in much participation in regional production chains. The conditions necessary to attract such investments were not present: predictable policies, transparent and consistent application of rules, supportive exchange rate and trade systems, infrastructure and human capital. Since Myanmar's population of over 50 million represented a substantial market, albeit with limited purchasing power, FDI was biased towards the urban market in electronics, motor vehicles and consumer electrical goods.[15]

Import-replacement industries dominate Myanmar manufacturing and FDI in this sector, already low at about 15 percent in the late 1990s, has fallen below 10 percent.[16] This stands in sharp contrast to well-integrated economies – China and the original ASEAN countries – as well as the newer members of ASEAN. Another measure of integration, the Grubel–Lloyd index (Figure 9.3),[17] confirms Myanmar's low participation in regional trading networks.

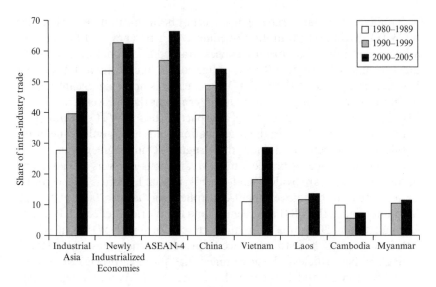

Sources: United Nations Comtrade database; and authors' calculation.

Figure 9.3   Share of intra-industry trade by region/country (Grubel–Lloyd Index)

One exception was Myanmar's textile industry, which grew rapidly in the 1990s on access to GSP preferences into the US market in particular. US sanctions in 2003 and the end of the Multi-Fibre Arrangement in 2005 set the sector back. According to official figures, the industry declined by 49 percent after its peak in 2002 as it also faced irregular power supplies, shortage of skilled labour and rigid government procedures.[18]

Agriculture and agri-business received priority in government policy by 2000. Subsequently, the fishing and marine products industries quickly grew into an export-capable sector, producing food products meeting international health and sanitation standards and attuned to international demands for quality control, stylish packaging and presentation and timely delivery. Firms in this sector are almost entirely owned by local entrepreneurs connected directly to their markets in Southeast Asia and beyond (including Australia). Plans were also approved to produce palm oil for Malaysia, market crops for Thailand from Southern Shan State and plantation crops and rice for China's Yunnan Province from the Wa Special Area.

To extract and export off-shore gas to Thailand international operators assembled a significant skilled labour force of engineers and managers. Skills and technology were transferred to local workers. To some extent

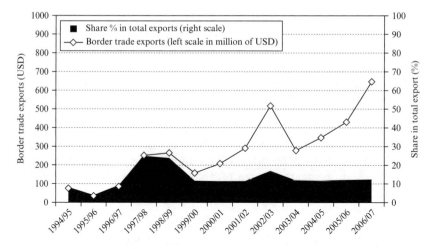

Sources: IMF, International Financial Statistics; World Bank, World Development Indicators; and authors' estimates.

Figure 9.4   *Border trade exports in US dollars and its share of total exports*

members of this workforce can join Myanmar's small pool of professionals in the related maritime transportation sector,[19] but the impact of the development of this sector on the wider economy is limited.

Myanmar craftsmanship and the natural quality of products such as teak and lacquer have successfully translated the processed timber products and furniture industry into competitive advantage. Here again, local entrepreneurs have demonstrated innovativeness in design and quality and operated successfully with foreign customers to set up marketing outlets in and beyond the region. Generally, little processing or other value-adding occurs and the returns to Myanmar have so far not been great.

Progress has been slow in implementing the 2000 government policy to set up Special Economic Zones (SEZ) for investors from the region to increase regional trade linkages. The SEZ law has still not been promulgated, and although streamlined border trade procedures (expedited customs checks, account payments arrangements and so on) have been introduced they still lag behind regional neighbours. Border trade has increased significantly in absolute terms but has not yet contributed to significant integration into regional production networks (Figure 9.4).

The Myanmar Government has worked hard to promote tourism from the early 1990s but earnings are modest compared to its neighbours and absolute levels are well short of neighbouring Thailand. Despite some modern facilities comparable to international standards, Myanmar's infrastructure remains underdeveloped. Many hotels, resorts and tourist services are part of international or regional chains and workers in this sector have begun to work in the tourism sector of other countries. The authorities have shown surprisingly little concern for any adverse spillover from tourism, although they have criticized the effects of sex tourism in other countries.

Overall, partly because of the importance of the unrecorded informal economy, the impact of globalization has been greater than official data would suggest. But whether this will continue to be the case will depend increasingly on a greater degree of political openness than is currently observed in Myanmar.[20]

8   CONSTRAINTS WORKING AGAINST GLOBALIZATION OF THE ECONOMY: WEAK POLICIES VERSUS SANCTIONS

With many economic reforms blocked by conservative interests in the military, a pattern of slowness to change and reluctance to reform emerged. Designated to direct the privatization programme, the army remained too reliant on its economic revenues to relinquish control over much of the economy. Additionally, ceasefire agreements with ethnic groups contained economic concessions in areas such as mining, tourism, construction and hotels, over which the central authorities thereafter exercised little control. But many of these ventures, located in sensitive border areas, had national security implications. The state proved reluctant to relinquish control and thus undermined the commitment to economic reform.

Moreover, some government practices worked against the spirit if not the letter of many of the post-1988 economic reforms. For example, in the early 1990s the army established Myanmar Economic Holdings and Myanmar Economic Corporation, which, by taking minority shareholdings in many joint ventures ensure *de facto* army control over businesses. There is no transparency about the financial affairs of MEH and MEC and almost no information about their operations is ever made public, even though their financial affairs are audited.

Furthermore, Myanmar operates a highly regulated (albeit non-discriminatory) trade regime. For example, SPDC Deputy Chair, Vice Senior General Maung Aye, headed the Trade Committee for many years and authorized imports and exports licences for all goods and for repatriation of funds or profits. Military leaders also control other business activities by issuing operating permits. Decisions on these matters are neither transparent, consistent, nor contestable, all being made by various committees headed by high-level military officers who comprise SPDC.

The state's controlling role in economic activity detracts from the positive impacts of globalization and retards genuine market-oriented development. SOEs, for example, still control some of the country's main natural resources (most minerals, the lucrative gem trade, and so on). And, as late as 2001, the unofficial UN Directory of the Myanmar Government listed more than 50 state-owned enterprises. Many operated in the red and required subsidies from the central authorities. Nor does it help the performance of Myanmar's SOE's that military officers without relevant business expertise are routinely kicked sideways to head SOEs.[21]

From the mid-1990s, most observers consider the SPDC's economic reforms lost their momentum. Almost no large-scale privatization was undertaken under the Privatization Committee (chaired by a high-ranking general), although a goldmine was listed in 2007. Unable to transform themselves into entrepreneurial corporates, SOEs still operate much as they have always done, subject as much to non-commercial military demands as market imperatives. In the macro-economy, liberalization measures were largely suspended or reversed after the mid-1990s as the authorities found it increasingly difficult to sustain foreign exchange reserves, to control inflation and to fund their fiscal deficits. More recently, some progress has been made in increasing the state's revenue collection, removing restrictions on banks imposed during the crisis and liberalizing agriculture.

Another major constraint on globalization is the complex exchange rate system which consists of:

1. An official exchange rate pegged at 8.5 kyat per SDR since 1977. The government sets other exchange rates for various purposes, such as customs valuation.
2. The Foreign Exchange Certificate (FEC) rate. The FEC is a certificate issued by the central bank in exchange for foreign currency and is the only legal means to undertake large international transactions. FECs can be exchanged into kyat, but the volume of FEC-denominated transactions is relatively modest, with the stock of FECs around US$374 million in recent years.
3. A market-determined rate based on the large illegal parallel market that exchanges foreign currencies with kyats at a slight premium over the FEC rate.

The official currency rate is grossly overvalued with a premium 150–200 times the market-determined exchange rate in recent years. The exchange rate system evolved as a means for the government to preserve its foreign exchange. The system is also supported by restrictive controls to limit the use of, and conserve, foreign exchange. For instance, Myanmar maintains exchange restrictions on the purchase of foreign exchange by residents. However, the exchange rate system has become unworkable: a fact tacitly accepted by the authorities as they have effectively allowed private transactions to be carried out at the informal market-determined rate.

The current system is not transparent and a well-functioning foreign exchange market has not developed. Foreign investors cite high transaction costs, rent-seeking and corruption as key impediments. The government knows of the exchange rate problems but has done almost nothing to address this barrier to greater international and regional integration.

Developments in the banking sector provide another example of the tension between the stated policy desire to modernize on the one hand and weak policies and international sanctions on the other. The 2003–04 banking crisis derailed the development of the sector. Under day-to-day supervision of banking operations, authorities imposed restrictions on withdrawals and emergency liquidity from the central banks and pressured borrowers into early repayment of their loans. They also introduced *ad hoc* administrative measures, such as extremely tight limits on the deposit-to-capital ratio and required bank-owners to increase capital. Notably, the government did not communicate with the public in order to maintain confidence. These measures – non-transparent, administrative, non-conventional – stemmed the run on banks, but at a high cost to banks, public confidence and the economy. They eventually led to the closure of several private banks and a temporary reversion to old-fashioned forms of lending and credit (see Figure 9.5). As a result, private banks no longer act as intermediaries but rather merely as providers of payment services.

Since the crisis, however, the authorities became more interested in applying modern banking regulation and supervision. One tangible sign of progress was the improvement in the Anti-Money Laundering and Combating of Financing of Terrorism framework, which led the Western-dominated Financial Action Task Force to drop Myanmar from its black-list of non-cooperating countries in 2006. Despite their attempts to develop a modern banking system,[22] private banks had not recovered commercially from the 2003–04 crisis when in 2007 they found themselves faced with a new wave of targeted financial sanctions which, in practice if not intent, affected the wider private sector as much as government activities.

Sanctions on trade and investment – largely imposed by Western nations – reduce the overall impact of globalization. Macroeconomic instability, erratic government decision-making, intrusive and unwieldy government licensing, unpredictable import regulations and restrictive

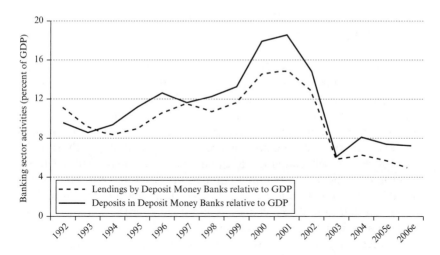

Sources: IMF, International Financial Statistics; and authors' estimates.

Figure 9.5   Banking sector activities relative to nominal GDP, 1992–2006

foreign exchanges procedures all contribute to an unfavourable climate for industries manufacturing and processing for regional markets.[23] While the authorities are quick to blame the country's economic malaise on sanctions, Myanmar's poor economic performance pre-dates sanctions by years if not decades. It remains to be seen whether the tougher 2007 financial sanctions will have a bigger impact, but since important sectors (such as oil) are exempt their impact might be limited although some vulnerable sectors may be hit hard. However, at a broad level the post-2007 financial sanctions at least discourage, and perhaps make impossible, financial linkages that underpin trade and investment flows.

Corruption is often mentioned as a constraint on foreign investment and business. According to Transparency International, in 2006 Myanmar ranked 160th out of 161 countries on the perceptions of corruption index, scoring only 1.9 out of a possible 10. This is hardly a surprising result given anecdotal evidence of both large-scale and petty corruption. But it is difficult to confirm the accuracy of this ranking when, generally speaking, international perceptions of Myanmar are often biased, ill-informed and based on hearsay. Without a doubt, the desire to expedite or ensure favourable bureaucratic decisions creates opportunities for corruption, blatant rent-seeking and the maintenance of networks of crony businesses.[24]

9   ECONOMIC OUTLOOK AND THE WAY FORWARD

The arguments here – that, by and large, policy choices have constrained the benefits of globalization – suggest considerable potential on the part of Myanmar to respond to many of the economic challenges of globalization. It remains to be seen whether Myanmar can overcome the unnecessary and burdensome limitations on telecommunications and the heavy regulatory and supervisory demands imposed by the Myanmar authorities to establish a genuinely enabling trade and investment environment without being left behind by its regional competitors. Country risk factors will inevitably continue to affect Myanmar adversely and in some situations may again lead to sudden collapse, as happened after the banking crisis of 2003–04 and the political crisis of 2007.

Whether Myanmar's private sector's responsiveness can prosper under the unwieldy and sometimes uninformed nature of regulatory policy also remains questionable. Clearly, success depends on innovative entrepreneurship with greater flexibility and acceptable business ethics. Transformational change would be helped enormously and perhaps critically by policy shifts like those in Myanmar's neighbours. Globalization's benefits will generally not be outweighed by costs in Myanmar because of the general conservatism of government policy and public behaviour but the benefits may not be fully realized if the many constraints affecting development in Myanmar are not addressed soon.

Policies enabling Myanmar to benefit from globalization are dissimilar from those undertaken by other transition economies, including regional neighbours such as China and Vietnam. Firstly, the government needs to address chronic macroeconomic instability, improving public finances, introducing monetary policy and reforming the exchange rate system. Reform also needs to focus on the financial system. Secondly, measures will be needed to create a conducive investment environment with transparent, clear and predictable rules. Efforts to streamline export–import licence requirements need to be deepened and rules facing foreign investors applied consistently. Further liberalizing agriculture can bring significant benefits to a large proportion of the Myanmar population. Thirdly, decades of underinvestment in human capital and physical infrastructure need to be reversed.

Without such changes Myanmar will continue to suffer from incomplete economic policies and poor economic performance, despite the country's rich resources and considerable potential. Under current policies macroeconomic stability is expected to be elusive, with economic growth below the long-term average and little progress in poverty reduction. Economic growth will remain well below historical levels and the experience of neighbouring countries. Inflation will remain high, fuelled by continued fiscal deficits. Structural weakness will impede both domestic and foreign investment. Business and public confidence will remain low, making it even more difficult for the authorities to bring about macroeconomic stability and economic growth. The economy will remain vulnerable to adverse shocks. A poor harvest, political turmoil, or a new financial crisis could cause severe economic disruption. A sharp decline in gas prices, or lower than expected production, will also adversely affect the external balance.

Effective policy responses to these pressures will, as always, depend to a great extent on the political state of the country. As any changes in economic policy are introduced, ensuring appropriate governance and accountability will be critical, and capacity building to align business practices more closely with practices now widely accepted internationally, and especially regionally, will be essential if the economic benefits of globalization are to be realized.

But progress in development still depends fundamentally on reaching some form of overall political settlement between the various parties. Any lasting settlement must involve a significant role for the military, at least as a transitional arrangement. However, the gradual but targeted demilitarization of the economy should be implemented carefully in order to avoid instability but should be begun without delay. While the military may need assurances about certain protection of their economic interests, as David Steinberg has argued (Steinberg 2005a), they must step back from the highly *dirigiste* role they have been playing, particularly in the internationally competitive productive sectors of the economy oriented to regional markets.

Recent tightening of sanctions by some countries is not expected to have a large direct impact on the overall economy, given restrictions already in place. Nevertheless, some sectors (for example, tourism) will be hit hard, while political uncertainty will likely adversely affect foreign direct investment inflows due to increasing political and reputational risk faced by investors.

NOTES

1. Official statistics are often unreliable and late, making it difficult to assess economic developments. In particular, estimates of the size and growth of GDP by official and other observers differ widely. Official data does not include an estimate of the large informal economy, while official growth estimates are generally much higher than those by other observers. Major reasons for these problems include capacity constraints, including the lack of technical skills as well as the more general nontransparent

governing environment. This chapter draws on both official data, where available, and authors' estimates where appropriate.

2. Myanmar maintains a multiple exchange rate system. The official exchange rate is pegged to the Special Drawing Right (SDR) at Kyat 8.5 per SDR. Formally, the official exchange rate applies only to transactions undertaken by the central government and state economic enterprises (SEEs). In practice, the government and SEEs use the official exchange rate for accounting purposes but its use in transactions is rationed. The authorities also issue Foreign Exchange Certificates (FECs) for external transactions; this FEC exchange rate is market-determined and currently stands around K1100 per US dollar. There is also an illegal but tolerated informal market that exchanges dollars with kyats at a small premium over the FEC rate. This informal market rate is widely used in transactions.

3. The data is for 2004. Myanmar ranks last in economic and social globalization and, perhaps surprisingly, ranks 114th in political globalization. See kof@kof.ethz.ch.

4. If one were to use official national accounts data, trade is less than 1 percent of GDP in 2006, much less than estimates based on more realistic market exchange rates. This is one example of how the multiple exchange rate system complicates economic analysis.

5. As examples: agricultural land was nationalized and redistributed, high tariffs were imposed on previously free trade and state marketing boards were established for most commodities and many manufactured products.

6. In effect, nationalization of the banks was carried to the extent of creating a single state-owned 'mono-bank', which directed the operations of a few specialized subsidiaries.

7. Initially the regime called itself the State Law and Order Restoration Council but changed its name in 1997 to State Peace and Development Council.

8. Speech by Khin Nyunt at the Third ASEAN Ministerial Meeting on Youth in Yangon, recorded in the Joint Press Statement, 2 November 2000.

9. Opening speech by Khin Nyunt at the Third BIMST–EC Trade/Economic Ministerial Meeting, in Yangon on 15 February 2001.

10. An interesting report by Nwe Nwe Aye in the *Myanmar Times*, 'Outside influences challenge Myanmar to adapt to the new' quoted an official from the Ministry of Culture saying: 'Owing to globalisation and the strong impact of media, young people are exposed to the outside world at the click of a computer mouse, and it is important they pick up only good things'. *Myanmar Times*, **12** (236), 4–10 October 2004.

11. The recently retired Director-General of Myanmar's National AFTA Office, U Maung Maung Yi, said in an interview that, 'Few of our businesses are enjoying the preferential trade arrangements offered through AFTA by the more developed ASEAN members'. See 'Trade expert warns of missed opportunities with ASEAN', *Myanmar Times*, **20** (389), 22–28 October 2007.

12. Myanmar became a member of the WTO by virtue of its prior membership of the GATT.

13. Alec Christie (July 2006), 'Myanmar's Legal System and Contract Law', DLA Phillips Fox.

14. Asia Law Brief (July 2003), *IP Review*.

15. Foreign firms investing in Myanmar in the import replacement category have included Toyota, Suzuki, Daewoo, British Tobacco.

16. FDI statistics are not completely reliable because they are generally based on FDI approvals.

17. This index attempts to measure the extent of intra-industry trade. The assumption here is that more integrated production chains across borders would result in a higher amount of intra-industry trading.

18. See paper by Myint Soe, Chairman of the Myanmar Garment Manufacturers Association prepared for a regional policy dialogue in 2007. Available at: www.unescap.org/tid/mtg/weaving_myan.

19. Along with doctors and civil engineers, Myanmar's merchant marine has always been excluded from the tightest restrictions on travel and transfer of funds.

20. See Sean Turnell and his Burma Economic Watch colleagues' presentation to the 2007 Myanmar/Burma Update conference in Canberra (forthcoming through ANU E-Press).
21. As a group, SOEs have been profitable since 2006 but mostly because they have been allowed to raise prices.
22. Myanmar appears to be a country that is under-banked. Currently, no foreign banks are permitted to operate in Myanmar, yet many private banks would like the opportunity to work with foreign investors to improve their capital and technological skills.
23. The obstacles facing business operations are well described by David Steinberg (2005b), pp. 86–116.
24. This is the reason why additional sanctions imposed by many OECD countries after September 2007 included known business associates of the Myanmar Government.

BIBLIOGRAPHY

East Asian Analytical Unit (1997), *The New ASEANs: Vietnam, Burma, Cambodia and Laos*, Canberra: Department of Foreign Affairs and Trade.
Economic Analytical Unit (2006), *ASEAN: Building an Economic Community*, Canberra: Department of Foreign Affairs and Trade.
Hlaing, Kyaw Yin, Robert H. Taylor and Tin Maung Maung Than (eds) (2005), *Myanmar: Beyond Politics to Societal Imperatives*, Singapore: Institute of Southeast Asian Studies.
Kudo, Toshihiro (2005), 'Stunted and distorted industrialization in Myanmar', Institute of Developing Economies discussion paper no 35, Tokyo.
Steinberg, David (2001) *Burma: The State of Myanmar*, Washington, DC: Georgetown University Press.
Steinberg, David (2005a), 'Burma/Myanmar: the role of the military in the economy', Sydney, NSW: *Burma Economic Watch*, 1.
Steinberg, David (2005b), 'Myanmar: the roots of economic malaise', in K.Y. Hlaing, R.H. Taylor and T.M.M. Than (eds), *Myanmar: Beyond Politics to Societal Imperatives*, Singapore: Institute of Southeast Asian Studies.
Taylor, Robert H. (2007), 'The legacies of the Second World War for Myanmar', in David Koh Wee Hock (ed.), *Legacies of WW II in East and South Asia*, Singapore: Institute of Southeast Asian Studies.
Than, Mya (2005), *Myanmar in ASEAN: Regional Cooperation Experience*, Singapore: Institute of Southeast Asian Studies.
Than, Tin Maung Maung (2007), *State Dominance in Myanmar: The Political Economy of Industrialization*, Singapore: Institute of Southeast Asian Studies.
Thein, Myat (2004), *Economic Development of Myanmar*, Singapore: Institute of Southeast Asian Studies.
Tucker, Shelby (2001), *Burma: The Curse of Independence*, London: Pluto Press.
Turnell, Sean, Alison Vicary and Wylie Bradford (2008), 'Migrant-worker remittances and Burma: an economic analysis of survey results', in *Dictatorship, Disorder and Decline in Myanmar*, Monique Skidmore and Trevor Wilson (eds), Canberra: ANU E-Press, pp. 63–86.

10. Cambodia: country case study

Matt Davies[1]

---

1 INTRODUCTION

Following the end of decades of ravaging conflict in the 1990s, Cambodia underwent an impressive renaissance. Besides political stability, economic growth and reducing poverty, the country also re-integrated with the international community, joining ASEAN and the WTO.

So many achievements in such a short time point to a bright future. However, Cambodia remains a distinctly poor country where rapid growth disproportionately favored the urban rich at the expense of the rural poor. Moreover, recent global economic developments reveal the fragility of macroeconomic stability in a narrowly based economy that is vulnerable to external shocks with key growth sectors facing increasingly intense international competition. The quality of governance remains basic and corruption is widespread.

This chapter reviews the reasons for Cambodia's economic success since 1995 and examines the extent to which it continues to drive growth and poverty reduction in the medium to long term. Will Cambodia exit low-income status in this generation and begin to catch up with its ASEAN partners or remain a poor relation within ASEAN subject to the vulnerabilities that face low-income countries?

The answers lie mostly in the policy choices made in the coming months and years. The chapter outlines some key reform priorities for Cambodia in Section 4, prior to which sections 2 and 3 attempt to understand how the Cambodia of today came about. Section 5 concludes.

2 THE HISTORICAL AND POLITICAL BACKDROP

Cambodia remains marked by the affects of the conflict in Indochina in the 1970s and by the genocidal regime of the Khmer Rouge. Its brutal bid to turn Cambodia into a Maoist, peasant-dominated agrarian cooperative resulted in the death of an estimated 2 million Cambodians (out of a total population of around 16 million) between 1975 and 1978. With the educated targeted for persecution and death, the population enslaved and currency abolished the country was almost entirely cut off from the outside world. Responding to recurring incursions into their border provinces, Vietnam invaded Cambodia in 1978 and ran the country throughout the 1980s on a central planning model heavily reliant on the Soviet Union for trade relations and aid.

The 1991 Paris Peace Accord ended almost 20 years of civil war and led to a transitional UN administration (UNTAC) that held power before elections in 1993 and oversaw the introduction of a new constitution and the reinstatement of the monarchy. The election resulted in a power-sharing arrangement between the royalist FUNCINPEC and the Hun Sen-led Cambodian People's Party (CPP), that emerged from the Vietnamese sponsored administration of the 1980s.

In 1997 the CPP assumed power amidst widespread violence but returned to a coalition with FUNCINPEC following the 1998 elections. The 2003 elections saw the CPP make further gains along with an emerging opposition, the Sam Rainsy Party. An inconclusive outcome led to a year-long political impasse, eventually resolved through a further CPP/FUNCINPEC coalition. Constitutional changes in 2006 enabled a government to be formed with a simple majority and in the 2008 elections the CPP gained full power.

3   GROWTH AND DEVELOPMENT (1995–2007)

3.1   Economic and Social Outcomes

Following the establishment of security and (relative) political stability in the 1990s. and despite upheavals in the regional and world economy (SARS, 1997 Asian crisis), Cambodia grew at an average 8.5 percent annually between 1995 and 2007. Growth peaked at 13.5 percent in 2005. Even with rapid population growth, per capita GDP (on a PPP basis) increased more rapidly than almost all of Cambodia's low-income peers. Inflation remained under control for the large part of the period, averaging less than 5 percent but increasing rapidly in the second half of 2007 in response to increases in world oil and food prices and surging domestic demand.

The garment and tourism industries accounted for nearly half of the total growth over the period.[2] Despite their contribution to growth, the industrial and services sectors employed only around a third of the labor force (Sida, 2006). Agriculture, which employed two-thirds of the labor force, accounted for only around a sixth of total growth between 1995 and 2005. In the early years, particularly between 1994 and 1998, unsustainable and mainly illegal forestry contributed to economic growth but imposed massive environmental and governance costs without contributing significantly to government revenues (IMF, 2004). Reforms in 1999 and a government-imposed moratorium in 2002 reduced impacts significantly but illegal forestry continued to concern many external observers (Global Witness, 2007).

Poverty, however, decreased substantially over the period, from 47 percent in 1994 to 35 percent in 2004 (World Bank, 2006). Access to water, provision of electricity, school enrollment and health also improved, including for the poorest. These gains, though notable, correspond with those made by other countries emerging from periods of conflict (ibid.). The pace of growth and its urban-centric nature did, however, lead to an increase in inequality – the Gini co-efficient rose from 0.35 in 1994 to 0.4 in 2004. The largest increase in inequality occurred in the mid-1990s when consumption in the urban areas grew considerably quicker than in rural areas. Since 1997 inequality has remained broadly stable.

Cambodia ranks 131 out of 177 countries on the United Nations Development Program Human Development Index and 124 on income. The poor face constraints to improving their livelihoods, including lack of secure land tenure, remoteness from markets, low levels of education and high dependency ratios (World Bank, 2006).

3.2   Sources of Growth[3]

Cambodia's population increase following the emergence from conflict led to a rapidly increasing labor force, still rising at around 200 000 people or 4 percent a year (Sida, 2006). The increase in the labor force contributed around 3.5 percentage points to annual GDP growth between 1995 and 2007.

The accumulation of physical capital per worker played an increasingly important role in underpinning growth of output – contributing around three percentage points to annual growth. In the early part of the period, around half of total investment was accounted for by public investment, mainly financed by aid (between 1995 and 2005, Cambodia received US$373 of aid per capita, over three times the average for low-income countries).[4] In latter years private investment picked up markedly, while public sector investment declined both as a share of GDP and of overall investment. The pick up in private investment was driven in part by substantial increases in foreign direct investment (FDI).

With labor and physical capital contributing around six percentage points to annual growth over the period, the remaining 2–3 percent must be due to improvements in productivity.[5] There were improvements in the education level of the workforce – in 2004 the younger cohorts of the workforce had substantially more education than older workers (Sida, 2006). Education levels, though, remain low compared to other East Asian economies. Similarly, while the increasing share of manufacturing and declining share of subsistence agriculture contributed to the increase in productivity, the sector remains labor-intensive and productivity is low by regional standards (World Bank, 2004).

3.3 Macroeconomic Policies

Fiscal policies

After the restoration of fiscal stability in the late 1990s, a strategy of avoiding domestic bank financing of the deficit – with some slippages around national elections – anchored fiscal policy. As a result, deficits varied with the availability/utilization of external finance, averaging around 5 percent of GDP (or 2 percent of GDP if grants are included as revenue). In recent years deficits declined reflecting moderating external finance, improved revenue collections and, in 2006, debt relief from the IMF.[6] The remaining public debt of around 30 percent of GDP was mostly external with limited risk of distress (IMF, 2007).[7]

Low levels of revenue collection remain the greatest weakness of fiscal policy. Revenues as a share of GDP averaged just over half the level of other PRGF-eligible countries between 2000 and 2004 (IMF 2007b). This reflected the very narrow tax base: the formal sector is small while generous investment incentives largely exempt the main growth sectors from taxes. Feeble enforcement and corruption further compromise tax collection. Cambodia's long and porous borders complicate the collection of taxes on trade, and smuggling is rife, particularly of petroleum products.[8] Poor management of state assets has also weakened non-tax revenue collections.

Recent improvements in administration, more commitment to enforcement and the growth of the formal economy helped revenue performance. Nevertheless revenues remained low and reliant on taxes on international trade in an environment of declining rates due to Cambodia's international obligations.

Low revenues, combined with the commitment to prudent fiscal balances, placed pressure on expenditure. Productive current expenditures were constrained in the late 1990s by the need to absorb military personnel. A demobilization program in 2001 helped reorient expenditure to priority areas, which doubled as a share of GDP between 1998 and 2003 (Lopez-Mejia and Hagemann, 2006). Nevertheless, improvements in the quality of expenditure were slow, due in part to the weak capacity of the public service and low public wages (IMF, 2007).

Spending was unable to keep up with the immense infrastructure needs. Low investment compared to many regional economies meant that Cambodia compared poorly with regional averages in terms of the road network, electricity generation and communications (ADB, 2004). Services were unreliable and expensive with phone and electricity costs higher than almost all regional economies (JETRO, 2007).

Expenditure management systems also undermined expenditure quality. Poor budgeting and execution led, until recently, to endemic cash shortages and the build up of domestic payment arrears. In response, the government and its development partners developed a comprehensive long-term public financial management reform program (PFRMRP) that is beginning to bear fruit. Budgeting is more credible – revenue collections are now able to finance the aggregate expenditure plan, which was not the case in the early 2000s – and expenditure control more effective – domestic payment arrears decreased by over 50 percent between 2005 and 2007. Significant problems remain: budget planning and forecasting is short term and open to significant error; cash management is rudimentary; and manual accounting and expenditure execution systems do not provide sufficient flexibility or control to budget managers.

Monetary and exchange rate policies
Cambodia remains highly dollarized. Although the riel is mainly used in rural and agricultural sectors and for small change in the cities, all major transactions are conducted in US dollars. Dollars make up around three-quarters of measured broad money and over 90 percent of the total estimated money supply.[9] Only around 5 percent of deposits and credit in the banking system are in local currency and the ratio is declining.

Dollarization delivered some benefits to the Cambodia economy between 1995 and 2007, helping to insulate it from the effect of external shocks – including the Asian crisis in 1997 – and encouraging export growth and financial re-intermediation. However, together with the incipient nature of the financial system, it restricted the role of monetary and exchange rate policy.

Money supply grew rapidly, from 8 percent of GDP in 1995 to 30 percent in 2007. Money growth was driven in particular by accumulation of foreign assets, reflecting the paucity of domestic investment opportunities for the growth in liabilities from dollarized re-intermediation and, latterly, accelerating foreign inflows. The level of financial intermediation remained well below that of comparator economies (IMF, 2007).

Dollarization forced the National Bank of Cambodia (NBC) to be largely a passive observer of the increasingly rapid rate of money growth. Price-based financial sector instruments barely existed – the NBC has no policy rate and no indirect instruments through which to control liquidity. In the face of generally moderate inflation, it left the instruments it did have at its disposal largely unchanged. Reserve requirements remained stable at 8 percent and capital adequacy ratios were eased slightly from 15 to 12 percent in 2005. Direct controls on credit growth in the early 2000s were dismantled. The surge in inflation and money growth that began in mid-2007, however, saw the NBC increase reserve requirements in early 2008 to 16 percent on dollar deposits in an attempt to slow credit growth that had exceeded 100 percent.

The exchange rate, which under dollarization affects the valuation of internal (rural–urban) more than external transactions, remained broadly stable and policy was necessarily largely passive. With the monetization of fiscal deficits eliminated and, in recent years, as the government actually withdrew local currency from circulation, intervention became the authorities' main tool for managing the level of riel in circulation and for building up international reserves. Despite their rapid enhancement near the end of the period, reserves remained low both in months of imports (around 2.5 months) and in terms of the dollar deposits of the banking system (around 80 percent and decreasing at the end of 2007).

Financial sector

Although commercial banking began in the early 1990s, the sector grew slowly until reforms in the early 2000s, which aimed at reducing the number of banks and ensuring those that remained were viable and able to comply with a tightened set of prudential regulations. Thereafter the banking sector grew rapidly. However, confidence in the sector was fragile with much of the population still hesitant to entrust their savings to banks and unable to seek credit as lack of land security frustrated their ability to offer collateral.

At the end of 2007 the financial sector remained rudimentary. There were 23 banks – a large amount for the sector's size – but most were very small – the largest five banks accounted for around 75 percent of all deposits. Interest rate spreads were very large and there were no functioning interbank market or government securities to act as collateral or investment vehicles. Banks were heavily exposed to individual sectors (particularly real estate) and customers and were aggressively expanding lending to them. Credit to the private sector was growing at an annual rate of 70 percent at the end of 2008. This growth represented a significant source of risk to the economy, particularly due to the buoyant real estate sector that was driven by foreign inflows sensitive to changing global economic conditions.[10] The global financial crisis of late 2008 showed that this risk was very real as the real estate and banking sector contracted.

External policy
Between 1995 and 2007 Cambodia became one of the most open economies in one of the most open regions in the world, with trade in goods and services reaching almost 150 percent of GDP. Although tourism and garments exports drove economic growth, net exports were an overall drag on growth due to the high imported content of Cambodia's exports.[11] The trade deficit averaged over 13 percent of GDP. The current account deficit was much smaller, averaging around 3 percent of GDP, reflecting surpluses in services (mainly tourism) and transfers (aid and remittances). Excluding official transfers, the current account deficit averaged around 10 percent of GDP. The terms of trade remained relatively stable, deteriorating by around 6 percent between 1998 and 2006.

Cambodia's international commitments from WTO and ASEAN membership anchored external policy. Tariffs on trade declined moderately from an average 18 percent in 1997 to 15 percent in 2007 but remain relatively high by regional standards. This reflects, in part, the fiscal sector's reliance on taxes on international trade, which constrain the speed at which the government can reduce tariffs. Under ASEAN agreements Cambodia has a commitment to reduce tariffs for the bulk of its imports to less than 5 percent by 2010.

There were also many administrative impediments to trade. The number of days to process a shipment in Cambodia was well above the regional average, informal payments were high and numerous agencies oversaw borders. Cambodia's accession to the WTO included commitments to implement new laws to facilitate trade, ranging from a commercial court to financial sector laws. However, progress was slow, due in part to the wide range of new legislation that the National Assembly had to consider (Ishikawa and Nakamura, 2006).

Governance and institutions
The quality of governance in Cambodia placed a drag on economic development. Public administration particularly suffered heavily from the destruction of human capital during the Khmer Rouge era. Burdensome bureaucratic procedures and heavy regulation also inhibited effective government and presented widespread opportunities for rent seeking. State assets were poorly managed with non-transparent contracting of franchises and leasing of public property reducing government revenue and diminishing public confidence in government (Table 10.1). Civil service and executive appointments were influenced by political patronage

Table 10.1   Cambodia: ranking in selected governance indicators, 2006–07

	Rank	Total No. of Countries
TI's Corruption Perception Index	162	179
Global Competitiveness Index	110	131
Business Competitiveness Index	114	127
WB's Governance Indicators		
Voice and Accountability	164	209
Political Stability	148	209
Government Effectiveness	180	212
Regulatory Quality	151	206
Rule of Law	185	211
Control of Corruption	192	207

Sources: Transparency International; 2007 World Economic Forum; and the World Bank.

– following the election in 2003 the new government consisted of 329 cabinet posts (Sjoberg and Sjoholm, 2005).

And then there is corruption (World Bank, 2004). In a 2005 survey, 80 percent of respondents ranked corruption as the most significant constraint on doing business in Cambodia (EIC, 2005). Inefficient government bureaucracy came a distant second. Although under development for a number of years, an anti-corruption law never reached the National Assembly.

The Khmer Rouge period and the subsequent period of central planning meant that the broader institutions of governance for a market economy did not exist in the mid-1990s. These institutions emerged slowly – basic laws such as a criminal procedures code were only placed on the books right at the end of the period and specialized institutions such as a commercial court were still under development. Law enforcement was also weak and there were widespread concerns over human rights violations and the lack of political impartiality of the police and the judiciary.

4   FUTURE PROSPECTS AND POLICY PRIORITIES

As specified in the National Strategic Development Plan (2006–10), Cambodia's long-term macroeconomic goals give priority to poverty reduction. If the record of recent years can be sustained and enhanced Cambodia could begin to catch up with the per-capita income levels of its ASEAN peers while rapidly reducing poverty. With a sustained 10 percent

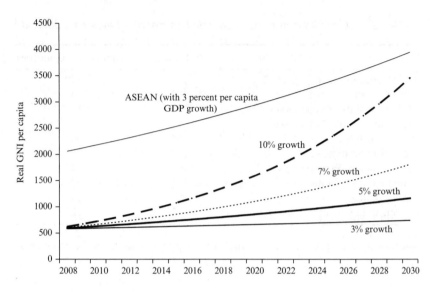

Figure 10.1   Alternative growth scenarios

yearly growth improvement (Figure 10.1) Cambodia could approach middle-income status in around ten years, whereas it would take a generation with 5 percent growth.

The year 2008 presented Cambodia with a more challenging international economic and financial environment and new challenges for domestic economic management. Inflation reached at a ten-year high on the back of rising international prices and surging domestic monetary growth. Meanwhile, external demand weakened and competition intensified in its crucial garment industry. The industry will face further tests as international demand shrinks at the same time as safeguard measures are removed. The global economic slowdown will also weaken the tourism industry and agriculture remains vulnerable to unpredictable weather.

Diversification of the economy is therefore vital not only for Cambodia to take advantage of the benefits of globalization but also to minimize exposure to the risks that come with it. It is also essential to absorb the rapidly growing workforce and allow the poor to move out of subsistence agriculture into more secure livelihoods. Achieving this diversification requires sustaining and improving in areas where Cambodia was successful over the last decade – macroeconomic policies, attracting investment – while improving performance in other areas – agricultural productivity, infrastructure, governance, social services – and avoiding setbacks in areas of potential risk – political instability and the financial sector.

Oil and gas production could improve the outlook. Cambodia has a number of offshore blocks under exploration in its own waters. These, and an area jointly owned with Thailand, could deliver substantial benefits in terms of growth and fiscal revenues. However, production would pose additional challenges to macroeconomic management. Translating the revenues into enhanced growth and poverty reduction while avoiding the pitfalls that have befallen many resource rich nations will require prudent macroeconomic management and improved public expenditure policy and management.[12]

4.1 Macroeconomic Management

Macroeconomic stability is essential for continued poverty reduction and for increasing integration into the global and regional economy. With continued dollarization and an underdeveloped financial sector, fiscal policy will remain the dominant ingredient in the macroeconomic policy mix. It is also crucial to finance improvements in social services and public infrastructure. The increasing demand pressures that became evident in late 2007 and continued in 2008, despite restrained recent fiscal policy, suggest that Cambodian authorities will face trade-offs. Continued commitment to prudent fiscal balances with non-inflationary financing will certainly be important in maintaining the macroeconomic stability of recent years. However, that in itself is unlikely to provide enough flexibility for the government to achieve the increased expenditure essential for continued growth.

Increased and broader-based revenue must therefore be a fiscal policy priority, both to allow increases in public expenditure and to allow flexibility in macroeconomic policy. Recent performance is encouraging – revenues reached 12 percent of GDP in 2007 for the first time since the peace accords. However, reforms to broaden the tax base, such as property taxation, VAT reform and reducing income tax exemptions remain essential. A more modern, broad-based tax system will also ultimately provide demand management tools to the authorities.

Revenue growth will be needed to finance investment in infrastructure and human capital, particularly education and training. This in turn will promote private sector investment and improve productivity. Improving expenditure quality and management must remain a priority, particularly in terms of planning expenditure in a medium-term context, enhancing fiscal reporting and improving cash management. It will also require sustained attention to civil service reform, including establishing a more meritocratic career progression, decreasing the scope and incentive for rent-seeking and steadily and sustainably increasing public sector wages.

Dollarization and the unsophisticated financial system will continue to constrain monetary and exchange rate policy. To manage liquidity the authorities need to establish market infrastructure, such as treasury bills, and an interbank foreign exchange market. In the short term, NBC will need to continue to build up its international reserves particularly to remain a credible lender of last resort to a dollarized and fragile banking system increasingly exposed to international financial flows.

Ultimately, declining levels of dollarization would benefit Cambodia, particularly in increasing flexibility in macroeconomic management. However, international experience shows few examples of successful dedollarization, particularly from levels as high as Cambodia's (Abdelati, 2006). The few successes, for instance Poland and Israel, have been based around sound macro fundamentals rather than coercive administrative measures. Development of local currency financial sector instruments will be essential in laying the foundation for future dedollarization.

4.2 International Integration

Cambodia's geographic position, in the heart of one of the most dynamic regions in the world, between two rapidly growing neighbors and well-connected to China and India, makes it ideally placed to take advantage of globalization. In fact, given its position and policies it has little option but to participate fully in globalization. Nevertheless, participation will test the resilience of Cambodia's weak institutional and policy environment. The challenges of managing an open economy are much greater once investors begin taking advantage of that openness. These challenges became more apparent with the pick up in international capital flows to Cambodia in recent years and their reversal with the downturn in economic conditions in the second half of 2008.

Cambodia's garment industry represents the basic entry-level to the production network type of industrialization seen in the rest of East Asia (see Chapter 2). With continued macroeconomic stability Cambodia is certainly a potential location for production network-related investment focused on the export of final products and low-level processing of intermediate products.

Moving its exports up the value chain by entering these production networks will place Cambodia in fierce competition with other Mekong economies as well as the regional powerhouses of China and India (see Chapter 3). Improving competitiveness will require addressing the low levels of education and productivity of the workforce, the poor infrastructure that increases the costs of doing business and the poor quality of governance, including the trade institutions and architecture, that reduces certainty for investors and, through corruption, increases their costs.

Cambodia's openness and macroeconomic stability places it in a good position to take advantage of international financing for economic development. However, at present, the unsophisticated financial sector and limited domestic investment opportunities have confined non-FDI inflows to the real estate sector. Cambodia did receive weak speculative grade sovereign credit ratings in 2007 but the government has no intention in the short term to use them for public sector financing, indicating that it intends them to provide a benchmark for private sector financing.

In the short term, banking sector stability is the crucial foundation that will allow Cambodia to take greater advantage of international financial markets while keeping the attendant risks under reasonable control. A high-profile bank failure could rapidly erode recent gains in confidence, leading to reversals in growth and a rapid decline in credit opportunities. Avoiding this requires NBC to improve banks' adherence to prudential regulations, particularly through more effective bank supervision. In the medium term a more sophisticated banking sector will be needed to make effective use of foreign finance, this should include securities and interbank markets and improved payment systems.

More broadly, the authorities' ambitious Financial Sector Blueprint, prepared with the support of the Asian Development Bank, contains a number of important initiatives that will assist in addressing the risks of greater international financial integration.

4.3 Ensuring the Poor Share in Growth[13]

Reducing poverty cannot rely on development of the manufacturing and financial sectors alone. These cannot absorb the 200000 people that will enter the workforce in each of the coming years. This requires addressing the agriculture sector that supplies the bulk of the population with its livelihood. World Bank (2006) estimates suggest that growth of 7 percent for a decade with the same composition as Cambodia's recent growth would reduce poverty but not by enough to achieve the halving of poverty rates targeted in the Cambodian Millennium Development Goals. In contrast, growth of 7 percent coupled with 4 percent annual agricultural growth would allow this goal to be substantially exceeded.

The macroeconomic and structural reforms highlighted above will also benefit the agricultural sector. Certainly, low inflation combined with improvements in infrastructure, social services, governance and financial intermediation are as essential for growth in agriculture as they are for improvements in services and manufacturing.

They are by no means enough. The main constraint to growth in the agriculture sector is access to adequate and secure land tenure. Land is highly unequally divided in Cambodia – the Gini co-efficient of land ownership of 0.65 (with 1 being perfect inequality) is one of the worst in the region. In addition, many small farmers work on land for which they have no security of tenure, which discourages lumpy investments with longer-term pay offs and prevents them accessing credit markets. Titling of land therefore needs to be accelerated as much as possible with priority given to areas in which smaller, poorer farmers predominate. In addition, increasing access to irrigation, fertilizers and extension services will assist in improving agriculture's low productivity.

Development of an agri-business sector that can build upon improved agricultural output will be crucial in better integrating the rural and urban sectors. The primary constraints to this are broadly similar to those facing the manufacturing and service industries – high costs of doing business particularly due to poor governance and infrastructure.

5   CONCLUDING REMARKS

Cambodia's significant progress since emerging from conflict in the early 1990s has improved aggregate living standards markedly. However, growth has been narrowly based and much of the population remains poor and dependent on subsistence agriculture, just as they were in the early 1990s.

To catch up with its ASEAN partners, Cambodia needs to maintain the growth rates of the 1995–2006 period while markedly accelerating the pace of poverty reduction. Both aspects will require a diversification of the productive base. Diversification must include rural sector improvements to reduce poverty and inequality. Additional manufacturing and service diversification will provide additional employment for those seeking to exit the agricultural sector and will also help mitigate the risk of shocks excessively derailing growth.

Lack of progress made in broadening the base for growth testifies to the difficulties. Growth requires more attention to macroeconomic stability, increasing government revenues, improving the quantity and quality of government expenditure and developing the nascent financial sector. Ensuring that these gains are matched by improvements in governance and in reducing costs of doing business will be crucial in providing an environment that encourages the domestic and international private sectors to provide the increased investment that Cambodia needs to maintain growth of around 10 percent and improve its inclusiveness.

NOTES

1. The views expressed in this chapter are entirely the author's and do not represent the views of the IMF. Thanks are due to Luis Valdivieso for his insightful comments, Suchitra Kumarapathy for invaluable research assistance and to Debra Loucks and Claudia Isern for editorial assistance. All errors remain, of course, solely those of the author.
2. Tourism was responsible for substantial proportions of the growth in services and construction.
3. Estimates of the contribution of each factor in this section follow the methodology of Bosworth and Collins (2003).
4. Almost half of the aid was received as technical assistance, mainly in the form of payments to foreign experts (IMF, 2004).
5. A possible source is errors in measurement – as productivity is a residual in the growth accounting framework it is "a measure of our ignorance" (Abramowitz, 1956).
6. Debt levels benefited from Paris Club rescheduling in 1995. However, 13 years later Cambodia has yet to finalize bilateral agreements, and is not servicing the associated debts, with the United States and Russia needed to complete this process. See IMF (2007b), Chapter V for details.
7. Cambodia's full outstanding obligations to the IMF (US$82 million) were written off as part of the Multilateral Debt Relief Initiative (MDRI).
8. Prices of petroleum products are lower in both of Cambodia's neighboring countries, reflecting their lower taxes and administered prices.
9. There is little information on the amount of dollars held outside the banking system. De Zamaroczy and Sa (2003) estimated that $2.9 billion were in circulation in 2001 – this reflected the effects of UNTAC, international aid flows, return of Cambodians abroad and large scale investment in the garment industry.
10. It has been estimated that up to half of banks' lending portfolios depended on the continued profitability of the real estate and construction sectors (IMF 2007b).
11. See Chapter 3 this volume on China and the Mekong countries for further information on the composition and structure of Cambodia's trade.
12. See IMF (2007b) Chapter 2 for a detailed description of the possible impacts of a successful oil sector.
13. This section draws mainly on the comprehensive work on poverty and inequality undertaken by the World Bank (2006 and 2007).

REFERENCES

Abdelati, W. (2006), 'Determinants of growth in Cambodia and other low-income countries in Asia: evidence from country panel data', in D. Coe et al. (eds), *Cambodia: Rebuilding for a Challenging Future*, Washington, DC: International Monetary Fund.

Asian Development Bank (ADB) (2007), *ADB's Infrastructure Operations: Responding to Client Needs*, March, ADB.

Bosworth, B. and S. Collins (2003), 'The empirics of growth: an update', *Brookings Papers on Economic Activity*, **2**.

De Zamaroczy, Mario and Sophana Sa (2003), 'Economic policy in a highly dollarized economy: the case of Cambodia', International Monetary Fund occasional paper no 219, Washington, DC.

Economic Institute of Cambodia (EIC) (2005), *Cambodia Economic Review*, October–December, Phnom Penh.

Global Witness (2007), *Cambodia's Family Trees*, Global Witness report, June, London.

International Monetary Fund (IMF) (2004), *Cambodia: Ex Post Assessment of Longer-Term Program Engagement*, country report no 04/234, Washington DC: IMF.

IMF (2007), *Cambodia: 2007 Article IV Consultation*, country report 07/290, Washington DC: IMF.

International Monetary Fund (2007b), *Cambodia: Selected Issues and Statistical Appendix*, country report no 07/291, Washington DC: IMF.

Ishikawa, S. and K. Nakamura (2006), 'Cambodia's accession to the WTO', in D. Coe et al. (eds), *Cambodia: Rebuilding for a Challenging Future*, Washington, DC: International Monetary Fund.

Japan External Trade Organisation (JETRO) (2007), 'The 17th survey of investment-related cost comparison in major cities and regions in Asia', March, Overseas Research Development.

Lopez-Mejia, A. and R. Hagemann (2006), 'Fiscal development and challenges', in D. Coe et al. (eds), *Cambodia: Rebuilding for a Challenging Future*', Washington, DC: International Monetary Fund.

Swedish International Development Cooperation Agency (Sida) (2006), 'Employment and growth in Cambodia – an integrated economic analysis', *Country Economic Report*, **2**, Stockholm.

Sjoberg, O. and F. Sjoholm (2005), 'The Cambodian economy: ready for take off?', Stockholm School of Economics working paper 209, April.

World Bank (2004), *Cambodia: Seizing the Global Opportunity: Investment Climate Assessment and Reform Strategy for Cambodia*, report no 27925-KH, Washington, DC: World Bank.

World Bank (2006), 'Cambodia: halving poverty by 2015?', in *Poverty Assessment*, Washington, DC: World Bank.

World Bank (2007), 'Sharing growth: equity and development in Cambodia', in *Equity Report*, Washington, DC: World Bank.

PART III

Political economy of reform in the Mekong

11. Historical and cultural constraints on development in the Mekong region

Martin Stuart-Fox

All states in the Mekong region seek economic development. However, owing to differences in the structure of Mekong economies, in resource availability and in stages of development, not all governments promote development equally effectively. Differences in development also arise from differences in the provision of institutional support systems, including enforcement of legal codes and regulations, or to insufficient investment in education, leading to shortages of trained personnel. While government policy can address such matters not all governments are equally willing to undertake reform measures.

Other factors also affect the rate and direction of development. These include how a developing society is structured, relations between different social groups, forms of political institutions and how power is exercised, systems of justice, and on the kinds of freedoms enjoyed by citizens.

No-one escapes the history of their own society, or the culture in which they were raised. But culture is not fixed; cultures evolve. Understanding how history and culture shape beliefs and institutions permits us not to escape history but to plan and direct it in beneficial ways.

The period since 1975, that most momentous year for the ruling regimes of the three countries of the former Indochina – Cambodia, Laos and Vietnam – has had the most immediate impact on development. But history did not begin in 1975. For Burma/Myanmar the crucial year was 1962 when the military first seized power. For Thailand the events of 1973–75 set the pattern of recent politics, though, as a relatively developed country, Thailand will not be a focus in this chapter.

The cultural differences that characterize different peoples and nation-states have deep historical roots. In terms of political culture the principal contrast is between Vietnam, whose cultural debt is to China, and the four Theravada Buddhist countries, whose cultural values derive from India.

1   THE BURDEN OF HISTORY

The colonial period for the states of mainland Southeast Asia was but a brief interlude in their histories.[1] In Laos and northern Vietnam it lasted only about 60 years; in Cambodia, southern Vietnam and in upper and lower Burma around twice as long. Yet in terms of changes wrought and opportunities lost its impact was considerable: new taxation systems commercialized agriculture; monopolies accorded to French and British capital impeded industry; and corvee labour and local taxes built and financed a basic infrastructure of ports, roads and railways. Meanwhile the development of human resources was mainly limited to a Francophone and largely Francophile elite in the three Indochinese states and to an English-educated elite in Burma.

The most pernicious impact of French colonialism, however, resulted not so much from the distortions of colonial policy, but from the manner in which France surrendered power. The comparison with Burma is instructive: the British left in 1948 after good-natured negotiations and without bloodshed.[2] In Indochina France precipitated a war that dragged on for eight years, marked by deceit and destruction. Only victory by the Vietminh at Dien Bien Phu forced the French to leave.

Independent Burma faced two major challenges: to rebuild an economy and infrastructure shattered by the Second World War; and to defeat a series of communist and ethnic rebellions threatening its very integrity. Nation-building had barely begun when the military seized power in 1962. For the next quarter of a century, the Burmese military pursued policies that were both authoritarian and socialist.[3] Burma's 'strict neutralism' in foreign relations and the refusal of the government to accept any aid it considered might compromise its non-alignment led to isolationism both regionally and internationally. Meanwhile the military budget devoted to quelling internal rebellion absorbed a disproportionate amount of Burma's limited resources, to the detriment of economic development.

In the three countries of Indochina, the Second Indochina War inflicted its own terrible legacy not just in the form of blighted lives and physical destruction and of unexploded ordnance and Agent Orange, but of lost opportunities and failed development programmes.

The revolutions of 1975 that concluded the Second Indochina War took place in the context not just of the Cold War, but also of Sino–Soviet animosity. The Khmer Rouge revolution was the most radical and uncompromising, the Lao the most peaceable, while the Vietnamese amounted to a belated extension of the revolution of 1954 from north to south. All three, however, had as their immediate political goal the imposition, in one form or another, of a communist regime. In contrast to Burma's non-alignment, all three Indochinese revolutions tied their respective countries to a single powerful international patron – Vietnam and Laos to the Soviet Union, and Cambodia to China – with all the limitations that entailed for sources of development aid. The Khmer Rouge aimed at first to be self-sufficient, but after 1979 Cambodia too came to depend on Soviet aid, via Vietnam. In the end, the total burden was more than Moscow was prepared to bear.

A second serious outcome of the three Indochinese revolutions was the loss of human resources. Laos lost as much as 90 percent of its educated class (who were either incarcerated in remote re-education camps, or fled as refugees). So did Cambodia, a large proportion of whose educated elite was murdered. Vietnam was better off because it could bring cadres from the north to administer the south, but it too lost or wasted too many human resources. Laos and Cambodia had to produce a new educated class almost from scratch, and in both countries it remains pitifully small.

Burma too suffered from the lack of an educated middle class. In colonial times many educated professionals were Indian, most of whom fled during the Second World War. Burmese eventually took their place but education suffered when the military closed down almost all private schools in the 1960s. After the military crushed the democratic movement in 1988, large numbers of educated Burmese again sought refuge abroad. As students have been in the forefront of opposition to the military in Burma, universities have been closed at various times thus further reducing the already small, educated middle class. Burma, like Laos and Cambodia, has failed to devote sufficient resources to education. Only in Vietnam has education been accorded greater priority.

Communist revolutions also had a positive agenda – to create fairer, more just societies offering improved living standards. This was a commendable ideal but necessary also for economic development. Revolution, however, failed to bring expected economic benefits. So too did the 'Burmese Way to Socialism'. The first ten years in power for the Lao People's Democratic Republic was a lost decade in terms of development as the economy went backwards. Policy was inept, targets were unmet and cooperatives collapsed. Similar failures occurred in the first ten years of the unified Socialist Republic of Vietnam, exacerbated by the costs of war and reconstruction in Cambodia, which was agonizingly slow in the face of continuing insecurity. When Vietnamese forces finally left Cambodia at the end of the 1980s, the ravages of revolution were still very evident. Meanwhile, draconian military controls stifled economic development in Burma.

The third factor that slowed development in the Indochinese states after 1975 was the Third Indochina War, which grew out of antagonism between the Khmer Rouge regime and Vietnam, and between Vietnam and China – not to mention continuing support by the West and ASEAN six for Cambodian insurgent groups operating out of Thailand. This conflict diverted a disproportionate amount of economic resources to the military, and slowed development still further. Once again Cambodia suffered most, though Vietnam had to bear the added cost of stationing forces in both Cambodia and Laos.

By the mid-1980s economic considerations forced the realization that some kind of political solution to the 'Cambodian problem' was essential. At the same time both Vietnam and Laos decided to move towards a more open, free-market economy, allow foreign investment, and mend relations with ASEAN, China and the West. Changes in economic policy produced almost immediate results in Laos and Vietnam, which enjoyed governmental continuity. Cambodia underwent yet another change of political institutions, which permitted it to benefit from increased non-governmental aid and to take advantage of new development opportunities.

In Burma the military regime also changed direction. In response to student-led demonstrations in 1988 the military formed the State Law and Order Restoration Council (SLORC), which two years later held free and remarkably fair elections, which were resoundingly won by the National League for Democracy under the leadership of Aung San Suu Kyi. This unforeseen outcome so shook the military that it annulled the results and has refused to relinquish power ever since. While keeping control of military-owned enterprises, the regime moved to diffuse popular discontent by freeing up the economy, though not to the same extent as in China and the Indochinese states. Foreign investment was permitted, under strict controls, and Burma was opened to tourism.

The 1990s were a period of economic growth in the Indochinese states, at least until the Asian economic crisis towards the end of the decade. Economic reform encouraged foreign investment and development. It was a time of renewed economic hope in the face of a rearguard ideological struggle, especially in Vietnam. Over this period, sources of economic assistance became more diversified, and more generous – except for Burma, which suffered from Western sanctions imposed on the military in response to its refusal to restore democracy. The inclusion of all three Indochinese states and Burma in ASEAN marked a new beginning in regional relations. The challenge over the past decade has been to move from inclusion to integration in order for the full benefits of membership in a larger economic community to be realized – a project encouraged by the Asian Development Bank through its Greater Mekong Sub-region scheme.

The new millennium has seen more flexible economic policy. Foreign direct investment has been welcomed, and the economies of all three Indochinese countries have experienced substantial rates of growth. In Burma too the military has continued to open the economy. The benefits, however, have not been evenly spread: in fact disparities of wealth have greatly increased. In all four countries, instead of being used to develop human resources, an increasing proportion of the resources of the state finds its way into the pockets of a political-economic elite (in Burma a military-crony capitalist elite). Pleas from aid donors and international lenders for improved governance and financial transparency have been deftly deflected or just ignored.

The burden of the past is much more pervasive than the above brief overview of historical events indicates. Increasingly the new elites in the three Indochinese states are coming to resemble the pre-revolutionary elites swept aside in 1975 in their attitudes to power and social privilege. Culturally entrenched, these attitudes lead to political behaviour that limits development opportunities for the majority of the population. The same is true in Burma, where the military has refused to relinquish any power. In this way, the presence of the past is felt in every aspect of the present, not least in matters of culture.

2 POLITICAL CULTURE IN THERAVADA BUDDHIST COUNTRIES

Within mainland Southeast Asia a significant cultural divide runs between Vietnam on the one hand, and the four Theravada Buddhist countries on the other. Buddhism forms a bridge, but the political culture of Vietnam owes far more to Confucian China than to distant India.

For the majority of people in the four Theravada countries Buddhism shapes their worldview. Key elements include the notions of karma and rebirth. No one can escape karma's natural moral law: one's deeds will inevitably be rewarded or punished, whether in this lifetime, or the next, or the next. This is one reason why there is a general lack of interest in Cambodia over the trial of Khmer Rouge leaders, for Cambodians do not doubt they will suffer their just deserts in future lifetimes.

Rebirth and karma imply that social position has been earned in previous existences. In other words the rich and powerful have a moral right to their wealth and power and to use it for their personal benefit. Of course, how they use them will have its own karmic repercussions but that is their concern. Thus karma legitimizes and underpins social hierarchy.[4] Karma also undermines the notion of equality. For Buddhists, people are evidently not born equal and karma explains why. In popular belief women are not equal to men in terms of karma, though they have an equal chance of being reborn male. These beliefs do not preclude notions of gender equality or the equal rights of citizens, but they make it difficult for them to be universally applied in practice.[5]

Given the reality of rebirth for Theravada Buddhists, and the significance of karma as the determining factor, it is not surprising that people should seek to increase the balance of good over bad karma through the accumulation of merit. Merit is made through moral action with respect to all sentient beings but especially towards monks. Giving to monks makes merit for the giver, not the receiver – which is why the military in Burma were so concerned when monks reversed their begging bowls and refused to accept gifts from army personnel.

The legitimizing of power elites through social hierarchy receives reinforcement from two other aspects of Theravada Buddhist political culture – the value accorded to social order and use of patronage as the primary means by which to concentrate and exert political power. Buddhists value social order for the opportunity it provides for individuals to pursue their own spiritual paths, enabling people to produce, give for religious purposes, and make merit.[6] For this reason ideals of social order tend to override individual rights in Theravada Buddhist countries.

What is important to note about this system is the extent to which power rests upon patronage and personal relationships. One gains advantage through the favour of someone in a superior position in the social hierarchy, while those in superior positions increase their social power and wealth through expanding the network of those dependent upon them. The more powerful one's patron, the greater one's own power and prestige. For a patron to build a power network he must have resources to disburse, most commonly access to the resources and power of the state. Examples of patronage range from intervention to secure a job or win a court case to the bestowal of monetary benefit in the form of access to resources, awarding of contracts, reduction of taxes, provision of loans, and so on. One important form of obligation takes the form of political support when this is required. Because transparent and impartial operation of political or financial processes threaten to eliminate sources of patronage moves to introduce them tend to be resisted.[7]

Political parties in Theravada Buddhist countries do not override the political culture of patronage and hierarchy – they incorporate it. For example, the structure of the Lao People's Revolutionary Party is hierarchical; so is its mode of operation (democratic centralism). But within the Party power is exercised through patronage networks that centre on key figures, usually members of the Politburo. Positions within the Party apparatus, the government, the judiciary and the bureaucracy are allocated as a result of negotiation between leaders of powerful networks that combine family, region and revolutionary credentials. The power even of top officials, such as ministers or departmental heads, depends not on the office alone and much less on formal statements of responsibilities or personal qualifications. It depends rather on where occupants fit within patronage networks, which determines who they can call upon for political support, for instance for promotion, or to back decisions that might conflict with the interests of others.[8]

In Cambodia, all political regimes and parties have functioned, and continue to function, as patronage networks. This was true of Sihanouk and his Sangkum party, of the Lon Nol regime, and of the dominant Cambodian People's Party today. Even the Khmer Rouge regime provides a striking example of how deep the roots of the political culture of patronage and hierarchy really go. The Khmer Rouge determined to do away entirely with traditional Cambodian culture in its entirety, and to build a new revolutionary culture. But Angkar, the supreme authority, was a strictly hierarchical power structure, which, though it purported to act on behalf of the people, never consulted them in any way. Within the organization, hierarchy was ensured through absolute discipline and unquestioning loyalty. But that loyalty was highly personalized, focused on the tiny top echelon of the Party, on Angkar Loeu, and ultimately on Pol Pot himself.[9]

In Burma it might be thought that the military command structure would preclude patronage politics, as it does in Western armies. Nevertheless, patronage networks are still important. An indication of this came with the fall of Prime Minister General Khin Nyunt, head of military intelligence, in October 2004. Not only were his sons sentenced along with their father to long prison terms but also dozens of officers in military intelligence were dismissed, along with civil servants associated with them. For the Burmese military leadership, as for Pol Pot, the entire opposing patronage network had to be rooted out.

The political culture of patronage and hierarchy has significant implications both for the structure of political parties in Theravada Buddhist countries and for political stability. Parties do not, even in a relatively long-established democratic system as in Thailand, stand primarily for a set of political principles, or represent the interests of particular social classes. Rather they form through and cohere around powerful and charismatic leaders who use them to build political patronage networks. Resistance to them builds at the point where a patronage network begins to threaten other powerful interests. The rise of opposition to Thai prime minister Taksin Shinawatra provides a classic example.[10] In Cambodia, all three principal parties are organized as patronage networks centred on significant leaders. In Burma, the concept of the *min laung*, or 'ruler-in-waiting' endowed with powerful karma, tends to reinforce the hierarchical structure of parties, as in the case of the National League for Democracy with Suu Kyi as its charismatic figurehead.

Parties organized as patronage networks in a democratic system generate political instability because so much depends on the role of the leader and the potential for patronage he represents. Personalized parties lack a strong institutional base. No-one doubts that the Republican and Democrat parties will survive the departure of any leader from politics in the United States, but political parties have proved far more ephemeral in democratic Thailand, and in Cambodia too. Only when a ruling party enjoys a complete monopoly of power, as in Laos, is it likely to be more durable.

3   POLITICAL CULTURE IN VIETNAM

Vietnamese political culture is very different from those of the Theravada Buddhist Mekong states; but this very difference provides some enlightening comparisons. Vietnam's cultural borrowing was from China with its Confucian philosophy of government, conception of social order and organization of society. While the emperor ruled with absolute power, the Confucian mandarinate administered the country on behalf of both emperor and people. Mandarins owed their positions not to birth but to their own talent in meeting a set of criteria for selection to public office, tested by a triennial examination open to all. They could be removed from office at any time at the emperor's whim. In other words, they owed their power both to the institution they served, as in any modern bureaucracy, and to imperial absolutism.

Unlike the tributary power structure of Theravada Buddhist polities, power in the Confucian system was centralized and delegated. Mandarins were appointed to administer provinces on behalf of the emperor, preferably not where their families resided in order to reduce the temptations of nepotism. Their primary duty was to ensure society functioned peacefully and efficiently, in other words, to maintain social order.[11]

Like Theravada Buddhist societies, Vietnamese Confucian society was hierarchical. Social order depended on each knowing his or her place in the social hierarchy. But this position was determined not by the karma of previous existences, but rather by a combination of birth and achievement (education and wealth). Society consisted of the two interacting spheres of court and village. Villages were communal and self-governing, responsible for their own affairs. Each owed its establishment to royal decree but the writ of central administration extended only to the village boundary. Taxes were centrally determined, but locally collected. This engendered a strong sense of communal identity and solidarity undiluted by the individuality that is inseparable from the notion of karma.

The imprint of French colonialism penetrated more deeply into the intellectual life of Vietnam than in either Cambodia or Laos. Nevertheless it was not Western liberalism but Marxism-Leninism that won greater allegiance from the Vietnamese elite. Not only did it offer more ideologically powerful opposition to colonialism, but also its political institutions were more compatible with the ideal of Confucian administration that Vietnamese took for granted. The Vietnamese Communist Party (VCP) comprised a political elite, hierarchically organized and ideologically trained for the exercise of power, with a similarly strong moral commitment, not to the individual rights proclaimed by the French Revolution, but to a concept of bureaucratic management and social order carried over from Confucianism applied to improving the welfare of the masses.

Even after the revolution had triumphed and the VCP had established an orthodox set of Marxist–Leninist political institutions, the family remained the core of Vietnamese social structure and family values continued to dominate Vietnamese thinking. An extraordinary 97 percent of respondents to the first World Values Survey conducted in Vietnam in 2001 affirmed that a principal goal in life was to make one's parents proud.[12] Filial commitment is not underpinned by religion (whether Mahayana Buddhism or Catholicism): it is a Confucian value. Social contact is primarily with family members and Vietnamese are wary about extending trust outside the family circle.

The Confucian legacy in modern Vietnamese Marxist–Leninist political culture assisted in the transition from a socialist centrally-directed economy to a free market economy without any loosening of political control, for a divide always existed in traditional Vietnamese society between the political elite and the commercial class. Confucian administration left open opportunities for economic entrepreneurs – indeed its role was to create conditions for production and trade to flourish by maintaining social order. The VCP today can be understood to have assumed a similar role, in that it claims to be guiding the economic development of the country to the point where an eventual transition to socialism becomes possible.[13]

The institutionalization of the VCP and the way political decisions are made are less personalized than in the numerically much smaller LPRP. Exercising an unchallengeable monopoly of power, however, opens VCP members, as in any other single ruling party, to temptations to expropriate state resources by and for themselves and their families. Party leaders are well aware of the danger this poses for the legitimacy of the Party and there is a greater resolve to govern effectively and to limit corruption to 'manageable' levels, in order to maintain public respect and confidence. Several senior Party officials have been convicted of corruption in Vietnam; none have been in Cambodia or Laos. Yet in Vietnam corruption convictions have not been used, as the conviction of Khin Nyunt for corruption was in Burma, as an excuse to destroy a whole patronage network: only criminal associates were pursued.

4   CONSTRAINTS ON DEVELOPMENT IN THE MEKONG REGION

The more obvious legacies of history that have constrained development in the Mekong region are gradually being overcome: infrastructure is being constructed, industry established, agriculture encouraged. Others are more difficult to deal with. These include unresponsive institutions that fail to make the best use of human resources; a continuing lack of technical and managerial skills; the costs of ideologically-driven policy decisions (such as subsidies to non-performing state-owned or military-owned enterprises); and the continuing influence of political cultures that limit the competitiveness, flexibility and modernizing potential of economies.

Two other legacies of post-colonial conflict and revolution require mention. The first is a propensity to use force to coerce and intimidate, rather than depend upon the rule of law. In the countries of Indochina united and disciplined revolutionary movements seized power by force (or in the case of Laos, the threat of force). In Vietnam and Laos opponents were efficiently disarmed. Thereafter the coercive power of the state was used in support of a single ruling party, not only to suppress all political opposition but also to curtail the activities of civil society with the effect of limiting consideration of alternative development policies.

In Cambodia, the Vietnamese-installed People's Republic of Kampuchea faced armed opposition from three different groups, all of which had to be accommodated in any solution to the conflict. Even after the UN-supervised settlement and the elections that concluded the Cambodian peace process arms were still freely available. Donor-supported disarmament programmes have not just collected weapons but had the effect of concentrating them in the hands of military forces loyal to the CPP. Particularly in the rural areas weapons are still used in extra-legal ways to coerce and intimidate. In Phnom Penh this is less evident and some debate over policy alternatives does take place.

In Burma the Tatmadaw (Burmese military) has monopolized coercive power in the name of national unity and security to defeat communist and ethnic insurgencies. Although the BCP insurgency disintegrated in 1989 and ceasefire agreements have been signed with all ethnic insurgencies (except for the Karen) weapons remain in the hands of ethnic militia and drug cartels. In the Burman heartland the military has been ruthless in using its coercive power to repress all popular and political dissent, with the result that civil society hardly exists and no public policy debate on development is possible.

Meanwhile, in Cambodia, a psychological legacy of revolution and civil conflict results in a widespread sense of impending threat and fear that uncontrollable forces of social disorder may at any time again disrupt people's lives. Given the tragic events of the last 35 years such fears are understandable. They manifest themselves in what might be called a 'survival mentality' characterized by suspicion of others and anxious concern for personal and family welfare and protection in the face of an uncertain future.

In Laos and Vietnam, by contrast, ruling regimes have now been in power for three decades, and people have become socialized to accept them. This has both a positive and a negative side, however. In both countries people understand how the ruling party functions, and what is expected of them. The hierarchical structure of the ruling parties and the lack of any recourse to independent institutional protection (in the form of an ombudsman, or an independent legal system) make it risky to challenge authority. Professors and students toe the party line. Public servants, concerned not to draw adverse attention to themselves, are reluctant to make decisions or to suggest innovations. Referring decisions up the bureaucratic and Party hierarchy makes government sluggish, however, and suppression of innovation limits capacity to respond to novel circumstances.

The attitudes and responses of citizens to government reflect and express prevailing political culture. Their cumulative social and economic impact affects the implementation of policy decisions and directives. Here lies the crucial link between political culture and economic development. Political culture, despite having deep historical roots, is not immutable. Shaped by the institutions of political power it can change when new institutions are introduced, either constitutionally through legislation, or by imposition. But legislating or imposing change is never sufficient in itself: any new institution has to be accompanied by the political will to make it work.

Political culture constrains and limits economic development in a variety of ways. In single party states there tends to be a confluence of interests between the party and the state. In the case of Laos, for example, it is usual for the president of the Lao People's Revolutionary Party to also be head of state. Membership of the government is decided by the party and endorsed by the National Assembly (NA).[14] All legislation is in accordance with party policy. Though there is some discussion of policy in the upper echelons of the Party and some debate on legislation in the NA the government functions essentially as the executive arm of the party. Not surprisingly, therefore, government policy takes primary account of the interests of the party. In a similar way the bureaucracy functions as the administrative arm of the party while the party closely controls all permitted mass organizations, notably the Lao Front for National Construction. So no institution balances the power of another.

Parties constructed as hierarchical patronage networks require the appropriation of resources from the state. Resources that would otherwise be used for the benefit of all citizens are directed preferentially to favoured recipients. The larger the network, the more resources are diverted. In the case of Burma, estimates of the military share of the budget go as high as 40 percent,[15] though how this breaks down (new arms purchases, running costs, and so on) is unknown, as no accurate figures are ever published. In addition to its massive involvement in the economy through military business enterprises,[16] the Tatamadaw has created its own privileged community with access to schools, hospitals, housing and other facilities unavailable to the rest of the population.

Patronage operates within the Vietnamese Communist Party (VCP), but to a lesser extent than in the Theravada Buddhist countries, and with a different effect. While personal connections are important in determining how resources are shared, power is more institutionalized. Vertical patronage networks are less dependent on family connections than in the LPRP.[17] What is similar, and this is true for all single-party states, is the capacity the VCP has for control over the resources of the state. Internal party methods of supervision and control limit the extent to which party members take advantage of this but a substantial amount of state resources still ends up in private hands, which current control procedures seem incapable of preventing.[18]

In the case of a multi-party state like Cambodia, competition between parties organized as hierarchical patronage networks inevitably takes the form of competition for control over state resources. The more resources one party can control, the more it has to offer as inducements to villagers to change their vote, and the more likely it is to win an electoral contest. As one party becomes dominant, as the CPP has done, the resources sequestered by the party are used to reward members in much the same way as in a single-party state. The political goal in a multi-party democratic system in which a patrimonial political culture predominates is for a party to extend its patronage network at the expense of other parties in order to shift the balance of power in its favour – to the point eventually of eliminating any possibility of other parties doing the same. For this ever more state resources must be appropriated, which will eat even more into the revenues of the state. This results in the de facto end of democratic competition: elections become legitimizing exercises, not opportunities to change the government, which is pretty well already the case in Cambodia.[19] Because power depends on the capture of state resources by the dominant party's patronage network, resistance to reforms aimed at retaining state resources for the fair and equal benefit of all citizens is likely to be even more sustained than in single-party states. One indication of this is the Cambodian government's reluctance to introduce effective anti-corruption legislation.

The diversion of state resources into private hands is one definition of corruption, though this can take many additional forms. Corruption varies from the plunder of natural resources (mainly timber and wildlife in Burma, Laos and Cambodia), to the granting of concessions (land for plantations, mining leases) and contracts in return for private payments, to diversion or reduction for a consideration of sources of government revenue (in the form of reduction of taxes for favoured clients, customs duties, and so on), to payments demanded for services, whether legal (registration of a business) or illegal (provision of forged documents, such as land titles).[20] All of these impact on development because they divert resources that could otherwise be spent on measures to build the economy (infrastructure, communications, and so on), and on services designed to create a critical mass of educated and informed citizens, who could contribute more fully to developing a modern economy.

Because revenue sources available to developing economies are limited by comparison to those of developed economies it is essential to make full use of them. The principal sources of revenue include business, income and other taxes; customs duties, tariffs and government fees, payments made under international agreements (such as overflight rights), and licences paid for rights to exploit natural resources. In Cambodia and Laos in particular, revenue collection by the state is insufficient to meet recurrent expenditure plus development projects. Grants and concessionary loans provided by foreign donors and NGOs make up the shortfall. In Vietnam greater efforts have been made to introduce reforms in taxation, revenue collection and public administration, and there is less dependency on foreign aid. In Burma, most of whose outside assistance now comes from China, increase in revenue requires reducing the flow of funds to loss-making military-owned enterprises, a move urged by international lending organizations but resisted by the SPDC.

International financial institutions have also been urging the Lao and Cambodian governments to increase revenue collection by decreasing losses due to corruption. In both countries officials see revenue payments of all kinds as opportunities for graft. Reductions in taxes are negotiated in return for payments to obliging finance ministry officials. Customs duties, meanwhile, are reduced by declaring only a proportion of imports: customs officers and importers share the savings. Logging, land and mining concessions require making payments (sometimes to overseas bank accounts) in order to be concluded. Private business must pay inflated transaction costs, and payments for political protection may be demanded on an ongoing basis.

Another area of corruption is financial. The commonest form is provision of loans through state-controlled banks, which will never realistically be repaid. Loans may be to well-connected individuals, to state-owned enterprises, or to enterprises run by the military. As non-performing loans mount, banks lose the capacity to lend for economically viable business ventures – to the point eventually where they require re-capitalization, as in Laos. Governments bear the cost, effectively transferring state resources into private hands.

All forms of corruption reduce funds available for education and health, agricultural services, and infrastructure maintenance. The flow-on effect on the economy diminishes human resources, lowers productivity, increases transport costs, and so on. More insidious effects of corruption include the risk of donor anger and fatigue when corrupt practices siphon substantial funds. Donors urge adoption of greater financial transparency and improved governance backed by more or less explicit threats to reduce funding, or withhold aid until reforms are initiated, or require oversight of all expenditure.[21] If governments want development aid to continue, enacting desirable reforms would seem to be a rational response. The political culture of patronage, however, delays reform.

Opportunities for corruption vary with position in the hierarchy of patronage networks. It is possible to regard small-scale corruption as a way of supplementing inadequate salaries, but where corruption becomes ubiquitous and accepted it not only undermines the moral fibre of society but also disadvantages the competitiveness of the economy. For example, where entry into preferred schools and results of examinations are obtained through payment of bribes to teachers, better students are disadvantaged.[22] The state thus fails to make use of the full potential of its own citizens. The same applies when appointment to public office is either bought or made on the basis of political or family connections instead of open competition.

High-level corruption not only provides a poor example for party members and civil servants, it also results in excessive consumption in place of investment. In the worst case the movement of funds offshore into private accounts deprives the country of any positive effect in the form of employment and consumption.[23] The importance of leadership on the part of those with the capacity to appreciate the larger national interest is thus vital.

The institution best capable of restraining the excesses of patronage politics is the legal system. All governments of Mekong region states recognize the rule of law as essential to maintain social order and political legitimacy and have stated their commitment to the rule of law. What is not so readily recognized is the importance of assuring the independence and integrity of the judiciary. In democratic societies, the constitutionally guaranteed independence of the judiciary constrains the power of executive government, for no member of government is immune from the law. In single party states independence of the judiciary is compromised, both because immediately following the revolutionary seizure of power the ruling party in effect was the law (through its control over people's courts), and because of the continuing overlap of high offices of the party, the state and the judiciary.

In all the Mekong countries ruling elites are reluctant to accept the judiciary as a constraint on its monopoly of power and they interfere in judicial proceedings. Interference is usual where a judicial case has political implications but it is common too in civil cases, especially where power is exercised through patronage networks. The judicial system is another arena for patronage. Court cases (for example in Laos and Cambodia over land disputes) are consistently determined not on the basis of principles of justice but on which side can call upon the most influential political connections. In Burma judicial interference is just as blatant.[24]

Failure to establish an independent judiciary adversely affects economic development in several ways. Foreign companies already worried over lack of transparency in gaining commercial rights or concessions (which might put them at a disadvantage with respect to competitors) are reluctant to invest where there is no recourse to an independent judiciary in the event of litigation. Domestic investment is also affected as an independent judiciary provides the only means of minimizing corruption. In both cases continuing demands for 'donations' to ruling party coffers cut into profit margins that because of cost structures are already only marginally competitive.[25]

Donor countries and international lending institutions can legitimately attempt to ensure that aid is properly used. They can express concern over human rights abuses. But civil judicial procedures are an internal matter for states and foreign pressure can easily be ignored. NGOs, the media, civil society associations and public opinion have potentially more influence but all are constrained in all the Mekong states.[26] Judicial independence can only come about, therefore, through a decision of the ruling party. This is more likely in a bureaucratic than in a patrimonial political culture because for the ruling party the courts are less valuable as an arena for patronage. Ironically such value is likely to increase as other avenues for patronage are closed off. It seems likely, therefore, that ruling parties in Laos and Cambodia will continue to be reluctant to establish genuinely independent judiciaries – unless and until the prevailing political culture changes. Meanwhile the possibility of an independent judiciary does not arise at all in Burma.

Prospects are more hopeful in Vietnam where power is less personalized. Already there is greater recognition within the ruling party of the need to curb corruption, partly because foreign direct investment is at higher levels than in Laos or Cambodia and investors need to be reassured, and partly because the VCP appears more concerned to preserve its legitimacy without recourse to coercion. Moreover the bureaucratic traditions of the VCP make it more likely that a decision to create a genuinely independent judiciary would be carried through. The crucial factor in all cases is the extent to which the legal system is seen as contributing to the power of the ruling party.

Finally I turn briefly to one possible policy response that has been canvassed to deal with the problem of how to reduce poverty, improve services and build human resources in rural areas as a means to stimulate development – decentralization. One would assume that to shift decision making closer to the village or community level would enable people better to take charge of their own affairs, improve transparency in service provision and encourage grassroots democracy. In practice, however, not only does this demand a level of education and skills in organization and financial management that is often entirely lacking, but the shift of power that accompanies decentralization also offers temptations that are not easily resisted. It is one thing for decentralization to be applied with the helpful support and assistance of a sympathetic NGO: it is quite another to be without that guidance and left to negotiate with the power apparatus of the state and its ruling party.

The experience of Laos when decentralization was first applied in the late 1980s in conjunction with the economic reform programme, the New Economic Mechanism, is instructive here. This decentralization was not to the village, but to the province level. The result could have been predicted. Regionalism has always been strong in Laos between the north, the centre and the south. Province party chiefs (now governors) always enjoyed a degree of autonomy from the central government in Vientiane that they jealously guarded. Decentralization greatly enhanced their power by placing new sources of revenue in their hands (external trade, tax collection, even appointment of managers of provincial branches of banks). Responsibility for service provision and payment of staff of central government ministries such as education and health was also transferred to the provinces. The result was that many teachers and health workers in more remote villages went unpaid for months as province chiefs used the resources under their control to expand their own political patronage networks. Within a few years recentralization became necessary to reinforce the authority of the central organs of the party.[27]

Electing village heads and village councils is preferable to having heads appointed by the ruling party, with no elected council (as in Laos). But the influence of political culture is impossible to avoid. In Cambodia, for example, councils with a majority of FUNCINPEC and SRP members have encountered difficulties in working with the ruling CPP. Where CPP-dominated councils were elected the pervasive nature of Cambodian political culture ensured that they would become drawn into the already existing party patronage network. The more resources are transferred to local councils, the more likely it is that they will be used not for the equal benefit of all villagers but to reinforce the power of village heads intent on building their own patronage networks within the village.

Because of the long tradition of village autonomy, solidarity and self-government, the outlook in Vietnam is more encouraging. The Grassroots Democracy Decree indicates the intention of the VCP to make its role at the commune level more accountable and transparent; that is, to take more account of commune members' views in planning and budgeting for grassroots projects and services. This is not yet democracy at the local level but it is moving in that direction. Implementation has been slow, partly because cadres are reluctant to relinquish any of their power but the tradition of communal involvement in village affairs helps the process along. If it is successful in Vietnam, this could serve as a model for other Mekong region states.

Finally, in Burma, although the military has presided over highly centralized governments, the ceasefire agreements it has concluded with ethnic minorities have gone some way towards decentralizing power. Regional parliaments, if enshrined in the new constitution, would formalize this devolution. However decentralization down to the level of local government would likely run into similar problems as in Laos, and is not envisaged.

5   CONCLUSION

History and political culture influence the extent to which political elites in different Mekong region countries are prepared to commit to reforms promoting further economic development. The impact of war, revolution and civil conflict in retarding development is hardly surprising, especially when comparison is made with those countries lucky enough to have escaped such turmoil. But less tangible burdens of the past are passed from one generation to the next through processes of acculturation and socialization. These components of cultural heritage may handicap a nation-state in the face of international competition. But though they are slow to change, even core beliefs are not immutable and culture constantly evolves to take account of new ways of doing things, new technologies and new patterns of consumption. The first stage in removing constraints is to understand why they are there and how they work.

In this chapter I have focused on beliefs about how social and political power can best be concentrated and applied. These beliefs are more likely to endure where they are not contested; that is, where power is mono-polized by a single party whose members benefit from the prevailing power structure. This is the case in Burma under military dictatorship and the single-party regimes of Laos and Vietnam. In Cambodia where interna-tional agreement imposed a multi-party system a single ruling party was prevailed upon to make room for other parties that it perceived as threat-ening its hold on power. Politics became not an arena for debate between parties championing alternative policies for the benefit of the Cambodian people but rather a struggle to concentrate power so as to lock out opposi-tion parties. And the form this took was competition between parties to expand hierarchical patronage networks centred on significant leaders.

Patronage politics views power as a means to preserve and maintain the party itself and to reward members who contribute to this end. Thus arises an inherent conflict of interests between the ruling party and the national good. Programmes and policies argued for on the grounds of their greater benefit for the nation-state, which at the same time threaten the structures by which the power monopoly of the party is sustained, will likely be resisted. Where civil society is very weak (Vietnam) or virtually non-existent (Laos, Burma) no forum for debate exists that might sway the thinking of party leaders. All debate takes place within the party itself (or the military in Burma), among members who agree that their interests are primarily served by preserving above all the vehicle of their rule. What this means is that alternative institutions that might answer more effectively to the competitive pressures of a global environment may never seriously be considered – especially if they are seen as threats to the ruling elite, rather than opportunities for the nation as a whole.

One consequence is that political thinking tends to be reactive rather than proactive; in response to pressures from outside powers and organi-zations rather than derived from the genius of free citizens of the nation-state seeking ways to be more competitive in pursuing their economic interests. In Cambodia, for example, calls for political change come almost entirely from NGOs (international and Cambodian), foreign governments and international lending institutions. The role of the CPP, by contrast, tends to be to resist any pressures that might undermine the basis of its power.

Patronage networks concentrate and retain power through manipulating state finances and law and through coercion. But while a powerful means of control, intimidation inevitably limits innovation and entrepreneurial talent and so handicaps the competitiveness of an economy. Moreover a larger-than-necessary military establishment is a heavy cost to any nation-state, especially if it is allowed freely to exploit significant national resources that would otherwise provide revenue for the state – as the Burmese have learned to their cost.

Loss of state revenues and failure to establish an independent legal framework both impact adversely on economic development. Loss of state revenue reduces the opportunities of the state to direct development in ways beneficial to the economy as a whole, such as investment in infrastructure or poverty alleviation to increase personal opportunities and improve living standards. Failure to establish the rule of law both limits free competition (for example, in the awarding of contracts) and reduces foreign investment.

My example of decentralization illustrates how political culture impacts desired policy outcomes. Participation in local government presupposes not just the necessary skills and appropriate attitudes and commitments, but also a set of checks and balances that prevent either a return to domination by the ruling party or local abuses of power.

Historical legacies and political culture are just two factors to take into account in trying to understand what influences the pace of economic development in the Mekong region. The success of these countries in overcoming the burden of their respective and intertwined histories has been striking. This chapter has attempted to explain why, beyond a certain point, ruling political parties (or the military in Burma) are reluctant to enact further reforms that would threaten the basis of their power. Vietnam may have the edge, but the political culture of patronage need not stand in the way of the development of the three Theravada Buddhist countries. Thailand provides an example of a Theravada Buddhist country that has been relatively successful in encouraging economic development, though even there political institutions have recently been buffeted by patronage politics. There is nothing to prevent other Mekong region states reaching Thailand's level of development. Just to understand where a problem lies is already to have moved some way towards overcoming it.

NOTES

1. A substantial literature exists on the histories of Vietnam, Cambodia, Laos, and Burma, and an even larger one on the First and Second Indochina wars. Useful background texts are Stanley Karnow (1984), *Vietnam: A History*, Harmonsworth: Penguin Books; David P. Chandler (1993), *A History of Cambodia*, 2nd ed., Boulder: Westview Press; Martin Stuart-Fox (1997), *A History of Laos*, Cambridge: Cambridge University Press; and David I. Steinberg (2001), *Burma: The State of Myanmar*, Washington: Georgetown University Press. And for Thailand, Chris Baker and Pasuk Phongpaichit (2005), *A History of Thailand*, Cambridge: Cambridge University Press.

2. Antagonism between ethnic groups that had been exacerbated by British colonial policies was left for the Burmese to sort out. The Burmese inability to do this is in large part responsible for the parlous state of Myanmar today.

3. The Burmese military created the Burma Socialist Programme Party in 1962 to promote the 'Burmese Way to Socialism'. At first BSPP membership was almost entirely limited to the military, and even after membership was expanded in the 1970s the military remained dominant.

4. Cambodian reformers blame belief in karma for the 'fatalistic outlook' of most Cambodians in accepting their lot in life, though one's karma can be improved through individual effort. See Abdulgaffar Peang-Meth (1991), 'Understand the Khmer: Sociological-Cultural Observations', *Asian Survey*, **31**, 442–55.

5. By contrast with Mahayana Buddhism, a fully ordained order of nuns (*bhikkhunis*) died out long ago in Theravada Buddhism. Its resuscitation might go some way to restoring equal gender status in Theravada societies. On the other hand, the possibility of rebirth of men as women, and vice versa, may well have worked against the more ingrained patriarchy of East Asia.

6. The ideal model of a polity ruled in accordance with Buddhist principles remains the empire of the third century BCE Indian king Ashoka.

7. As of writing, after years of drafting, Cambodia still had not passed an anti-corruption law. Meanwhile the Lao anti-corruption law has failed to produce any prosecutions of senior officials.

8. I have discussed the Lao case more fully in Martin Stuart-Fox (2005), 'Politics and Reform in the Lao People's Democratic Republic', Murdoch University Asia Research Centre, Working Paper No. 126.

9. David Chandler (2000), *Voices from S-21: Terror and history in Pol Pot's secret prison*, St Leonards, NSW: Allen & Unwin.

10. Taksin Shinawatra's Thai Rak Thai Party functioned as a patronage network, which threatened to eclipse patronage networks centred on the palace and the military – which is why they combined to overthrow him.

11. An interesting argument for the alternation of yin and yang forces throughout Vietnamese history can be found in Neil L. Jamieson (1993), *Understanding Vietnam*, Berkeley: University of California Press.

12. Russell J. Dalton and Nhu-Ngo (2001), *The Vietnamese Public in Transition: The World Values Survey: Vietnam 2001*, Irvine, CA: Center for the Study of Democracy, University of California.

13. This pretence provides the last shred of Marxist legitimacy for the VCP.

14. Officially the prime minister submits names of ministers to the National Assembly, which appoints the government. In fact, as the prime minister is always a member of the Political Bureau of the party, it is the party that names the government.

15. Taisamyone (6 July 2007), 'Disproportionate military expenditure in Burma, *Burma Digest*, Editorial, at http://burmadigest.wordpress.com/2007/07/06/editorial-disproportionate-military-expenditure-in-burma/, 1 July 2008.

16. Andrew Selth (1998), 'Burma's defence expenditure and arms industries', *Contemporary Security Policy*, **19** (2), 23–49.

17. 'A defining characteristic of the political system in Vietnam is the way in which policies

and decisions are arrived at through a complex process of vertical and horizontal consensus building. There is an important interplay between the vertical lines of authority, and the strong horizontal mechanisms of policy guidance, instruction and accountability. . .', E. Shanks et al. (April 2004), *Understanding Pro-poor Political Change: The Policy Process. Vietnam*, London: Overseas Development Institute, ix. In other words, in Vietnam procedures, even if informal, temper top-down decision making in a way that undercuts patronage, something much less in evidence in Laos.

18. Scott Fritzen (2006), 'Beyond "Political Will": How Institutional Context Shapes the Implementation of Anti-Corruption Policies', *Policy and Society*, **24** (3), 79–96.

19. Cf. Ronald Bruce St John (1 January 2006), 'Cambodia's Failing Democracy', Foreign Policy in Focus Commentary, www.fpif.org.

20. For examples of corruption in Cambodia see the damning Global Witness Report of June 2007, *Cambodia's Family Trees: Illegal logging and the stripping of public assets by Cambodia's elite*, and Adrien Levy and Cathy Scott-Clark (2 May 2008), 'Sale of the Century', *The Guardian Weekly*, 23-25. And for corruption in Laos see Martin Stuart-Fox (March 2006), 'The Political Culture of Corruption in the Lao PDR', *Asian Studies Review*, **30**, (1), 59–75.

21. In June 2006 the World Bank demanded repayment of US$7.6 million corruptly siphoned off from projects it was funding in Cambodia, http://news.bbc.co.uk/2/hi/business/5054984.stm, 13 August 2008. Pressure of this kind only works when it is concerted. Major aid donors like China that attach no conditions to their aid undermine such pressure for reform.

22. Corruption in education systems is endemic and provides a very poor example for children, a point made in the *Cambodian Corruption Assessment* prepared for USAID, May–June 2004. Party officials make sure their children attend the best schools in Laos. Higher degree students in Vietnam must pay thesis examiners to award their hard-earned degrees.

23. This is more common in Cambodia than Laos or Vietnam, though one Lao minister of finance did manage to transfer funds offshore and then flee the country and claim asylum abroad.

24. Roundtable Discussion with three Burmese lawyers (13 May 2007), *Radio Free Asia*, reprinted (September 2007), *Legal Journal on Burma*, **27**, 47–50.

25. This is true for the garment industries in both Laos and Cambodia, more especially the latter in relation to accession to the WTO. Moreover in Cambodia the industry accounts for a far larger percentage of exports than for Laos, where mining and hydropower are more important export earners.

26. NGOs are particularly numerous and active in Cambodia, but have been unable to prevent control of the magistracy by the Cambodian People's Party. Combined NGOs have called for fundamental reform of the Supreme Council of the Magistracy. *NGO Statement to the 2006 Consultative Group Meeting on Cambodia*, Phnom Penh, 2–3 March, 2006, p. 9. As for the media, reporting of corruption is relatively frequent in the Vietnamese language press, whereas in Cambodia and Laos it is virtually confined to the foreign language press. Investigation of particular cases and naming of names do not occur. In all three countries, civil society is 'underdeveloped', to say the least.

27. I have discussed centre–province relations in Martin Stuart-Fox (2005), *Politics and Reform in the Lao People's Democratic Republic*, Murdoch University, Asia Research Centre, Working Paper, No. 126. See also Patrick Keuleers and Langsy Sibounheuang (1999), 'Central–Local Relations in the Lao People's Democratic Republic: Historic Overview, Current Situation and Trends', in Mark Turner (ed.), *Central-Local Relations in Asia-Pacific: Convergence or Divergence?*, London: Macmillan, p. 204. For an analysis of the likely outcome of a new round of decentralization, see United Nations Development Program (2001), *National Human Development Report Lao PDR 2001: Advancing Rural Development*, Vientiane: UNDP, Chapter 7.

12. The political economy of policy reform: the future of reforms for the Mekong 4?

Hal Hill, Suiwah Leung and Trevor Wilson

1 INTRODUCTION

Reform means durable and significant policy change that improves aggregate socio-economic welfare. The literature focuses on major changes in policy, sometimes referred to as 'turning points'. Asian examples include China in 1978, India in 1991, Indonesia in 1966 and Vietnam in 1986. But some countries boast no such turning points. In Southeast Asia, policy reforms in Malaysia, Singapore and Thailand consist of incremental progress.[1] In Myanmar, political changes in 1988 generated new policy directions without far-reaching reforms.

The nature of reforms and their bureaucratic complexity also differs. Some measures are straightforward, stroke-of-the pen deregulations, such as introducing a floating exchange rate, replacing non-tariff barriers with tariffs, removing regulatory requirements, opening an industry to competition and abolishing corrupt agencies. These decisions require careful prior evaluation and a judgement that parties disadvantaged by reforms will not be able to sabotage them. But once this 'due diligence' has been undertaken, implementation is relatively straightforward.

By contrast, other reforms require a bureaucracy capable of implementing them. For example, successful tax reform depends on a competent and honest tax administration. This may be an interactive process, in the sense that the reforms are designed to lessen the scope for discretionary interventions (such as a value added tax that builds in an incentive for compliance, simpler tax rates and regulations). Another illustration is that while decentralization of resources and administrative authority empowers sub-national agencies, a strong central government committed to clear goals is required for successful implementation of reform.

Why do governments introduce reforms? Bhagwati (2002) posits that the literature on the political economy of trade liberalization – and reform more generally – emphasizes the interplay of 'ideas, interests, and institutions'. Reform ideas fall generally within the province of economists whilst political scientists concentrate on the study of coalitions and interest groups. Institutions, particularly in the context of the development of political cultures, are often within the purview of historians. Work at the intersection of all these three disciplines remains relatively unexplored territory. This is especially so in developing countries: political processes are more personalistic, political cultures more varied, outcomes more fluid, and the detailed case study literature on economic policy making in its infancy. The next section makes some conjectures about reform processes, illustrated by trade and central bank reforms in Indonesia and the Philippines in the 1980s. These are then used in later sections to assess the future of policy reforms in the Mekong 4.

2 THE POLITICAL ECONOMY OF REFORM: CONJECTURES

Effective reform requires a coherent intellectual agenda, an analysis of what needs to be done, how, and in what sequence. It also requires a process to mobilize a consensus for their implementation. Timing of reforms is also important, and successful reforms often have an element of opportunism in their implementation. However, ideas, as Keynes (1936) observed, are central:

> The ideas of economists and political philosophers . . . are more powerful than is commonly understood. Indeed the world is ruled by little else. Practical men, who believe themselves to be quite exempt from any intellectual influences, are usually slaves of some defunct economist . . . I am sure that the power of vested interests is vastly exaggerated compared with the gradual encroachment of ideas . . . soon or later, it is ideas, not vested interests, which are dangerous for good or evil.

Ideas are commonly associated with think tanks and economics faculties of leading universities. Often a key group of technocrats received training in leading universities abroad – Chile's 'Chicago Boys' and Indonesia's 'Berkeley Mafia' – but the channels of influence are in reality much broader. In some cases, the reform agenda is formulated and driven by observing successes abroad, most frequently in neighbouring countries. International agencies can play an effective role if there is a domestic interest in, and will for, reform (Krueger and Rajapatirana, 1999). However, in their absence externally-mandated reform attracts domestic opprobrium, implementation is likely to be spasmodic and the reforms transient. The 'revolving door' syndrome, referred to by Collier (2007) in the African context, illustrates that unless donors can impact the domestic consensus on policies, their role will be relatively limited. These arguments are also consistent with the cross-country econometric evidence that finds aid contributes to growth only when 'good policies' are present (Burnside and Dollar, 2000).

As for interest groups, technocrats, domestic and international, are generally politically powerless. To translate their ideas into policy, they need to convince political leaders of the case for reform, and to work with them to implement reform. These frequently involve building a constituency for reform to influence the leadership. In authoritarian regimes, the key is access to the president or ruling party. Here the technocrats engage in what Hadi Soesastro (1989) termed 'low politics' in the Indonesian case. That is, the technocrats seized the opportunity created by the sudden decline in international oil prices in the early 1980s to persuade President Soeharto to implement far-reaching reforms, but without having to engage in large-scale, high-profile public or parliamentary persuasion. In democratic regimes, where politicians have to persuade an electorate, the technocrats may have to engage in the public discourse, to persuade political and opinion leaders, and also to ameliorate or buy off potential opposition (and losers). Government bureaucrats may also become drivers of reforms where they realize that the system they are administering is dysfunctional.

The development of human capital and political cultures takes place in the long sweep of history. For instance, a history of wars leading to the devastation of educated elites could be expected to retard economic reforms. Also, a political culture that is reactive rather than proactive, resulting in part from ingrained patronage systems down the centuries, would also pose barriers to reforms that threaten to remove the economic rents so useful to the exercise of patronage.

In addition to the interplay of ideas, interests and institutions, there are two cross-cutting issues which have been found to be significant in the timing and pace of major reforms.

The first is the 'crisis hypothesis', which observes that significant events – major economic crisis, military defeat (or threat), cessation of external support, natural disaster – often trigger major reforms. For example, Lal and Myint (1996, p. 288) conclude that 'Turning points . . . are invariably associated with macroeconomic crises.' Of course, much depends on the nature of the crisis. In the case of 'twin crises', in the sense that a deep economic crisis is accompanied by, and may trigger, political turbulence, then these events may lead to political and institutional vacuums and incapacity to undertake effective reform. A major recent example is the collapse of the communist regimes in the former Soviet Union and Eastern Europe; political change in Indonesia in 1998 and the Philippines in 1986 are milder examples. More modestly, Burma's crisis of 1988 had both political and economic origins, so it was not surprising that its aftermath saw socialist economic policies ostensibly dropped and openness adopted.

The second is that successful reforms are invariably comprehensive, at least in design. Piecemeal reform undermines the entire process. The literature on the interaction between macroeconomic and trade policy illustrates the point, and also provides an intellectual rationale for the sequencing of reforms. As Rajapatirana (2001) and other analysts of successful trade liberalization point out, a willingness to allow a large depreciation boosts the competitiveness of tradable goods industries, and facilitates a lowering of protection. Krueger (1978, p. 231) goes further, arguing that the 'failure to devalue by a sufficient margin will prevent sustained liberalization'; moreover, a 'realistic real exchange rate [is] an essential condition for sustained liberalization'.

Examples of trade liberalization and central bank restructuring in Indonesia and the Philippines shed light on the above conjectures. For detailed discussion, see Boxes 12.1 and 12.2. In summary, trade liberalization in Indonesia and the Philippines in the 1980s depended on the intellectual ascendancy of openness as an engine of economic growth East Asia. The Berkeley Mafia in Indonesia and the academic and government economists in the Philippines pushed this idea to their respective political leaders. Foreign investors were in favour of trade liberalization once they decided to use these countries as part of the production network exporting to the rest of the world rather than as domestic markets behind high tariff walls. The threat posed by the substantial reduction in oil revenue, as well as the political stability in Indonesia under the Soeharto regime since the 1960s, helped speed up the reform process. In contrast, political uncertainty in the Philippines in the 1980s, and the absence of a specific threat to export revenues, meant that trade liberalization took about 15 years to achieve.

The idea of central bank independence came from the intellectual ascendancy of the importance of central banks in targeting inflation in order to be competitive in export-led growth. To do this, central banks need to be freed from the pressure of printing money to finance budget deficits. Technocrats in the two countries, supported by the IMF, foreign investors, business interests and political leaderships pushed this argument while recognizing macroeconomic stability as the cornerstone of economic development and political stability.

BOX 12.1   POLITICAL ECONOMY OF TRADE
REFORM: INDONESIA AND THE
PHILIPPINES IN THE 1980s

Both Indonesia and the Philippines implemented major trade reforms in the 1980s and transformed their economies from inward-looking to significantly open regimes. In Indonesia fiscal policy remained prudent, with immediate adjustment on the expenditure side, and a series of effective tax reform measures that lifted revenue (Hill 2000). Donors responded quickly and generously. Two large nominal exchange rate depreciations occurred in 1983 and 1986 and these, combined with low inflation, provided a major boost to competitiveness.

After securing macroeconomic stabilization, the government turned to microeconomic measures and implemented a comprehensive reform package. Most NTBs were gradually removed and tariffs lowered and unified. Exporters were placed on a free-trade footing through an effective duty exemption and rebate system. A sweeping reform of customs sidelined the deeply corrupt and obstructive import/export procedures. Foreign investment restrictions were relaxed. The financial sector was deregulated and the stock market reactivated. Many regulatory barriers to entry were removed, particularly in sectors formerly dominated by SOEs, such as the strategically important inter-island shipping industry.

What explains the success of these reforms?[1] As most analysts of this episode note, strong opposition to the reforms was to be expected. The influential policy community distrusted liberalism and vested interests had built up around the complex system of controls and intervention, in the business sector, the SOEs and the bureaucracy. There was by contrast a weak export sector and a tiny, marginalized intellectual community calling for reforms.

Success lay with an able, coherent and powerful group of reformers known as the 'technocrats'. This so-called Berkeley Mafia had occupied all the major economic policy portfolios since the beginning of the Soeharto era. Although lacking political party support, they had strong technical credentials. Importantly, they had developed close relations with Soeharto before he came to power and they had overseen the spectacular stabilization and recovery in the second half of the 1960s.

External actors also helped. Relations with Japan were exceptionally close. As the country's major donor and investor, Japan viewed Indonesia as a strategically crucial partner. Indonesia's relations with the US were also very close. The IFI's provided useful policy and analytical advice on a range of issues. And, since the reforms were not part of any formal IMF and World Bank conditionality, they were easier to sell domestically.

Three additional facilitating factors enabled the reforms to be introduced with little opposition and boosted their effectiveness. Firstly, the Soeharto regime, in spite of its authoritarian bent and controversial accession to power, had by then delivered almost two decades of rapid economic growth and improved living standards. Secondly, domestic vested interests opposed to reform had limited independent power; notable also was the absence of the Soeharto family business empires that were soon to become greedily all-powerful. Thirdly, most of East Asia was liberalizing and world markets were becoming increasingly open. The 'fear of China' syndrome as a cause for export pessimism had yet to emerge.

The Philippine trade liberalizations were eventually just as effective and apparently durable as Indonesia's. But they were much slower, spanning about 15 years, a deep crisis, a transition from authoritarian rule to democracy and three administrations. The case for reform was comprehensively argued in three major academic publications from the late 1960s, and by the country's leading academic economics department, whose graduates have traditionally dominated the main economic policy institutions of government.[2] The major international agencies were also heavily involved, both in advocacy and conditions-based lending programmes. The slow pace of reform therefore attests to the strength of the opposition, and especially the role of several key veto players.

Halting and piecemeal reform began in the 1970s. By the late 1970s, the intellectual battle for liberalization was largely won. Average tariff rates and their dispersion around the mean began to fall from 1980, and import licensing was relaxed. A major political and foreign exchange crisis from 1983 to 1986 temporarily set back the reforms, but by the end of the decade the original trade liberalization programme was back on track. A sharp, real exchange rate depreciation provided a major boost for tradables. Reforms continued through the 1990s, during both the Aquino and Ramos administrations, and with only a brief and temporary halt in the wake of the 1997–98 Asian economic crisis. The result is that the Philippines is now a largely open economy, with relatively few quantitative restrictions concentrated in some remaining sensitive sectors.

Bautista and Tecson (2003), both significant players in these reforms, emphasize the key role of the professional economics community, which staffed major economics agencies by the 1980s. Economists at the University of the Philippines were the key actors here, combined with a quasi-independent government agency, the Philippine Institute for Development Studies, which employed many of its graduates. The export lobby was too small to push for these reforms, while the agricultural lobbies were poorly organized or in some cases bought off by special sector-specific concessions, as in sugar and coconuts. Thus, 'these "technocrats" . . . became the de facto political representative of export producers' (p. 143).

Three other factors supported this intellectual foundation. Firstly, World Bank programmes in the late 1970s and early 1980s provided financial and human capital resources, particularly during the adjustment phase. Secondly, a realization by the late 1970s that the Philippines was both growing and liberalizing more slowly than its East Asian neighbours allowed competitive liberalization to became a factor of some influence. Thirdly, the reformist Ramos administration (1992–98) inherited the trade liberalization agenda and implemented it vigorously, not only by completing the schedule of tariff cuts and decontrol but also by a range of other major policy advances, including macroeconomic stabilization, the floating of the currency, and the removal of many regulatory barriers to competition. Perhaps most importantly, the faster growth over this period was the most significant reform dividend, for a country where 'growth pessimism' had become widespread owing to decades of poor performance.

Notes
1. For political economy explanations by Indonesia's leading economists, see Azis (1994), Soesastro (1989), and the collection of interviews with the key ministerial policy makers of the era in Thee (ed, 2003).
2. See for example Power and Sicat (1971), Baldwin (1975), Bautista, Power and Associates (1979), Medalla et al. (1995) and Bautista and Tecson (2003).

BOX 12.2 CENTRAL BANK RESTRUCTURING: INDONESIA AND THE PHILIPPINES IN THE 1990s

In both Indonesia and the Philippines, central bank restructuring followed a devastating economic crisis, a brief episode of very high inflation and occurred during the transition from authoritarian to democratic rule. In the Philippines in particular, macroeconomic policy had historically been neither especially prudent nor adventurous, and in both countries, the central banks had been seen as an arm of government and subject to its priorities. In both reforms, the IMF played a role, although the reform had a strong domestic constituency.

The transformation was most pronounced in the Philippines (Gochoco-Bautista, 2003). The new central bank, BSP, was established in 1991 with clearly defined autonomy and objectives. Macroeconomic policy outcomes since then clearly illustrate the success of the reforms. Inflation has been appreciably lower than historical norms and almost always single-digit. Moreover, the BSP has achieved these outcomes in spite of particularly challenging domestic and external circumstances.

The adoption of central bank independence in Indonesia is more recent and remains a work-in-progress.[1] The measure was implemented in 1999, as part of the LOI with the IMF. There is not yet the same contrast in macroeconomic outcomes as is evident in the Philippines: inflation rates are broadly similar to the pre-independence period (putting aside the aberrant hyperinflation of 1998), although BI is gradually fine-tuning its framework of inflation-targeting in the context of a floating exchange rate.

Notwithstanding the Indonesian qualifications, these reforms have been both desirable and successful. The central banks wanted the reforms and they generally had the support of the finance ministry. There was also a consensus among key political actors that, given an emerging and still fragile democracy, central bank independence would insulate macroeconomic policy from political pressures and provide a reassuring signal to investors. In addition, there was no strong constituency with a vested interest to oppose the reforms.

Note
1. See the two key references on Indonesian macroeconomic policy over this
    period, by two former BOI governors, respectively Djiwandono (2005) and
    Boediono (2005).

---

3   FUTURE OF REFORMS IN THE MEKONG 4

Chapter 7 identified the creation of modern institutions as one of the
major challenges facing Vietnam in order to become a fully-fledged emerging market economy. This agenda requires a strong and independent
central bank capable of formulating monetary policy as well as administering prudential oversight of financial institutions. A new State Bank of
Vietnam (SBV) needs to be supported by, and work in conjunction with, a
revamped Ministry of Finance that is capable of administering an effective
fiscal policy agenda. These ideas are well-accepted in the region, as well
as among economists and technocrats within the Vietnamese government
and universities.[2] Vietnam's dependence on foreign capital also enhances
the voice of foreign investors who form part of the interest groups in
support of strong macroeconomic institutions. International institutions,
such as the IMF, are also working to mould a consensus on these reforms.
However, despite the balance of arguments moving in favour of modernizing these key institutions, there is not yet a full consensus on moving
these reforms forward.

Consensus decision-making in Vietnam involves conducting small controlled experiments within the country, which are then appraised by
sections of the leadership before applying the changes elsewhere (Rama
2008). In the case of macroeconomic reforms, however, successful examples from other countries are needed, and the BSP in the Philippines is a
clear example of how a relatively small group of professional staff with the
right leadership and incentives can succeed in building a respected institution in the midst of a rather disorganized and corrupt bureaucracy. The
fact that Bank Indonesia has followed in its footsteps is a further example.
Pessimists argue that the powers of the large SOEs are too strong, and
the level of corruption within the upper echelons of government too
entrenched for any effective powers to be given to the SBV and MOF. On
the other hand, the macroeconomic crisis in mid-2008, not to mention
recession in the global economy, have demonstrated the importance
of increasing the sophistication of economic management to maintain
macroeconomic stability, job-growth and social stability in the country.

Therefore the ingredients should exist and the conditions seem ripe in Vietnam for major revamps of its key macroeconomic institutions.

The nature of reforms in the legal and judiciary system as well as of public administration more broadly will necessarily take some time. However, judging by the themes of study groups and visiting delegations from Vietnam, ideas are being gathered from Australia and elsewhere for judiciary and public administration reform. Furthermore, the literature reviewed above indicates that, once the key macroeconomic institutions are strengthened, the task of institutional building in other parts of the public service becomes easier. Still, the task is challenging, and resources will inevitably be diverted in the short term to manage the economy at a time of global recession. Furthermore, the veto power on the part of the Vietnamese Communist Party could mean long time-lags in decision making. Nevertheless, the task is achievable and the crisis may strengthen the political will towards deepening reforms.

Lao PDR faces many of the same challenges in modernizing its institutions as Vietnam, but is at an earlier stage of development and faces a number of additional obstacles. Institutionally, the quality of governance is weaker and the relatively small number of trained personnel/technocrats remains a serious constraint on moving the reform process forward. Moreover a highly decentralized political structure poses a formidable challenge to mobilizing a consensus for reforms. This is especially true in the area of fiscal management, where the recentralization of tax administration and treasury management, two key ingredients in the modernization process, faces many obstacles.

Finally, Lao dependence on minerals and hydroelectricity exports is potentially a further complicating factor. Although there are examples within the region of ways of managing rents from resources, such as the offshore petroleum fund of East Timor, the Lao political culture of acquiring resources for patronage (as well as for individual/family consumption) makes it difficult to establish an effective operation of a fund in the nation's interest.

Nevertheless, the current prime minister is relatively young and is said to be well-disposed to the technocrats. Moreover, incremental reforms in public financial management and banking have taken place, and the economy is being opened up to foreign capital albeit through a somewhat slow and uncertain process. Successful accession to the WTO could help move the process of reform and Lao's integration into the regional and global economy forward. This would be particularly so if the more advanced ASEAN countries and China were to move up the value chain and establish brand name products for their own domestic consumption. Places at the bottom of the manufacturing chain could then be opened up for low-cost producers. Whether Lao PDR will be sufficiently competitive to attract and retain those investments and whether those investments will generate future economic growth depends a great deal on the reforms that are undertaken in the meantime. The role of the donor community, whether through policy advice or capacity building, is to continue to try and move the balance of arguments in favour of deeper institutional reforms.

The political economy context for reform in Cambodia remains tied to its turbulent political past that left severe holes in both institutions and human capacity. Key economic institutions, particularly in the financial system, ceased to exist or became moribund. Years of conflict depleted the pool of talented and experienced public servants. Despite recent progress in improving institutional and human capacity, gaps remain and present significant challenges to maintaining reform momentum.

In contrast to Vietnam and Laos, Cambodia has approached reform in a more complex political environment. For a large majority of the post UNTAC period a fragile formal coalition between CPP and FUNCINPEC formed the government. Officials from the two parties divided civil service posts. However, in effect the CPP held the balance of power throughout most of the period. Reforms required building consensus within the party more than with coalition partners. This remains the key for economic reforms. Close linkages between senior officials across the administration based on political affiliations, marriage and family[3] ensure that economic reformers cannot drive reform without convincing broader interest groups in the party.

Nevertheless, the international community can also influence reform. Cambodia has actively integrated with the international community particularly by joining global and regional organizations such as the WTO and ASEAN. The fixed obligations of membership of these bodies, such as legislative requirements and tariff reductions, will continue to underpin reforms in the coming years. Technical and political cooperation in the context of these groupings could also provide support to reform.

With the furthest to go in achieving true economic reforms, Myanmar lacks the institutions capable of overseeing reforms in its banking and financial systems. Its technocrats are almost entirely disempowered and there are no clear, consistent or properly communicated principles of governance. Government intervention in business activities goes beyond legal frameworks. At the moment, there is also no evidence of the political will either to reduce drastically the roles of a multiplicity of SOEs or to distance the army from its chronically interventionist role throughout the economy, especially through its military-run investment corporations.

Reform for Myanmar would include giving real meaning to policies purporting to uphold a 'market-oriented economy', expediting privatization measures, strengthening legal protections for corporate entities in the already growing private sector, and stronger penalties for breaches of business rights and entitlements and for corruption. Other changes would focus on the exchange rate, taxation, property rights and the labour market. A programme of planned and structured 'demilitarization' would be desirable. In sum, a comprehensive infusion of good governance principles is called for to lift Myanmar to a more competitive position with its neighbours and with comparable economies. Considerable assistance could be required to ensure these changes are carried out effectively but assistance would need to be delivered sensitively and gradually.

NOTES

1. See Lal and Myint (1996, p. 288) for an attempt to apply policy turning points to a large sample of developing countries.
2. A group of Western-trained economics PhDs have returned to Vietnam since 1997 and are currently employed in senior positions in the bureaucracy and universities, principally the CIEM within the Ministry of Planning and Investment and the National Economics University, amongst others. There is significant professional cohesion amongst this group who affectionately call themselves the 'ANU Mafia'. In addition, there are programmes being put in place at the ANU for training the staff of the SBV in macroeconomic policy and management.
3. *Cambodia's Family Trees*, Global Witness, London 2007.

REFERENCES

Azis, I. (1994), 'Indonesia', in J. Williamson (ed.), *The Political Economy of Reform*, Washington DC: Institute for International Economics, pp. 385–416.

Baldwin, R.E. (1975), *Foreign Trade Regimes and Economic Development: The Philippines*, Cambridge, MA: Ballinger.

Bautista, R.M., J.H. Power and Associates (1979), *Industrial Promotion Policies in the Philippines*, Makati: Philippine Institute for Development Studies.

Bautista, R.M. and G. Tecson (2003), 'International dimensions', in A.M. Balisacan, and H. Hill (eds), *The Philippine Economy: Development, Policies and Challenges*, New York: Oxford University Press, pp. 136–71.

Bhagwati, J. (2002), 'Introduction: the unilateral freeing of trade versus reciprocity', in J. Bhagwati (ed.) *Going Alone: The Case for Relaxed Reciprocity in Freeing Trade*, Cambridge, MA: MIT Press.

Boediono (2005), 'Managing the Indonesian economy: some lessons from the past', *Bulletin of Indonesian Economic Studies*, **41** (3), 309–24.

Burnside, C. and D. Dollar (2000), 'Aid, policies, and growth', *American Economic Review*, **90** (4), 847–68.

Collier, P. (2007), *The Bottom Billion*, Oxford: Oxford University Press.

Djiwandono, J.S. (2005), *Bank Indonesia and the Crisis: An Insider's View*, Singapore: Institute of Southeast Asian Studies.

Gochoco-Bautista, M.S. (2003), 'Monetary and exchange rate policy', in A.M. Balisacan and H. Hill (eds), *The Philippine Economy: Development, Policies and Challenges*, New York: Oxford University Press.

Hill, H. (2000), *The Indonesian Economy*, 2nd edn, Cambridge: Cambridge University Press.

Keynes, J.M. (1936), *The Collected Writings of John Maynard Keynes*, Cambridge: Cambridge University Press.

Krueger, A.O. (1978), *Foreign Trade Regimes and Economic Development: Liberalization Attempts and Consequences*, Cambridge, MA: Ballinger.

Krueger, A.O. and S. Rajapatirana (1999), 'The World Bank's policies towards trade and trade policy reform', *World Economy*, **22** (6), 717–40.

Lal, D. and H. Myint (1996), *The Political Economy of Poverty, Equity and Growth*, Oxford: Oxford University Press.

Medalla, E.M., G.R. Tecson, R.M. Bautista, J.H. Power and Associates (1995/96), *Philippine Trade and Industrial Policies: Catching Up With Asia's Tigers*, vols I and II, Makati: Philippine Institute for Development Studies.

Power, J.H. and G.P. Sicat (1971), *The Philippines: Industrialization and Trade Policies*, London: Oxford University Press.

Rajapatirana, S. (2001), 'Developing-countries' trade policies in the 1990s: back to the future', in D. Lal and R. Snape (eds), *Trade, Development and Political Economy: Essays in Honour of Anne O. Krueger*, London: Palgrave.

Rama, M. (2008), 'Making difficult choices: Vietnam in transition', Commission on Growth and Development working paper no 40, Hanoi.

Soesastro, M.H. (1989), 'The political economy of deregulation in Indonesia', *Asian Survey*, **29** (9), 853–69.

Thee K.W. (ed) (2003), *Recollections: The Indonesian Economy, 1950s-1990s*, Singapore: Institute of Southeast Asian Studies.

Index